ACCLAIM FOR FRITJOF CAPRA'S

The Science of LEONARDO

FRITJOF CAPRA

The Science of LEONARDO

Fritjof Capra, Ph.D., physicist and systems theorist, is a founding director of the Center for Ecoliteracy in Berkeley, California, which promotes ecology and systems thinking in primary and secondary education. Dr. Capra is the author of four international bestsellers, *The Tao of Physics* (1975), *The Turning Point* (1982), *Uncommon Wisdom* (1988), and *The Web of Life* (1996). His previous book, *The Hidden Connections*, was published in 2002. Capra has been the focus of over fifty television interviews, documentaries, and talk shows in Europe, the United States, Brazil, Argentina, and Japan, and has been featured in major international magazines and newspapers. He was the first subject of the BBC's new documentary series "Beautiful Minds."

www.fritjofcapra.net

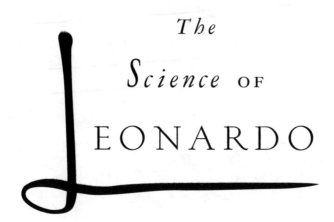

The

Science OF

EONARDO

Inside the Mind

of the

Great Genius

of the

Renaissance

The Science of

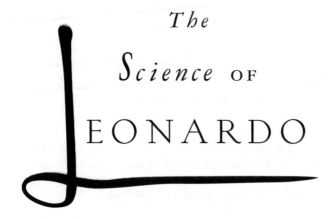

Leonardo

FRITJOF

CAPRA

ANCHOR BOOKS

A DIVISION OF RANDOM HOUSE, INC.

NEW YORK

To Elizabeth and Juliette

FIRST ANCHOR BOOKS EDITION, DECEMBER 2008

Copyright © 2007 by Fritjof Capra

The Library of Congress has cataloged the Doubleday edition as follows:
Capra, Fritjof.
The science of Leonardo : inside the mind of the great genius of the Renaissance / Fritjof Capra.
p. cm.
Includes bibliographical references.
1. Leonardo, da Vinci, 1452–1519. 2. Leonardo, da Vinci, 1452–1519—Notebooks,
sketchbooks, etc. 3. Scientists—Italy—History—To 1500—Biography. 4. Scientists—
Italy—History—16th century—Biography. 5. Science, Renaissance. I. Title.
Q143.L5C37 2007
509.2—dc22 [B] 2007002461

Anchor ISBN: 978-1-4000-7883-7

Author photograph © Karl Grossman
Book design by Ellen Cipriano (with Terry Karydes and Donna Sinisgalli)
Diagrams in appendix by Jeffrey L. Ward

www.anchorbooks.com

Printed in the United States of America
10 9 8 7 6 5 4 3 2 1

First I shall do some experiments before I proceed farther, because my intention is to cite experience first and then with reasoning show why such experience is bound to operate in such a way. And this is the true rule by which those who speculate about the effects of nature must proceed.

—LEONARDO DA VINCI, C. 1513

CONTENTS

ACKNOWLEDGMENTS

When I began my research for this book, I entered a field that was completely foreign to me, and I am grateful to many friends and colleagues for helping me orient myself in the world of Leonardo scholarship.

I am especially grateful

to my wife, Elizabeth Hawk, for helping me identify the leading contemporary scholars, research institutions, and special libraries;

to Claire Farago for clarifying many basic questions about Leonardo's language and about the scholarly editions of his Notebooks, and especially for introducing me to the Elmer Belt Library at the University of California, Los Angeles;

to Carlo Pedretti for valuable conversations and correspondence about the history and dating of Leonardo's drawings and texts;

to Domenico Laurenza for his encouragement and support, for illuminating discussions and correspondence about various aspects of Leonardo's science, and for valuable help in translating certain passages from the original manuscripts;

to Linda Warren, Head Librarian of the Elmer Belt Library, and to Monica Taddei, Head Librarian of the Biblioteca Leonardiana in Vinci, for giving me unrestricted access to their collections of the complete facsimile editions of Leonardo's manuscripts, and for their generous help with bibliographical research;

to Eduardo Kickhöfel for valuable research assistance at the Biblioteca Leonardiana, and for many interesting discussions of Leonardo's science;

to Franco Bulletti at Giunti Editore in Florence for a fascinating discussion of the production process of their facsimile editions of Leonardo's manuscripts;

to Clara Vitulo, curator at the Biblioteca Reale in Turin, for arranging a special viewing of Leonardo's self-portrait, the Codex on the Flight of Birds, and other original drawings in the library's collection;

to Rowan Watson, Head of Documentary Materials at the Victoria and Albert Museum, for showing me the Codices Forster in the collection of the National Art Library, and for an interesting discussion of their history;

and to Françoise Viatte, Director of the Department of Graphic Arts at the Louvre, for her encouragement and for helpful discussions and correspondence about Leonardo's works in the Louvre's collection.

During my research and writing, I discussed various areas of contemporary science and technology and their relevance to Leonardo's work with colleagues and friends. I am especially indebted

to Pier Luigi Luisi for inspiring conversations during the very early stages of the project, and for his warm hospitality in Zurich and Rome;

to Ugo Piomelli for numerous enlightening discussions of Leonardo's fluid dynamics;

to Ann Pizzorusso for informative correspondence about the history of geology;

to Brian Goodwin for illuminating discussions of morphogenesis in botany;

to Ralph Abraham for a critical reading of the chapter on Leonardo's mathematics;

to George Lakoff for many inspiring conversations about contemporary cognitive science;

and to Magdalena Corvin, Amory Lovins, and Oscar Motomura for stimulating discussions on the nature of design.

I am also very grateful to Satish Kumar for giving me the opportunity to teach a course on Leonardo's Science of Quality at Schumacher College in England during the spring of 2006, and to the participants in the course for many critical questions and helpful suggestions.

I wish to thank my literary agents, John Brockman and Katinka Matson, for their encouragement and valuable advice.

I am deeply grateful to my brother, Bernt Capra, for reading the entire manuscript and for his enthusiastic support and numerous helpful suggestions. I am also very grateful to Ernest Callenbach, Amelia Barili, and to my daughter, Juliette Capra, for reading portions of the manuscript and offering many critical comments.

I am indebted to my assistant, Trena Cleland, for her careful and sensitive editing of the first draft of the manuscript, and for keeping my home office on an even keel while I was concentrating on my writing.

I am grateful to my editor Roger Scholl at Doubleday for his support and advice, and for his superb editing of the text.

Last but not least, I wish to express my deep gratitude to my wife, Elizabeth, for countless discussions on Renaissance art, for helping me select the book's illustrations, and for her patience and enthusiastic support during many months of strenuous work.

PHOTOGRAPHIC
ACKNOWLEDGMENTS

The Royal Collection © 2007, Her Majesty Queen Elizabeth II (Figs. I-1, 2-1, 2-2, 3-1, 4-1, 4-2, 4-5, 5-1, 6-1, 6-2, 6-3, 6-4, 7-2, 7-3, 7-7, 8-2, 9-1, 9-4, E-1)

Réunion des Musées Nationaux/Art Resource, NY, Bibliothèque de l'Institut de France, Paris, France (Figs. 2-5, 6-6, 6-7, 7-1, 7-4, 8-5, 8-6, 8-7, 9-2)

Réunion des Musées Nationaux/Art Resource, NY, Louvre, Paris, France (Figs. 1-2, 2-4, 4-3)

Biblioteca Ambrosiana, Milano (Figs. 2-3, 8-1, 8-3)

Biblioteca Reale, Torino, with permission from Ministero per i Beni e le Attività culturali (Figs. P-1, 4-4, E-2)

Laboratorio Fotográfico, Biblioteca Nacional de España, Madrid (Figs. 6-5 *left*, 7-6)

Polo Museale Fiorentino (Figs. 1-1, 3-2)

V&A Images/Victoria and Albert Museum, London (Fig. 7-5)

The British Library Board (Fig. 8-4)

Klassik Stiftung Weimar (Fig. 9-3)

Archivio Fotografico IMSS Firenze, Fotografia de Eurofoto (Fig. 6-5 *right*)

Archivio Fotografico IMSS Firenze, Fotografia di Simon Hazelgrove (Fig. 6-8)

Museo d'Arte Antica, Castello Sforzesco, Milano (Fig. 2-6)

PREFACE

Leonardo da Vinci, perhaps the greatest master painter and genius of the Renaissance, has been the subject of hundreds of scholarly and popular books. His enormous oeuvre, said to include over 100,000 drawings and over 6,000 pages of notes, and the extreme diversity of his interests have attracted countless scholars from a wide range of academic and artistic disciplines.

However, there are surprisingly few books about Leonardo's science, even though he left voluminous notebooks full of detailed descriptions of his experiments, magnificent drawings, and long analyses of his findings. Moreover, most authors who have discussed Leonardo's scientific work have looked at it through Newtonian lenses, and I believe this has often prevented them from understanding its essential nature.

Leonardo intended to eventually present the results of his scientific research as a coherent, integrated body of knowledge. He never managed to do so, because throughout his life he always felt more compelled to expand, refine, and document his investigations than to organize them in a systematic way. Hence, in the centuries since his death, scholars studying his celebrated Notebooks have tended to see them as disorganized and chaotic. In Leonardo's mind, however, his science was not disorganized at all. It gave him a coherent, unifying picture of natural phenomena—but a picture that is radically different from that of Galileo, Descartes, and Newton.

Only now, five centuries later, as the limits of Newtonian science are becoming all too apparent and the mechanistic Cartesian worldview is giving way to a holistic and ecological view not unlike Leonardo's, can we begin to appreciate the full power of his science and its great relevance for our modern era.

My intent is to present a coherent account of the scientific method and achievements of the great genius of the Renaissance and evaluate them from the perspective of today's scientific thought. Studying Leonardo from this perspective will not only allow us to recognize his science as a solid body of knowledge. It will also show why it cannot be understood without his art, nor his art without the science.

As a scientist and author, I depart in this book from my usual work. At the same time, however, it has been a deeply satisfying book to write, as I have been fascinated by Leonardo da Vinci's scientific work for over three decades. When I began my career as a writer in the early 1970s, my plan was to write a popular book about particle physics. I completed the first three chapters of the manuscript, then abandoned the project to write *The Tao of Physics*, into which I incorporated most of the material from the early manuscript. My original manuscript began with a brief history of modern Western science, and opened with the beautiful statement by Leonardo da Vinci on the empirical basis of science that now serves as the epigraph for this book.

Since paying tribute to Leonardo as the first modern scientist (long before Galileo, Bacon, and Newton) in my early manuscript, I have retained my fascination with his scientific work, and over the years have referred to it several times in my writings, without, however, studying his extensive Notebooks in any detail. The impetus to do so came in the mid-1990s, when I saw a large exhibition of Leonardo's drawings at The Queen's Gallery at Buckingham Palace in London. As I gazed at those magnificent drawings juxtaposing, often on the same page, architecture and human anatomy, turbulent water and turbulent air, water vortices, the flow of human hair and the growth patterns of grasses, I realized that Leonardo's systematic studies of living and nonliving forms amounted to a science of quality and wholeness that was fundamentally different from the mechanistic science of Galileo and Newton. At the core of his investigations, it seemed to me, was a persistent exploration of patterns, interconnecting phenomena from a vast range of fields.

Having explored the modern counterparts to Leonardo's approach, known today as complexity theory and systems theory, in several of my previous books, I felt that it was time for me to study Leonardo's Notebooks in earnest and evaluate his scientific thought from the perspective of the most recent advances in modern science.

Although Leonardo left us, in the words of the eminent Renaissance scholar Kenneth Clark, "one of the most voluminous and complete records of a mind at work that has come down to us," his Notebooks give us hardly any clues to the author's character and personality.[1] Leonardo, in his paintings as well as in his life, seemed to cultivate a certain sense of mystery. Because of this aura of mystery and because of his extraordinary talents, Leonardo da Vinci became a legendary figure even during his lifetime, and his legend has been amplified in different variations in the centuries after his death.

Throughout history, he personified the age of the Renaissance, yet each era "reinvented" Leonardo according to the zeitgeist of the time. To quote Kenneth Clark again, "Leonardo is the Hamlet of art history whom each of us must recreate for himself."[2] It is therefore inevitable that in the following pages I have also had to reinvent Leonardo. The image that emerges from my account is, in contemporary scientific terms, one of Leonardo as a systemic thinker, ecologist, and complexity theorist; a scientist and artist with a deep reverence for all life, and as a man with a strong desire to work for the benefit of humanity.

The powerful intuition I had in that London exhibit, that the Leonardo I describe above is indeed "the Leonardo of our time," was confirmed by my subsequent research and exploration of the Notebooks. As art historian Martin Kemp wrote in the catalog of an earlier exhibit of Leonardo's drawings in the Hayward Gallery in London:

> It seems to me that there is a core to [Leonardo's] achievement, however imperfectly transmitted and received by different generations, that remains intuitively accessible. What has been sensed is that his artistic productions are more than art—that they are part of a vision embracing a profound sense of the interrelatedness of things. The full complexity of life in the context of the world is somehow implied when he characterises any of its constituent parts. . . . I believe that his vision of the totality of the world as

a kind of single organism does speak to us with particular relevance today, now that our technological potential has become so awesome.[3]

Kemp's portrait of the Leonardo of that exhibit, characterized so eloquently in the passage above, mirrors my own. It is this Leonardo who will emerge from my exploration of his unique synthesis of science and art.

Fritjof Capra
Berkeley, December 2006

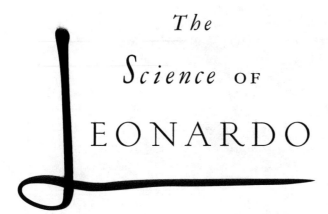

The

Science OF

LEONARDO

Figure P-1: Leonardo's Self-Portrait, c. 1512, Biblioteca Reale, Turin

An Interpreter of Nature

In Western intellectual history, the Renaissance—a period stretching from the beginning of the fifteenth to the end of the sixteenth century—marks the period of transition from the Middle Ages to the modern world. In the 1460s, when the young Leonardo da Vinci received his training as painter, sculptor, and engineer in Florence, the worldview of his contemporaries was still entangled in medieval thinking. Science in the modern sense, as a systematic empirical method for gaining knowledge about the natural world, did not exist. Knowledge about natural phenomena, some accurate and some inaccurate, had been handed down by Aristotle and other philosophers of antiquity, and was fused with Christian doctrine by the Scholastic theologians who presented it as the officially authorized creed. The authorities condemned scientific experiments as subversive, seeing any attack on Aristotle's science as an attack on the Church.

Leonardo da Vinci broke with this tradition. One hundred years before Galileo and Bacon, he single-handedly developed a new empirical approach to science, involving the systematic observation of nature, logical reasoning, and some mathematical formulations—the main characteristics of what is known today as the scientific method. He fully realized that he was breaking new ground. He humbly called himself *omo sanza lettere* ("an unlettered man"), but with some irony and with pride in his new method, seeing himself as an "interpreter between nature and humans." Wherever he turned there were new discoveries to be made, and his scientific creativity, combining passionate intellectual curiosity with great patience and experimental ingenuity, was the main driving force throughout his life.

For forty years, Leonardo collected his thoughts and observations in his celebrated Notebooks, together with descriptions of hundreds of experiments, drafts of letters, architectural and technological designs, and reminders to himself about future research and writing. Almost every page in these Notebooks is crowded with text and magnificent drawings. It is believed that the entire collection ran to 13,000 pages when Leonardo died without having sorted them, as he had intended. Over the subsequent centuries almost half of the original collection was lost, but over 6,000 pages have been preserved and translated from the original Italian. These manuscripts are now widely dispersed among libraries, museums, and private collections, some in large compilations known as codices, others as torn pages and isolated folios, and a few still as notebooks in their original bound forms.[1]

THE SCIENCE OF PAINTING

Leonardo was gifted with exceptional powers of observation and visual memory. He was able to draw the complex swirls of turbulent water or the swift movements of a bird with a precision that would not be reached again until the invention of serial photography. He was well aware of the extraordinary talent he possessed. In fact, he considered the eye as his principal instrument as both a painter and a scientist. "The eye, which is said to be the window of the soul," he wrote, "is the principal means whereby sensory awareness can most abundantly and magnificently contemplate the infinite works of nature."[2]

Leonardo's approach to scientific knowledge was visual. It was the approach of a painter. "Painting," he declares, "embraces within itself all the forms of nature."[3] This statement, in fact, is the key to understanding Leonardo's science. He asserts repeatedly, especially in his early manuscripts, that painting involves the study of natural forms, and he emphasizes the intimate connection between the artistic representation of those forms and the intellectual understanding of their intrinsic nature and underlying principles. For example, in the collection of his notes on painting, known as *Trattato della pittura (Treatise on Painting)*, he writes:

> The science of painting extends to all the colors of the surfaces of bodies, and to the shapes of the bodies enclosed by those surfaces. . . . [Painting] with philosophic and subtle speculation considers all the qualities of forms. . . . Truly this is science, the legitimate daughter of nature, because painting is born of nature.[4]

For Leonardo, painting is both an art and a science—a science of natural forms, of qualities, quite different from the mechanistic science that would emerge two hundred years later. Leonardo's forms are living forms, continually shaped and transformed by underlying processes. Throughout his life he studied, drew, and painted the rocks and sediments of the earth, shaped by water; the growth of plants, shaped by their metabolism; and the anatomy of the animal (and human) body in motion.

THE NATURE OF LIFE

Nature as a whole was alive for Leonardo. He saw the patterns and processes in the microcosm as being similar to those in the macrocosm.

He frequently drew analogies between human anatomy and the structure of the Earth, as in the following beautiful passage from the Codex Leicester:

> We may say that the Earth has a vital force of growth, and that its flesh is the soil; its bones are the successive strata of the rocks which form the mountains; its cartilage is the porous rock, its blood the veins of the waters. The lake of blood that lies around the heart is the ocean. Its breathing is the increase and decrease of the blood in the pulses, just as in the Earth it is the ebb and flow of the sea.[5]

While the analogy between microcosm and macrocosm goes back to Plato and was well known throughout the Middle Ages and the Renaissance, Leonardo disentangled it from its original mythical context and treated it strictly as a scientific theory. Today we know that some of the analogies in the passage quoted above are flawed, and in fact Leonardo himself corrected some of them late in his life.[6] However, we can easily recognize Leonardo's statement as a forerunner of today's Gaia theory—a scientific theory that views the earth as a living, self-organizing, and self-regulating system.[7]

At the most fundamental level, Leonardo always sought to understand the nature of life. This has often escaped earlier writers, because until recently the nature of life was defined by biologists only in terms of cells and molecules, to which Leonardo, living two centuries before the invention of the microscope, had no access. But today, a new systemic understanding of life is emerging at the forefront of science—an understanding in terms of metabolic processes and their patterns of organization. And those are precisely the phenomena Leonardo explored throughout his life.

A SYSTEMIC THINKER

Leonardo da Vinci was what we would call, in today's scientific parlance, a systemic thinker.[8] Understanding a phenomenon, for him, meant connecting it with other phenomena through a similarity of patterns. When he studied the proportions of the human body, he compared them to the proportions of buildings in Renaissance architecture. His investigations of muscles and bones led him to study and draw gears and levers, thus interlinking animal physiology and engineering. Patterns of turbulence in water led him to observe similar patterns in the flow of air; and from there he went on to explore the nature of sound, the theory of music, and the design of musical instruments.

This exceptional ability to interconnect observations and ideas from different disciplines lies at the very heart of Leonardo's approach to learning and research. At the same time, it was also the reason why he often got carried away and extended his investigations far beyond their original role in the formulation of a "science of painting," exploring almost the entire range of natural phenomena known at his time as well as many others previously unrecognized.

Leonardo's scientific work was virtually unknown during his lifetime and remained hidden for over two centuries after his death in 1519. His pioneering discoveries and ideas had no direct influence on the scientists who came after him, although during the subsequent 450 years his conception of a science of living forms would emerge again at various times. During those periods, the problems he had struggled with were revisited with increasing levels of sophistication, as scientists advanced in their understanding of the structure of matter, the laws of chemistry and electromagnetism, cellular and molecular biology, genetics, and the critical role of evolution in shaping the forms of the living world.

Today, from the vantage point of twenty-first-century science, we can recognize Leonardo da Vinci as an early precursor of an entire lineage of scientists and philosophers whose central focus was the nature of organic form. They include Immanuel Kant, Alexander von Humboldt, and Johann Wolfgang von Goethe in the eighteenth century; Georges Cuvier, Charles Darwin, and D'Arcy Thompson in the nineteenth; Alexander Bogdanov, Ludwig von Bertalanffy, and Vladimir Vernadsky in the early twentieth; and Gregory Bateson, Ilya Prigogine, and Humberto Maturana in the late twentieth century; as well as contemporary morphologists and complexity theorists like Brian Goodwin, Ian Stewart, and Ricard Solé.

Leonardo's organic conception of life has continued as an undercurrent of biology throughout the centuries, and during brief periods came to the fore and dominated scientific thought. However, none of the scientists in that lineage were aware that the great genius of the Renaissance had already pioneered many of the ideas they were exploring. While Leonardo's manuscripts were gathering dust in ancient European libraries, Galileo Galilei was being celebrated as the "father of modern science." I cannot help but argue that the true founder of modern science was Leonardo da Vinci, and I wonder how Western scientific thought would have developed had his Notebooks been known and widely studied soon after his death.

SYNTHESIS OF ART AND SCIENCE

To describe nature's organic forms mathematically, we cannot use Euclidean geometry, nor the classical equations of Newtonian physics. We need a new kind of qualitative mathematics. Today, such a new mathematics is being formulated within the framework of complexity theory, technically known as nonlinear dynamics.[9] It involves complex nonlinear equations and computer modeling, in which curved shapes are analyzed and classified with the help of topology, a geometry of forms in movement. None of this was available to Leonardo, of course. But amazingly, he experimented with a rudimentary form of topology in his mathematical studies of "continuous quantities" and "transmutations," long before this important branch of modern mathematics was developed by Henri Poincaré in the early twentieth century.[10]

Leonardo's principal tool for the representation and analysis of nature's forms was his extraordinary facility of drawing, which almost matched the quickness of his vision. Observation and documentation were fused into a single act. He used his artistic talent to produce drawings that are stunningly beautiful and at the same time serve as geometric diagrams. For Leonardo, drawing was the perfect vehicle to formulate his conceptual models—a perfect "mathematics" for his science of organic forms.[11]

The dual role of Leonardo's drawings—as art and as tools of scientific analysis—shows us why his science cannot be understood without his art, nor his art without his science. His assertion that "painting embraces in itself all the forms of nature" cuts both ways. In order to practice his art, he needed the scientific understanding of the forms of nature; in order to analyze the forms of nature, he needed the artistic ability to draw them.

In addition to his keen intellect and powers of observation, his experimental ingenuity, and his great artistic talents, Leonardo also had a very practical bent. As he pursued his investigations of nature's forms, beholding them with the eye of a scientist and painter, the useful applications of his discoveries were never far from his mind. He spent a major part of his life conceiving machines of all kinds, inventing numerous mechanical and optical devices, and designing buildings, gardens, and cities.

When he studied water, he saw it not only as the medium of life and the driving force of nature, but also as a source of power for industrial systems, similar to the role that steam—another form of water—would play in the Industrial Revolution three centuries later. His extensive investigations of the flows of air and wind and the flight of birds led him to invent various flying machines, many of them based on sound aerodynamic principles. Indeed, Leonardo's achievements as a designer and engineer are on a par with his accomplishments as an artist and scientist.

THE EYE AND THE APPEARANCE OF FORMS

In his *Treatise on Painting*, Leonardo makes clear that painting is the unifying perspective and integrating thread that runs through all his fields of study. From this work, a coherent conceptual structure emerges, which he might have intended to use for the eventual publications of his Notebooks.

Like all true scientists, Leonardo based his science on systematic observation. Hence his starting point is the human eye. His careful investigations of the anatomy of the eye and the origin of vision were unparalleled in his time. He paid particular attention to the connections between the eye and the brain, which he demonstrated in a series of beautiful drawings of the human skull. Using brilliant anatomical dissections, Leonardo displayed for the first time the complete path of vision through the pupil and lens to the optic nerve, and all the way to a specific cavity in the brain, known to neurologists today as the third cerebral ventricle.[12]

This is where he located the "seat of the soul," where all sense impressions meet. Leonardo's concept of the soul comes very close to what cognitive scientists today call "cognition," the process of knowing.[13] His theory of how sensory impulses travel along the nerves from the sense organs to the brain is so ingenious that I doubt if neuroscientists today could conceive of anything better, were they given the restrictions of having to work without any knowledge of electromagnetism, biochemistry, and microbiology.

Leonardo saw his discoveries in optics and the physiology of vision as the grounding of his science of painting, beginning with the science of perspective, the outstanding innovation of Renaissance art. "Painting is based on perspective," he explains, "and perspective is nothing else than a thorough knowledge of the function of the eye."[14] From perspective, he moved on to explore the geometry of light rays (known today as geometrical optics), the effects of light falling on spheres and cylinders, the nature of shadow and of contrasts, and the juxtaposition of colors.

These systematic studies, illustrated in long series of intricate drawings, were the scientific basis of Leonardo's extraordinary artistic ability to understand and render the most subtle visual complexities. Most renowned was his invention and mastery of a special art of shading—a melting of shades, known as sfumato—which delicately blurs the outlines of bodies. In the words of art historian Daniel Arasse,

> The supreme expression of the science of painting and of its divine character, Leonardo's *sfumato* was the power behind the poetry of his paintings and the mystery that seems to emanate from them.[15]

Eventually, these sophisticated studies of the effects of light and shade led Leonardo to thoroughly investigate the very nature of light. With only the most rudimentary instruments, he used his phenomenal powers of observation, his ability to recognize similarities of patterns, and the great intuitive understanding of light he had acquired as a painter to formulate concepts that were diametrically opposed to the ideas of his contemporaries, but were almost identical to those Christian Huygens would propose two hundred years later in his famous wave theory of light.[16]

THE LIVING FORMS OF NATURE

Leonardo's studies of living forms began with their appearance to his painter's eye, and then proceeded to detailed investigations of their intrinsic nature. In the macrocosm, the main themes of his science were the movements of water and air, the geological forms and transformations of the Earth, and the botanical diversity and growth patterns of plants. In the microcosm, his main focus was on the human body—its beauty and proportions, the mechanics of its movements, and how it compared to other animal bodies in motion, in particular the flight of birds.

The science of living forms, for Leonardo, is a science of movement and transformation, whether he studies mountains, rivers, plants, or the human body. To understand the human form means to understand the body in motion. Leonardo demonstrated in countless elaborate and beautiful drawings how nerves, muscles, tendons, bones, and joints work together to move the limbs; how limbs and facial expressions perform gestures and actions.

As always, Leonardo used the insights he gained from this extensive research in his paintings. In the words of Daniel Arasse,

> From the early *Madonnas*, through the portraits, to *St. John the Baptist*, Leonardo caught the figure in motion. The immediate and exceptional impact of *The Last Supper* was largely due to the fact that Leonardo replaced the traditional arrangement with a rhythmical composition that considerably changed the very idea of the subject.[17]

As a painter, Leonardo felt that he should use gestures to portray the frames of mind and emotions that provoked them. He asserted that, in the painting of a human figure, the most important task was to "ex-

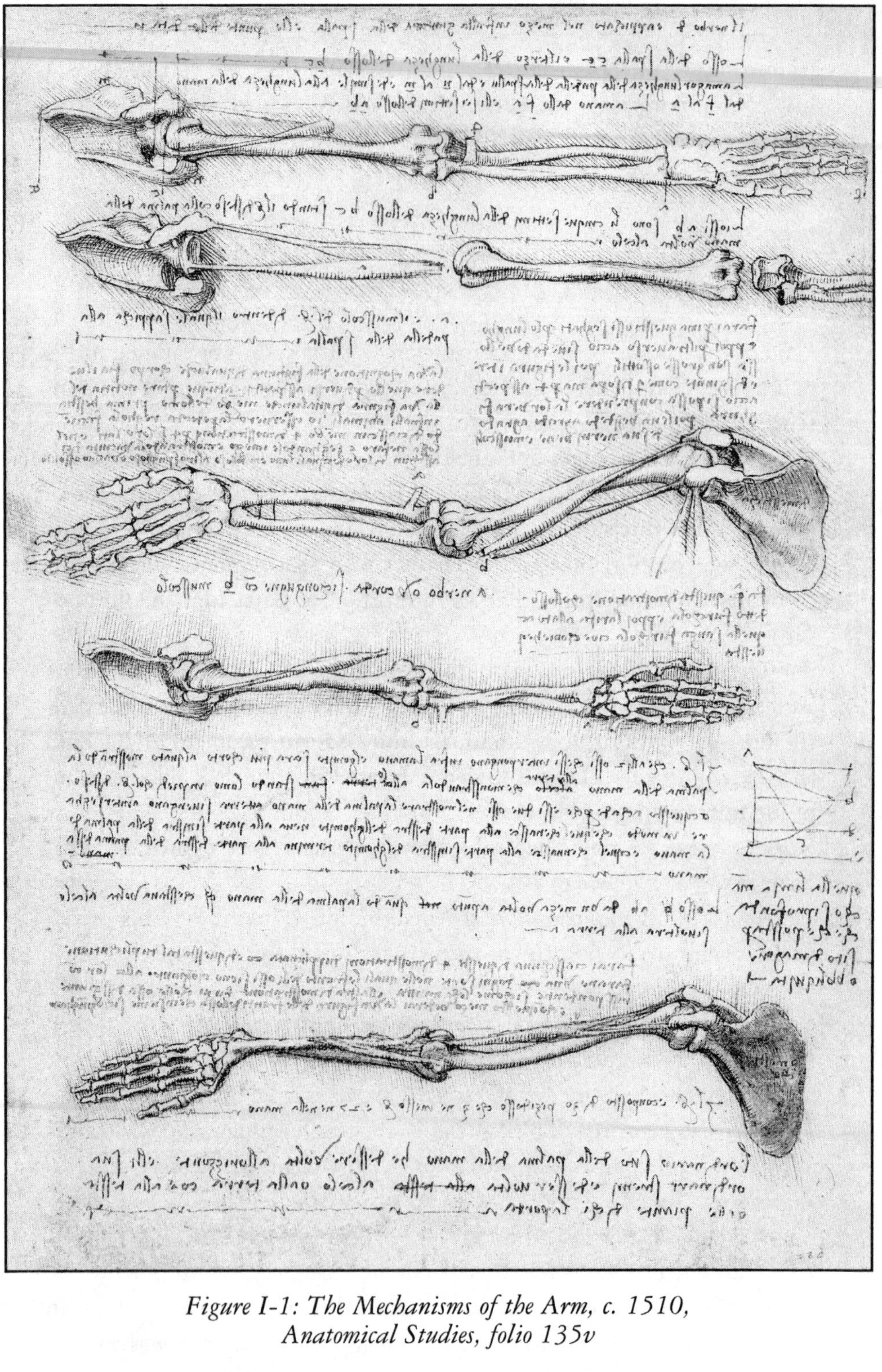

Figure I-1: The Mechanisms of the Arm, c. 1510,
Anatomical Studies, folio 135v

press in gesture the passion of its soul."[18] Indeed, to portray the body's expression of the human spirit was the artist's highest aspiration, in Leonardo's view. And it was one in which he himself excelled, as the paintings of his mature period attest. As art historian Irma Richter explains in the introductory comments to her classic selections from the Notebooks, for Leonardo, "the human body was an outward and visible expression of the soul; it was shaped by its spirit."[19] We shall see that this view of soul and spirit, unmarred by the mind-body split that René Descartes would introduce in the seventeenth century, is perfectly consistent with the conception of the "embodied mind" in today's cognitive science.[20]

Unlike Descartes, Leonardo never thought of the body as a machine, even though he was a brilliant engineer who designed countless machines and mechanical devices. He clearly recognized, and documented in superb renderings, that the anatomies of animals and humans involve mechanical functions (see Fig. I-1). "Nature cannot give movement to animals without mechanical instruments," he explained.[21] But that did not imply for him that living organisms were machines. It only implied that, in order to understand the movements of the animal body, he needed to explore the principles of mechanics, which he did for many years in a thorough and systematic way. He clearly understood that the means of the body's movements were mechanical. But for Leonardo, their origin lay in the soul, the nature of which was not mechanical but spiritual.[22]

LEONARDO'S LEGACY

Leonardo did not pursue science and engineering to dominate nature, as Francis Bacon would advocate a century later. He had a deep respect for life, a special compassion for animals, and great awe and reverence for nature's complexity and abundance. While a brilliant inventor and designer himself, he always thought that nature's ingenuity was vastly superior to human design. He felt that we would be wise to respect nature and learn from her. It is an attitude that has reemerged today in the practice of ecological design.[23]

Leonardo's synthesis of art and science is infused with a deep awareness of ecology and systems thinking. It is not surprising that he spoke with great disdain of the so-called "abbreviators," the reductionists of his time:

> The abbreviators of works do injury to knowledge and to love. . . . Of what value is he who, in order to abbreviate the parts of those things of which he professes to give complete knowledge, leaves out the greater part of the things of which the whole is composed? . . . Oh human stupidity! . . . You don't see that you are falling into the same error as one who strips a tree of its adornment of branches full of leaves, intermingled with fragrant flowers or fruit, in order to demonstrate that the tree is good for making planks.[24]

This statement is revealing testimony of Leonardo's way of thinking and is also ominously prophetic. Reducing the beauty of life to mechanical parts and valuing trees only for their lumber is an eerily accurate characterization of the mind-set that dominates our world today. In my view, this makes Leonardo's legacy all the more relevant to our time.

Our sciences and technologies have become increasingly narrow in their focus, and we are unable to understand our multifaceted problems from an interdisciplinary perspective. We urgently need a science that honors and respects the unity of all life, that recognizes the fundamental interdependence of all natural phenomena, and reconnects us with the living earth. What we need today is exactly the kind of thinking and science Leonardo da Vinci anticipated and outlined five hundred years ago, at the height of the Renaissance and the dawn of the modern scientific age.

PART ONE

LEONARDO, THE MAN

ONE

Infinite Grace

The earliest literary portrait of Leonardo da Vinci, and to me still the most moving, is that by the Tuscan painter and architect Giorgio Vasari in his classic book *Lives of the Artists*, published in 1550.[1] Vasari was only eight years old when Leonardo died, but he gathered information about the master from many artists who had known him and remembered him well, most notably Leonardo's close friend and disciple Francesco Melzi. An acquaintance of Leonardo, the surgeon and art collector Paolo Giovio, wrote a short eulogy, but it is unfinished and merely a page long.[2] Vasari's chapter, "Life of Leonardo da Vinci," therefore, is as close as we can come to a contemporary account.

Besides being an accomplished painter and architect,

Vasari was a keen collector of drawings by famous masters and of stories about them. The idea of writing a book on the history of Italian art from the thirteenth to the sixteenth centuries was suggested to him by Giovio during a dinner party in Rome.[3] The book became a bestseller when it was first published, and its wide popular appeal has endured over the centuries due to the author's lively and colorful portraits, replete with charming anecdotes. Through a series of engaging stories about the lives of its greatest artists, Vasari's *Lives* conveyed the revolutionary nature of the Italian Renaissance. In spite of many inaccuracies and a tendency toward referring to legends and idolizing, Vasari's work remains the principal source for anyone interested in that period of European art and culture.

QUALITIES AND APPEARANCE

The opening paragraphs of Vasari's chapter on Leonardo are an emphatic declaration of the master's exceptional qualities and appearance:

> In the normal course of events many men and women are born with various remarkable qualities and talents; but occasionally, in a way that transcends nature, a single person is marvelously endowed by heaven with beauty, grace, and talent in such abundance that he leaves other men far behind, all his actions seem inspired, and indeed everything he does clearly comes from God rather than from human art.
>
> Everyone acknowledged that this was true of Leonardo da Vinci, an artist of outstanding physical beauty who displayed infinite grace in everything he did and who cultivated his genius so brilliantly that all problems he studied he solved with ease. He possessed great strength and dexterity; he was a man of regal spirit and tremendous breadth of mind; and his name became so famous that not only was he esteemed during his lifetime but his reputation endured and became even greater after his death.

Vasari's effusive portrait of Leonardo may seem exaggerated, but his description is echoed in many contemporary accounts and references, in

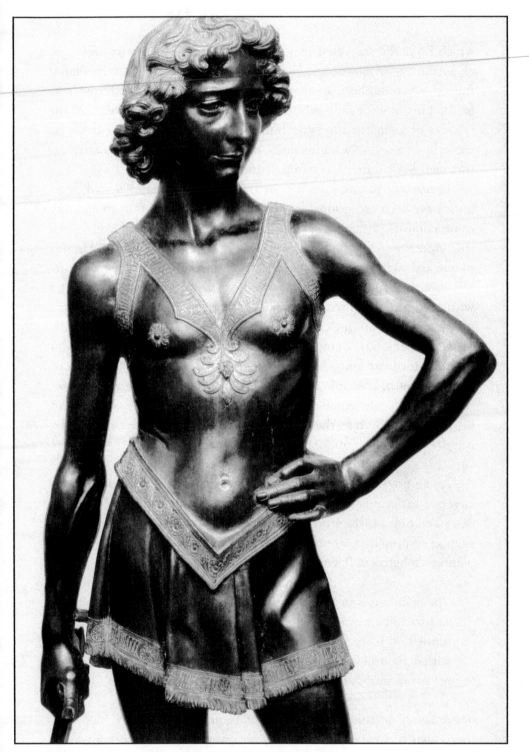

Figure 1-1: Andrea del Verrocchio, David, *Museo Nazionale, Florence*

which Leonardo was often compared to the classical geniuses and sages of antiquity—Archimedes, Pythagoras, and most frequently Plato.[4] Indeed, when Raphael, another great master of the Italian Renaissance, painted his fresco *The School of Athens* in the Vatican, he gave Plato the features of Leonardo, dressing him in a rose-colored toga (a color favored by Leonardo), with his index finger raised in a characteristic gesture well known from Leonardo's paintings.

Leonardo's physical beauty in his youth and middle-aged years must have been exceptional, as it is mentioned by all his contemporary commentators, even though this was not customary at the time. An anonymous writer called the Anonimo Gaddiano exclaimed, "He was so unusual and many-sided that nature seemed to have produced a miracle in him, not only in the beauty of his person, but in the many gifts with which she endowed him and which he fully mastered."[5] Others marveled at the unique combination of physical strength and grace he seemed to embody. Many authors, including Vasari, referred to him with the ultimate epithet—*il divino*.

As a youth, Leonardo liked to dress flamboyantly. "He wore a rose-colored cloak," the Anonimo Gaddiano tells us, "which came only to his knees, although at the time long vestments were the custom. His beard came to the middle of his breast and was well-combed and curled."

As he grew older, Leonardo apparently dressed more conventionally, but his appearance was always elegant and refined. Paolo Giovio described him as "the arbiter of all questions relating to beauty and elegance, especially pageantry." Leonardo's own description of the painter's inherent refinement is revealing as well:

> The painter sits in front of his work at great ease, well-dressed, and wielding a very light brush with delicate colors. He adorns himself with the clothes he fancies; his home is clean and filled with delightful pictures, and he is often accompanied by music or readers of various beautiful works.[6]

There exists no confirmed portrait of Leonardo as a young man, but legend has it that he was the model for several angels and other youthful figures portrayed by Renaissance artists. The most credible of them is the lovely adolescent *David* sculpted by Andrea del Verrocchio during the time Leonardo was his student (see Fig. 1-1). The slender figure, wavy hair, and strikingly handsome face certainly match the contemporary descriptions of the young Leonardo, and art historians have pointed out that several of the statue's facial characteristics seem to foreshadow those in the well-known portraits of the old master.[7]

There are quite a few portraits of Leonardo as an older man, most of them idealizing him as a venerable sage.[8] The most authentic is that which is considered the artist's only existing self-portrait, a captivating, highly detailed drawing in red chalk that he made when he was about sixty, although he appears older than his age (see Fig. P-1 on p. xxii). The drawing is housed in the Biblioteca Reale in Turin and is known as the Turin self-portrait. Unfortunately, it has been severely affected by centuries of exposure to air and light. The paper is now covered with "fox marks" (rusty-brown spots caused by excessive moisture and subsequent accumulation of iron salts), and the drawing is rarely exhibited in public.

In spite of its poor condition, the Turin self-portrait, which has been reproduced in countless posters and books, exerts a powerful effect on the viewer. This is even more true if one is fortunate enough to spend some time with the original, viewing it from different angles and distances, revealing the portrait's complex and subtle expressions. Leonardo drew this portrait at a time of personal uncertainty and discontent. He was well aware that the greater part of his life was behind him; his eyes had weakened and his health was failing. He was living in Rome at the time, where he was revered. But already he was beginning to become out of fashion as an artist, eclipsed by younger rivals like Raphael and Michelangelo, who were in their prime and were the favorites of the papal court.

In Leonardo's self-portrait, this unhappy time is reflected in a line of disillusionment, or perhaps contempt, around the mouth. Yet, under the bushy brows and majestic forehead, his eyes—the "windows of the soul"—have preserved the quiet intensity of his gaze as well as a deep serenity. The resulting expression, to me, is that of a powerful, critical intellect, tempered by wisdom and compassion.

Over the years, the Turin self-portrait has become not only the iconic image of Leonardo, but the model for the archetypal portrait of the old sage in the centuries after him. "This great furrowed mountain of a face," wrote art historian Kenneth Clark, "with its noble brow, cavernous eyes, and undulating foothills of beard is like the faces of all the great men of the nineteenth century as the camera has preserved them for us—Darwin, Tolstoy, Walt Whitman."[9]

A quality that is not visible in Leonardo's self-portrait but was always mentioned by his contemporaries was his kind and gentle nature, in the words of the duchess Isabella d'Este, "this air of sweetness and gentleness that is so characteristic of him." "Leonardo's disposition was so lovable that he commanded everyone's affection," Vasari writes. "He was so generous that he sheltered and fed all his friends, rich or poor." He was also eloquent and charming in conversation. In fact, Vasari claimed he was so persuasive that he could "bend other people to his own will."

Leonardo combined this gentle and charming disposition with great physical strength. In his younger years he was apparently quite an athlete, "most skillful in lifting weights," as the Anonimo Gaddiano tells us, and an excellent horseman. According to Vasari, "he was physically so strong that he could withstand any violence; with his right hand he would bend the iron ring of a doorbell or a horseshoe as if they were lead." Vasari may have exaggerated Leonardo's strength (and we know that Leonardo was left-handed), but his athletic prowess seems to have been well known.

During his years in Milan, he entertained the court with fables, songs, and charming conversation. "He sang beautifully to his own accompaniment on the *lira* to the delight of the entire court," we are told by Paolo Giovio. But Leonardo also pursued his scientific research with intense concentration and needed to escape frequently to spend long periods of time alone. "The painter or draftsman must be solitary," he wrote in the *Treatise on Painting*, "and most of all when he is intent on those speculations and considerations which, continually appearing before the eyes, give material to the memory to be well stored."[10] These frequent withdrawals into periods of solitude, spent in contemplation and sustained observations of nature, likely contributed to the air of mystery that surrounded him.

CHARACTER TRAITS

Throughout his life, Leonardo displayed an air of serene self-confidence, which helped him overcome professional setbacks and disappointments with equanimity and allowed him to calmly pursue his research even during times of great political turbulence. He was well aware of his unique genius and skill, yet he never boasted about them. Nowhere in his Notebooks does he vaunt the originality of his inventions or discoveries, nor does he flaunt the superiority of his ideas, even as he explains how they differ from traditional beliefs. This lack of arrogance and ego was remarkable indeed.

Another quality that distinguished him was his passion for life and for all living things. He immersed himself in the study of living forms not only intellectually, but emotionally as well. He held a great awe and reverence for nature's creativity, and felt particular compassion for animals. His love of horses was well known to his contemporaries, and can be seen in his drawings, in which he used his acute powers of observation to render the animals' movements and "noble proportions" in exquisite detail. Vasari claimed that Leonardo always kept horses. Equally touching is Vasari's famous story of Leonardo buying birds in the marketplace, so that he might set them free:

> Often when he was walking past the places where birds were sold he would pay the price asked, take them from their cages, and let them fly off into the air, giving them back their lost freedom.

His love of animals was also the reason Leonardo became a vegetarian—something unheard-of in Italy during the Renaissance, and therefore widely noticed. Leonardo's justification for his vegetarianism combines his firm moral stance with keen scientific observation. He argued that, unlike plants, animals are sensitive to pain because they are capable of movement, and he did not want to cause them pain and suffering by killing them for food:

Nature has ordained that living organisms with the power of movement should experience pain in order to preserve those parts which might diminish or be destroyed by movement. Living organisms without the power of movement do not have to strike against any opposing objects, so that pain is not necessary in plants, and hence when they are broken they do not feel pain as do animals.[11]

In other words, in Leonardo's mind, animals develop sensitivity to pain because it gives them a selective advantage in avoiding injury when they move about.

By all accounts, Leonardo was a man of unusual tenderness. He had tremendous compassion for the suffering of people and animals. He was vehemently opposed to war, which he called *pazzia bestialissima* ("most bestial madness"). In view of this, it seems contradictory that he should have offered his services as military engineer to various rulers of his time.

Part of the answer to this contradiction had to do with his pragmatic attitude when it came to securing a stable income that would allow him to pursue his scientific research. With his extraordinary talent for designing machines of all kinds, and in view of the endless political rivalries and conflicts on the Italian peninsula, Leonardo shrewdly recognized that employment as a consulting military engineer and architect was one of the best ways to secure his financial independence.

However, it is also clear from his Notebooks that he was fascinated by the destructive engines of war, perhaps in the same way that natural cataclysms and disasters fascinated him. He spent considerable time designing and drawing machines of destruction—bombards, explosive cannonballs, catapults, giant crossbows, and the like, even as he remained adamantly opposed to war and violence.

As biographer Serge Bramly points out, despite his many years of service as military engineer, Leonardo never participated in any offensive action. Most of his advice consisted of designing structures to defend and preserve a town or city.[12] During a conflict between Florence and Pisa, he proposed to divert the river Arno as a means to avoid a bloody battle. He went on to add that this should be followed up with the construction of a navigable waterway that would reconcile the combatants and bring prosperity to both cities.

Leonardo's most explicit condemnation of war consists of a long and detailed description of how to paint a battle, written when he was in his late thirties. Even a few excerpts from this text, which runs over several pages, reveal how vividly the artist intended to picture the horrors of war:

> You will first paint the smoke of the artillery, mingled in the air with the dust raised by the commotion of horses and combatants. . . . Let the air be full of arrows of all kinds, some shooting upwards, some falling, some flying level. The bullets from the firearms will leave a trail of smoke behind them. . . . If you show a man who has fallen to the ground, reproduce his skid marks in the dust, which has been turned into blood-stained mire. . . . Paint a horse dragging the dead body of its master, and leaving behind him in the dust and mud the track where the body was dragged along. Make the vanquished and beaten pale, with brows raised and knit, and the skin above their brows furrowed with pain. . . . Represent others crying out with their mouths wide open and running away . . . ; others in the agonies of death grinding their teeth, rolling their eyes, with their fists clenched against their bodies, and their legs contorted.[13]

A decade after he wrote this, Leonardo, who was then over fifty and at the height of his fame, received a commission for a huge mural, which gave him the opportunity to turn his words into action. The Signoria, the Florentine city government, had decided to celebrate the military glory of Florence by decorating its new council chamber with two large frescoes depicting its victories in two historic battles—against Milan at Anghiari and against Pisa at Cascina. The Signoria commissioned the former fresco from Leonardo and the latter from his young rival Michelangelo.

The Battle of Anghiari was the most important public commission Leonardo had ever received. He completed the huge cartoon (or sketch) within a year, as stipulated in his contract, and then spent over half a

Figure 1-2: Peter Paul Rubens after Leonardo, The Struggle for the Standard, *c. 1600–1608, Musée du Louvre, Paris*

year painting the fresco's central scene, a group of horsemen fighting for a standard. Because of technical problems that resulted in the rapid deterioration of the mural, he never completed the huge painting. (Michelangelo left Florence for Rome to paint the frescoes on the ceiling of the Sistine Chapel, without starting his *Battle of Cascina*.) The central part of Leonardo's composition, known as *The Struggle for the Standard*, remained on the wall of the council chamber in the Palazzo Vecchio for almost sixty years before the Signoria finally had its last traces removed. During those decades it dazzled spectators and was copied by several other Renaissance masters.

Leonardo left many preparatory drawings for *The Battle of Anghiari*, from which art historians have reconstructed the painting's general composition.[14] While he intended to present the unfolding of the battle with great clarity and historical accuracy, Leonardo used the central episode as a symbolic statement exposing the fury and "bestial madness" of war.

The superb copy of *The Struggle for the Standard* by Peter Paul Rubens (Fig. 1-2), now at the Louvre, shows Leonardo's incredibly tight composition of a confused melee in which, in Vasari's words, "fury, hate, and rage are as visible in the men as in the horses." Moreover, by dressing the combatants in unrealistic theatrical costumes rather than in battlefield armor, Leonardo enhanced the symbolic character of the scene, underscoring the artistic declaration of his abhorrence of violence. Had he completed the fresco, and had it survived, it might well stand alongside Picasso's *Guernica* as one of the art world's most forceful condemnations of the folly of war.

SECRECY AND CONTRADICTIONS

Biographers have often been exasperated by the illusive task of presenting a clear picture of Leonardo, the man. He was worldly, eloquent, and charming, but also solitary, accustomed to spending long periods in intense concentration. He had an eminently practical mind, yet delighted in fables, allegories, and fantasies.[15] He displayed physical strength and virile energy as well as refined elegance and feminine grace. As Serge Bramly comments wryly, "With Leonardo, everything seems to have two sides."[16]

Leonardo not only embodied a dynamic tension between contradictory paradoxes in his personality, but he himself was also fascinated by opposites throughout his life. While he searched for a canon of ideal human proportions, he was strangely attracted by grotesque appearances. "He so loved bizarre physiognomies, with beards and hair like savages," Vasari recounts, "that he would follow someone who had caught his attention for a whole day. He would memorize his appearance so well that on his return home he would be able to draw him as if he had him before his very eyes."[17]

Leonardo made many drawings of these "grotesques," which enjoyed great popularity in his time and were the forerunners of the famous caricatures of the eighteenth and nineteenth centuries. Perhaps the most typical of Leonardo's caricatures is a bald, resolute elderly man with a terrific frown and "nutcracker" nose, who is often juxtaposed on the same sheet of paper with a beautiful youth of soft, feminine features. Old age and youth, virility and grace, are examples of the interplay of opposites—of the yang and the yin as they are called in Chinese philosophy—that are so striking in Leonardo's personality and art.

The artist's fascination with grotesque forms also led him to devise the most extravagant, and often quite macabre, practical jokes, which delighted the courtiers in Milan and Rome. At the papal court in Rome, Vasari tells us that Leonardo obtained a large lizard to which he attached "with a mixture of quicksilver some wings, made from the scales stripped from other lizards, which quivered as it walked along. Then, after he had given it eyes, horns, and a beard he tamed the creature, and keeping it in a box he used to show it to his friends and frightened the life out of them." On another occasion, according to Vasari, Leonardo cleaned and scraped the intestines of a bullock and "made them so fine that they could be compressed into the palm of one hand. Then he would fix one end of them to a pair of bellows lying in another room, and when they were inflated they filled the room in which they were and forced anyone standing there into a corner." Reportedly, he perpetrated hundreds of follies of this kind.

The challenge of presenting a consistent portrait of Leonardo da Vinci is further complicated by the fact that he was very secretive about his personal thoughts and feelings. In the thousands of pages of manuscripts that have come down to us, there is barely a trace of Leonardo's emotional life. There are very few affectionate references to anyone, family or friends, and hardly any clues to his feelings about the people and events of his time. While he was a master at expressing subtle emotions in his paintings, it seems that Leonardo kept his own innermost feelings to himself.

This secrecy also extends to his sexuality. It is widely assumed that Leonardo was gay, but there is no definite proof of his homosexuality. Art historians have pointed to various features of his drawings and writings that might indicate that he was attracted to men, and it has often been noted that there is no record of any woman in Leonardo's life, while it was well known that he always seemed to be surrounded by strikingly beautiful young men.[18] But even though there were many openly homosexual and successful Florentine artists in the Renaissance,

Leonardo was as secretive about his sexuality as he was about other aspects of his personal life.

Leonardo was equally secretive about his scientific work. Although he intended to eventually publish the results of his investigations, he kept them hidden away during his entire life, apparently out of fear that his ideas might be stolen.[19] In Milan, he designed his studio so that the platform holding his work could be lowered through the floor to the story below, using a system of pulleys and counterweights, to hide it from inquisitive eyes whenever he was not working.[20]

Much has been made in this context of the fact that Leonardo, who was left-handed, wrote all his notes in mirror writing, from right to left. In fact, he could write with both hands and in either direction. But, like many left-handed people, he probably found it more convenient and faster to write from right to left when he jotted down his personal notes. On the other hand, as Bramly points out, this extraordinary handwriting also suited very well his taste for secrecy.[21]

The main reason Leonardo did not share his scientific knowledge with others, although he shared his knowledge of painting with fellow artists and disciples, was that he regarded it as his intellectual capital—the basis of his skills in engineering and stagecraft, which were the main sources of his regular income. He must have feared that sharing this body of knowledge would have diminished his chances of steady employment.

Moreover, Leonardo did not see science as a collective enterprise the way we see it now. In the words of art historian and classicist Charles Hope, "He had . . . no real understanding of the way in which the growth of knowledge was a cumulative and collaborative process, as was so evidently the case with the major intellectual enterprise of his time, the recovery of the heritage of classical antiquity."[22] Leonardo had no formal education and was not able to read the scholarly books of the time in Latin, but he studied Italian translations whenever he could obtain them. He sought out scholars in various fields to borrow books and elicit information, but he did not share his own discoveries with them—neither in conversations, as far as we know, nor in correspondence or publications.

This secrecy about his scientific work is the one significant respect in which Leonardo was not a scientist in the modern sense. If he had shared his discoveries and discussed them with the intellectuals of his time, his influence on the subsequent development of Western science might well have been as profound as his impact on the history of art. As it was, he had little influence on the scientists who came after him, because his scientific work was hidden during his lifetime and remained locked in his Notebooks long after his death. As the eminent Leonardo scholar Kenneth Keele reflected, "The intellectual loneliness of the artist-scientist Leonardo was not merely contemporary; it has lasted for centuries."[23]

SIGNS OF GENIUS

Since Leonardo da Vinci is widely viewed as the archetype of a genius, it is interesting to ask ourselves what we mean by that term. On what grounds are we justified in calling Leonardo a genius, and how does he compare with other artists and scientists known as geniuses?

During Leonardo's time, the term "genius" did not have our modern meaning of a person endowed with extraordinary intellectual and creative powers.[24] The Latin word *genius* originated in Roman religion, where it denoted the spirit of the *gens*, the family. It was understood as a guardian spirit, first associated with individuals and then also with peoples and places. The extraordinary achievements of artists or scientists were attributed to their genius, or attendant spirit. This meaning of genius was prevalent throughout the Middle Ages and the Renaissance. In the eighteenth century, the meaning of the word changed to its familiar modern meaning to denote these individuals themselves, as in the phrase "Newton was a genius."

Regardless of the term used, the fact that certain individuals possess exceptional and inexplicable creative powers beyond the reach of ordinary mortals was recognized throughout the ages. It was often associated with divine inspiration, especially in connection with poets. For example, in the twelfth century, the German abbess and mystic Hildegard von Bingen was famous throughout Europe as a naturalist, composer, visual artist, poet, and playwright. She herself, however, took no credit for the amazing range and depth of her talents but commented simply that she was "a feather on the breath of God."[25]

In the Italian Renaissance, the association of exceptional creative powers with divine inspiration was expressed in a very direct way by bestowing on those individuals the epithet *divino*. Among the Renaissance masters, Leonardo as well as his younger contemporaries Raphael and Michelangelo were acclaimed as divine.

Since the development of modern psychology, neuroscience, and genetic research, there has been a lively discussion about the origins, mental characteristics, and genetic makeup of geniuses. However, numerous studies of well-known historical figures have shown a bewildering diversity of hereditary, psychological, and cultural factors, defying all attempts to establish some common pattern.[26] While Mozart was a famous child prodigy, Einstein was a late bloomer. Newton attended a prestigious university, whereas Leonardo was essentially self-taught. Goethe's parents were well educated and of high social standing, but Shakespeare's seem to have been relatively undistinguished; and the list goes on.

In spite of this wide range of backgrounds, psychologists have been able to identify a set of mental attributes that seem to be distinctive signs of genius, in addition to exceptional talent in a particular field.[27] All these were characteristic of Leonardo to a very high degree.

The first is an intense curiosity and great enthusiasm for discovery and understanding. This was indeed an outstanding quality of Leonardo, whom Kenneth Clark called "the most relentlessly curious man in history."[28] Another striking sign of genius is an extraordinary capacity for intense concentration over long periods of time. Isaac Newton apparently was able to hold a mathematical problem in his mind for weeks until it surrendered to his mental powers. When asked how he made his remarkable discoveries, Newton is reported to have replied, "I keep the subject constantly before me and wait until the first dawnings open little by little into the full light."[29] Leonardo seems to have worked in a very similar way, and most of the time not only on one but on several problems simultaneously.

We have a vivid testimony of Leonardo's exceptional powers of concentration from his contemporary Matteo Bandello, who described how as a boy he watched the artist paint *The Last Supper*. He would see the master arrive early in the morning, Bandello tells us, climb up onto the scaffolding, and immediately start to work:

He sometimes stayed there from dawn to sundown, never putting down his brush, forgetting to eat and drink, painting without pause. He would also sometimes remain two, three, or four days without touching his brush, although he spent several hours a day standing in front of the work, arms folded, examining and criticizing the figures to himself. I also saw him, driven by some sudden urge, at midday, when the sun was at its height, leaving the Corte Vecchia, where he was working on his marvelous clay horse, to come straight to Santa Maria delle Grazie, without seeking shade, and clamber up onto the scaffolding, pick up a brush, put in one or two strokes, and then go away again.[30]

Closely associated with the powers of intense concentration that are characteristic of geniuses seems to be their ability to memorize large amounts of information in the form of a coherent whole, a single gestalt. Newton kept mathematical proofs he had derived for months in his mind before eventually writing them down and publishing them. Goethe is said to have entertained his fellow passengers on long coach journeys by reciting his novels to them, word for word, before committing them to paper. And then there is the famous story of Mozart, who as a child wrote out a note-perfect score of Gregorio Allegri's *Miserere*, a complex chant for a five-part choir, after hearing it only once.

Leonardo would follow people with striking facial features for hours, memorize their appearance, and then draw them when he was back in his studio, reportedly with complete accuracy. The Milanese painter and writer Giovanni Paolo Lomazzo tells the story of how Leonardo once wished to paint some peasants laughing:

He chose certain men whom he thought appropriate for his purpose, and, after getting acquainted with them, arranged a feast for them with some of his friends. Sitting close to them he then proceeded to tell the maddest and most ridiculous tales imaginable, making them, who were unaware of his intentions, laugh uproariously. Whereupon he observed all their gestures very attentively and those ridiculous things they were doing, and impressed them on his mind; and after they had left, he retired to his room and there made a perfect drawing which moved those who looked at it to laughter, as if they had been moved by Leonardo's stories at the feast.[31]

In subsequent chapters I shall recount the chronology of Leonardo's life, following its trajectory from Vinci, the little hamlet, to Florence, the thriving center of Renaissance art, to the Sforza court in Milan, to the papal court in Rome, and to his final home in the Loire valley in the palace of the king of France. However, the documentations of this rich and fascinating life contain hardly any clues to the sources of Leonardo's genius. Indeed, as classicist Penelope Murray observes in the introduction to her anthology *Genius: The History of an Idea*:

> There remains something fundamentally inexplicable about the nature of such prodigious powers. We attribute the extraordinary quality of, for example, Shakespeare's poetry, Mozart's music and Leonardo's paintings to the genius of their creators because we recognize that such works are not simply the product of learning, technique, or sheer hard work. Of course we can trace sources and influences . . . but no amount of analysis has yet been able to explain the capacities of those rare and gifted individuals who can produce creative work of lasting quality and value.[32]

In view of the persistent failure of scientists to shed light on the origins of genius, it would seem that, after all, Vasari's explanation may still be the best: "Occasionally, in a way that transcends nature, a single person is marvelously endowed by heaven with beauty, grace, and talent in such abundance that he leaves other men far behind, all his actions seem inspired, and indeed everything he does clearly comes from God rather than from human art."

The Universal Man

The intellectual climate of the Renaissance was decisively shaped by the philosophical and literary movement of humanism, which made the capabilities of the human individual its central concern. This was a fundamental shift from the medieval dogma of understanding human nature from a religious point of view. The Renaissance offered a more secular outlook, with heightened focus on the individual human intellect. The new spirit of humanism expressed itself through a strong emphasis on classical studies, which exposed scholars and artists to a great diversity of Greek and Roman philosophical ideas that encouraged individual critical thought and prepared the ground for the gradual emergence of a rational, scientific frame of mind.

In Florence, the cradle of the Renaissance, the humanists' enthusiastic embrace of discovery and learning gave rise to a new human ideal—*l'uomo universale*, the infinitely versatile "universal" man, educated in all branches of knowledge and capable of producing innovations in many of them. This ideal became so firmly associated with the Renaissance that later historians have commonly referred to it as the ideal of the "Renaissance man." In the Florentine society of the fifteenth century, not only artists and philosophers but also merchants and statesmen strove to become "universal." They became learned in Latin and Greek, conversant with the works of Aristotle, and familiar with classical treatises on natural history, geography, architecture, and engineering.[1]

The Florentine humanists were inspired by several individuals in their midst who seemed to perfectly embody the ideal of the *uomo universale*. One of the first and most famous was Leon Battista Alberti, born half a century before Leonardo, to whom he seems the perfect precursor.[2] Alberti, like Leonardo, was said to be blessed with exceptional beauty and great physical strength, and he was also a skilled horseman and gifted musician. Moreover, he was a celebrated architect and accomplished painter, wrote beautiful Latin prose, studied both civil and canonical law as well as physics and mathematics, and was the author of several pioneering treatises on the visual arts. As a young man, Leonardo was fascinated by Alberti: He read him avidly, commented on his writings, and emulated him in his own life and work.

In his later years, Leonardo, of course, surpassed Alberti in both the breadth and depth of his work. The difference between Leonardo and the other "universal men" of the Italian Renaissance was not only that he went much farther than anyone else in his inquiries, asking questions nobody had asked before, but that he transcended the disciplinary boundaries of his time. He did so by recognizing patterns that interconnected forms and processes in different domains and by integrating his discoveries into a unified vision of the world.

Indeed, it seems that this is how Leonardo himself understood the meaning of *universale*. His famous statement, *"Facile cosa è farsi universale"*—"It is easy to become universal"—has often been interpreted to mean that infinite versatility was easy to acquire. When we read his assertion within the context in which it was made, however, an entirely different meaning becomes apparent. While discussing the proportions of the body, Leonardo wrote in his *Treatise on Painting*,

> For a man who knows how, it is easy to become universal, since all land animals resemble each other in the parts of their body, that is, muscles, nerves, and bones, and differ only in length and size.[3]

For Leonardo, in other words, being universal meant to recognize similarities in living forms that interconnect different facets of nature—in this case, anatomical structures of different animals. The recognition that nature's living forms exhibit such fundamental patterns was a key insight of the school of Romantic biology in the eighteenth century. These patterns were called *Urtypen* ("archetypes") in Germany, and in England Charles Darwin acknowledged that this concept played a central role in his early conception of evolution.[4] In the twentieth century, anthropologist and cyberneticist Gregory Bateson expressed the same idea in the succinct phrase "the pattern which connects."[5]

Thus, Leonardo da Vinci was the first in a lineage of scientists who focused on the patterns interconnecting the basic structures and processes of living systems. Today, this approach to science is called "systemic thinking." This, in my eyes, is the essence of what Leonardo meant by *farsi universale*. Freely translating his statement into modern scientific language, I would rephrase it this way: "For someone who can perceive interconnecting patterns, it is easy to be a systemic thinker."

LEONARDO'S SYNTHESIS

Leonardo's synthesis of art and science becomes easier to grasp when we realize that in his time, these terms were not used in the sense in which we understand them today. To his contemporaries, *arte* meant skill (in the sense we still use today when we speak of "the art of medicine," or "the art of management"), while *scientia* meant knowledge, or theory. Leonardo insisted again and again that the "art," or skill, of painting must be supported by the painter's "science," or sound knowledge of living forms, by his intellectual understanding of their intrinsic nature and underlying principles.

He also emphasized that this understanding was a continual intellectual process—*discorso mentale*—and that painting itself, therefore, deserved to be considered an intellectual endeavor.[6] "The scientific and true principles of painting," he wrote in the *Trattato*," are understood by the mind alone without manual operations. This is the theory of painting, which resides in the mind that conceives it."[7] This conception of painting sets Leonardo apart from other Renaissance theorists. He saw it as his mission to elevate his art from the rank of a mere craft to an intellectual discipline on a par with the seven traditional liberal arts. (In the Middle Ages, the seven branches of learning known as the liberal arts were the "trivium" of grammar, logic, and rhetoric, whose study led to the Bachelor of Arts degree, plus the "quadrivium" of arithmetic, geometry, astronomy, and music, which led to the Master of Arts.)

The third element in Leonardo's synthesis, in addition to *arte* (skill) and *scientia* (knowledge), is *fantasia*, the artist's creative imagination. In the Renaissance, confidence in the capabilities of the human individual had become so strong that a new conception of the artist as creator had emerged. Indeed, the Italian humanists were so bold as to compare artistic creations to the creations of God. This comparison was first applied to the creativity of poets, and was then extended, especially by Leonardo, to the painter's creative power:

> If the painter wants to see beauties that make him fall in love, he is the lord who can generate them, and if he wants to see monstrous things that frighten, or funny things that make him laugh, or things that truly arouse compassion, he is their lord and God. . . . In fact, whatever there is in the universe, by essence, presence, or imagination, he has it first in his mind and then in his hands.[8]

For Leonardo, the artist's imagination always remains closely linked to his intellectual understanding of nature. "The inventions of his *fantasia*," explains Martin Kemp, "are never out of harmony with universal dynamics as rationally comprehended; they are fabulous yet not implausible, each element in their composition deriving from the causes and effects of the natural world."[9] At the same time, Leonardo insisted on the divine quality of the painter's creativity. "The godlike nature of the science of painting," he declared, "transforms the painter's mind into a resemblance of the divine mind."[10]

Leonardo realized that *fantasia* is not limited to artists, but rather is a general quality of the human mind. He called all human creations—artifacts as well as works of art—"inventions," and he made an interesting distinction between human inventions and the living forms created by nature. "Nature encompasses only the production of simple things," he argued, "but man from these simple things produces an infinity of compounds."[11]

From the modern scientific perspective, this distinction no longer holds, because we know that in the process of evolution, nature, too, produces living forms through an infinity of new compounds from cells and molecules. However, in a broader sense, Leonardo's distinction is still valid as a distinction between forms that emerge through evolution and forms created by human design. In contemporary scientific language, Leonardo's term "simple things" would be replaced by "emergent structures" and his notion of "compounds" by "designed structures."[12]

Throughout his life, Leonardo referred to himself as an inventor. In his view, an inventor was someone who created an artifact or work of art by assembling various elements into a new configuration that did not appear in nature. This definition comes very close to our notion of a designer, which did not exist in the Renaissance. (Leonardo's term *disegnatore*, sometimes incorrectly translated as "designer," always means "draftsman"; a better equivalent of "designer" is his term *compositore*.) The concept of design as a distinct profession emerged only in the twentieth century as a consequence of mass production and industrial capitalism.[13] During the preindustrial era, design was always an integral part of a larger process that included problem solving, innovation, form giving, decoration, and manufacturing. This process traditionally took place in the domains of engineering, architecture, crafts, and the fine arts.

Accordingly, Leonardo did not separate the design process—the abstract configuration of multiple elements—from the process of material production. However, he always seemed to be more interested in the process of design than in its physical realization. It is worthwhile to recall that most of the machines and mechanical devices he invented, designed, and presented in superb drawings were not built; most of his military inventions and schemes of civil engineering were not realized; and although he was famous as an architect, his name is not connected with any known building. Even as a painter he often seemed to be more interested in the solution of compositional problems—the *discorso mentale*—than in the actual completion of the painting.

It seems to me, then, that the wide-ranging activities and achievements of Leonardo da Vinci, the archetypal *uomo universale*, are best examined within the three categories of artist, designer, and scientist. In his own synthesis, the activities of the inventor, or designer, like those of the artist, are inextricably linked to *scientia*, the knowledge of natural principles. He referred to himself, in one of his most arresting expressions, as "inventor and interpreter between nature and humans."[14]

THE SUBLIME LEFT HAND

In practice, it was Leonardo's exceptional drawing facility that formed the link between the three domains of art, design, and science, as he himself recognized:

> Drawing, [the foundation of painting], teaches the architect to render his building agreeable to the eye; this is what teaches potters, goldsmiths, weavers, embroiderers. It has found the characters by which different languages are expressed; it has given the arithmeticians their ciphers and has taught geometers how to represent their figures; it instructs the experts in perspective, astronomers, machine builders, and engineers.[15]

With his acute powers of observation and his "sublime left hand" (as his friend, the mathematician Luca Pacioli, called it), Leonardo was able to draw, in exquisite detail, flowers, birds in flight, whirlpools, muscles and bones, and human expressions with unparalleled accuracy

Figure 2-1: Madonna and Child and other studies, c. 1478–80, Drawings and Miscellaneous Papers, Vol. III, folio 162r

(see Fig. 2-1). Writing about the studies for his early *Madonnas*, Kenneth Clark comments, "They show his matchless quickness of vision, which allowed him to convey every movement or gesture with the certainty and unconscious grace of a great dancer performing a familiar step."[16]

Leonardo's anatomical drawings were so radical in their conception that they remained unrivaled until the end of the eighteenth century, nearly three hundred years later. Indeed, they have been praised as the beginning of modern anatomical illustration.[17] To present the knowledge he had gathered from his extensive anatomical dissections, Leonardo introduced numerous innovations: drawing structures from several perspectives; drawing in cross sections and "exploded" views; showing the removal of muscles in successive layers to expose the depths of an organ or anatomical feature. None of his predecessors or contemporaries came close to him in anatomical detail and accuracy.

To the few of his contemporaries who were privileged to see them, Leonardo's anatomical manuscripts must have seemed almost miraculous. When the Cardinal of Aragon visited the old master in France in 1517, his secretary, Antonio de Beatis, wrote in his journal: "This gentleman has written a treatise on anatomy, showing the limbs, muscles, nerves, veins, joints, intestines, and everything that can be explained in the body of men and women, in a way that has never been done by anyone before."[18]

Leonardo called his anatomical drawings "demonstrations," adopting a terminology typically used by mathematicians to refer to their diagrams, and he proudly asserted that they gave "true knowledge of [various] shapes, which is impossible for either ancient or modern writers . . . without an immense, tedious and confused amount of writing and time."[19] Indeed, when looking through the Anatomical Studies, it is evident that Leonardo's main focus is on the drawings. The accompanying text is secondary, and sometimes absent altogether. In a way, these manuscripts are reminiscent of modern scientific papers in which the main statements are the mathematical equations, with a few explanatory lines between them (see Fig. 2-2).

Leonardo used the same innovative techniques that he perfected in his anatomical drawings in his vast collection of technical drawings of mechanisms and machines. A multitude of mechanical elements in dif-

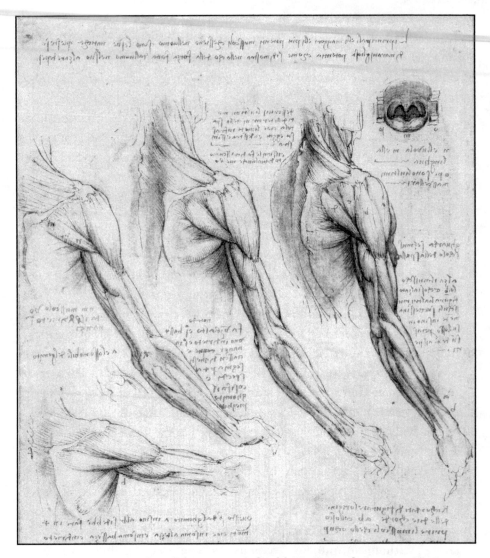

*Figure 2-2: Muscles of the arm and shoulder in rotated views, c. 1510,
Anatomical Studies, folio 141v*

ferent combinations are presented in cutaway or exploded views and
from many sides, with great mastery of visual perspective and subtle
renderings of light and shade (see Fig. 2-3). Drawings of similar machines were produced by other Renaissance engineers. However, as art

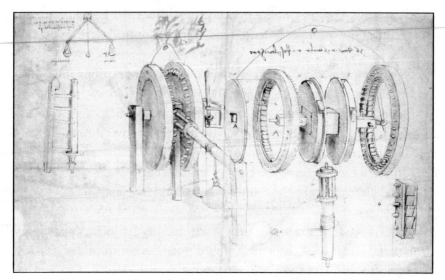

Figure 2-3: Two-wheeled hoist, Codex Atlanticus, folio 30v

historian Daniel Arasse points out, while theirs are merely explanatory, Leonardo's are *convincing*, persuading the viewer of the feasibility and soundness of the author's designs:

> His working drawings not only possess a rare elegance; they are visually put in context, and they have the concrete appearance of objects which exist: the angle or angles of view, the subtlety of the shadows and the treatment of the background itself on which they are drawn gives them an extraordinarily persuasive . . . effectiveness.[20]

As an artist, Leonardo introduced a novelty into the practice of preparatory drawing, which forms an intriguing counterpoint to the precision of his scientific and technical drawings.[21] In many studies for his paintings, he would go over the outlines of a figure again and again, sketching several alternative lines and variations of the figure's position, until he found the ideal form. These preparatory sketches have an extraordinary dynamic quality. One can almost feel the rhythm of Leonardo's "sublime left hand" as he tries out different possibilities, translating his *discorso mentale* into a blur of lines. In Leonardo's time, this technique was unprecedented, as Martin Kemp describes:

> Never before had any artist worked out his compositions in such a welter of alternative lines. The pattern-book drawing techniques of the fourteenth and fifteenth centuries, which Verrocchio had relaxed in some measure, have here been overthrown in a "brain storm" of dynamic sketching. Such flexibility of preparatory sketching became the norm for later centuries; it was introduced almost single-handedly by Leonardo.[22]

Sometimes—as, for example, in a study for his famous *Madonna and Child with Saint Anne*—Leonardo would push his technique of dynamic sketching to an extreme, producing what Arasse describes as "an unreadable blur. Nothing can any longer be distinguished in this chaos, but his eye has perceived in the movement of his hand the hidden, buried, latent form, straining to become a figure. Leonardo marks this with a stylus and, turning the sheet over, makes it visible with a distinct line."[23]

To me, this is a fascinating visual illustration of the process known to complexity theorists as "emergence"—the spontaneous emergence of new forms of order out of chaos and confusion.[24] According to complexity theory, creativity—the generation of new forms—is a key property of all life, and it involves the very process that Leonardo revealed in his exquisite preparatory drawings. I would argue that our most creative insights emerge from such states of uncertainty and confusion.

THE SOUL OF PAINTING

Although he kept his scientific ideas to himself, Leonardo freely shared his views on painting with his students and fellow artists. At his death he left over six hundred pages of detailed instructions for painters, covering all aspects of his science and art of painting. From this vast collection, scattered through eighteen of Leonardo's Notebooks (over half of which, as noted earlier, are now lost), his friend and disciple

Francesco Melzi compiled the famous anthology known as *Trattato della pittura (Treatise on Painting)*.[25] First published in 1651, it was soon translated throughout Europe, and remained a standard text for art students for three centuries.

The first part of the *Trattato*, known as the "Paragone" ("Comparison"), is a long polemical "debate" comparing painting to poetry, music, and sculpture.[26] This kind of polemic was fashionable in the fifteenth century, and Leonardo's highly original arguments in favor of painting are so lively and witty that we can easily imagine him presenting them in an actual debate.

"Painting serves a more noble sense than poetry," he argues, "and renders the figures of the works of nature with more truth than the poet does." He continues in a lighter vein: "Take a poet who describes the beauties of a lady to her lover, and take a painter who represents her, and you will see where nature will turn the enamored judge."[27] Music ought to be called "the younger sister of painting," Leonardo suggests, "since it composes harmony from the conjunctions of its proportional parts. . . . Yet painting excels and rules over music, because it does not immediately die after its creation the way the unfortunate music does."[28] What about sculpture? Surely, no painting endures as well as marble or bronze? True, he admits, "sculpture has the greatest resistance to time." Nevertheless, painting is far superior, because sculpture "will not produce lucid and transparent bodies like the veiled figures that show the nude flesh under the veils laid against it. It will not produce the minute pebbles of varied colors below the surface of transparent waters." Sculptors, he continues, "cannot represent . . . mirrors and similar lustrous things, nor mists, nor bad weather, nor infinite other things that I need not mention because it would be too tedious."[29]

The deeper purpose of Leonardo's lively polemic was to advance persuasive arguments for considering painting as a mental activity and a science, far above the rank of a mere craft. At the beginning of the Renaissance, painting was classified as a "mechanical art," together with crafts like gold and metal work, jewelry, tapestry, and embroidery. None of these mechanical arts stood out in terms of prestige, and their practitioners remained relatively anonymous. Commissions would typically specify the quality of the raw materials (gold leaf, lapis lazuli, etc.), which was more important to the patron than the name of the artist.[30]

When Florence became a major artistic center in the fourteenth century, its painters began to share their knowledge and experience, and collectively developed many technical innovations. They perfected the fresco technique (the art of painting *al fresco*, that is, on freshly spread moist plaster), introduced panel painting, and, a century later, pioneered perspective and oil painting. The Florentine painters and sculptors also established an elaborate apprenticeship system, with strict quality control under the supervision of professional guilds, all of which enhanced their prestige and gradually elevated their professions above the anonymous world of craftsmen.

Leonardo committed himself to advancing this process of emancipation, to convince society that painting should be considered an intellectual enterprise, a true liberal art. To distinguish painting from manual labor, Alberti, in his 1435 book *De Pictura (On Painting)*, had already discussed the importance of mathematics, one of the liberal arts of the time, as the foundation of perspective and the geometry of shadows, and by implication as the intellectual core of painting as a whole.[31] Leonardo followed in Alberti's footsteps but then went beyond him by promoting painting as an intellectual discipline based not only on mathematics but on the theoretical knowledge of "all the qualities of forms."[32]

As a painter, Leonardo excelled especially in modeling subtle gradations of light and dark, known to art historians as chiaroscuro. He revolutionized painting by completely reconceptualizing traditional techniques. "In his use of light and shade, Leonardo was the precursor of all subsequent European painting," writes Kenneth Clark."[33]

The essence of Leonardo's innovation lies in his use of shadow as a unifying element, a theme that brings out different qualities of tone and color. As Martin Kemp explains in his discerning analysis of Leonardo's *Virgin of the Rocks*,

> From [the] soft substratum of velvety shadow emerge the colors, revealed only by the presence of light. . . . Within this unity of shadow an infinite subtle series of adjustments are made to ac-

commodate the inherent tonal values of different colors, from the lightest yellow to the deepest of blues.[34]

One of the hallmarks of a master painter in the Florentine tradition was the ability to represent figures in apparent three-dimensional relief. "The first task of the painter," writes Leonardo, "is to make a flat surface appear as a body in relief, standing out from that surface, and he who surpasses the others in that skill deserves most praise."[35] As Kenneth Clark explains, Leonardo was not content to achieve this effect by "the subtle combination of drawing and surface modeling which the painters of the quattrocento [fifteenth century] had brought to perfection. He wished to achieve relief through the scientific use of light and shade."[36] According to Leonardo, such an achievement is "the soul of painting."[37]

Leonardo's technique of using light and shade to give his figures "great vigor and relief," as Vasari put it, culminated in his celebrated creation of sfumato, the subtle melting of shades that eventually became the unifying principle of his paintings. "Leonardo's *sfumato* was the power behind the poetry of his paintings," Arasse claimed, "and the mystery that seems to emanate from them."[38]

It is clear from Leonardo's writings on the use of light and shade that he derived his knowledge from a series of systematic experiments with lamps shining on a variety of geometrical solids. He drew numerous complex diagrams showing the formation, projection, intersections, and gradations of shadows in endless combinations. As I will show later in the book, his detailed investigations of vision, the nature of light and shadow, and the appearance of forms were the gateway to his science of painting.[39]

Leonardo's earliest existing notes on shadow and light date from around 1490,[40] but it is evident from his *Virgin of the Rocks* (1483–86) that he had thoroughly mastered the basic concepts several years earlier. His power of observation, combined with his intuitive understanding of light, allowed him to render not only the most subtle gradations of chiaroscuro, but also complex secondary effects of light— reflected sheens, areas of diffused light, subtle glows, and the like— with unprecedented mastery. According to Kemp, "No one until the nineteenth century was to achieve a comparable level of intensity in depicting the elusive complexities of visual phenomena."[41]

DISCORSO MENTALE

Leonardo could not have developed his mastery of chiaroscuro, nor his characteristic sfumato style, without a major advance in Renaissance painting—the use of oil-based paints. Oil painting makes it possible to put layers of paint on top of each other without blurring the colors (provided the layers are allowed to dry individually), to go back over work again and again, and to mix paints at ease, all of which were essential for Leonardo to achieve his special effects of relief and sfumato.

Oil painting is said to have been invented by the Flemish master Jan van Eyck. According to Vasari, the technique was introduced in Italy first in Naples, Urbino, and Venice before eventually reaching Florence, where it caused a sensation. When Leonardo was an apprentice in Verrocchio's workshop, the Tuscan painters had not yet fully mastered the technique of oils. Leonardo became a major figure in its perfection, together with his fellow student Perugino, who passed their secrets on to Raphael.[42]

Over the years, Leonardo achieved a sublime mastery in applying the finest layers of paint to create the luminous color tones that give his paintings their special magic. As Serge Bramly describes it, "The light passes through his paintings as if through stained glass, straight on to the primed surface beneath, which reflects it back, thus creating the impression that it emanates from the figures themselves."[43]

The slow and careful process of painting that is required by oils was ideal for Leonardo's approach. He could spend weeks between layers of paint, and could rework and refine his panels for years, reflecting on every detail of their conception, engaging in the mental discourse that he saw as the essence of his art and science. This *discorso mentale*, the intellectual process of painting, was often more important to Leonardo than the actual completion of the work. Consequently, the total output of his life as a painter was relatively small, especially in view of the profound impact he had on the subsequent history of European art.

On the other hand, Leonardo's completed masterpieces always involved radical innovations at several levels—artistic, philosophical, and scientific. For example, the *Virgin of the Rocks* (Fig. 2-4) was not

Figure 2-4: Virgin of the Rocks, *c. 1483–86, Musée du Louvre, Paris*

only revolutionary in its rendering of light and dark. It also represented a complex and controversial meditation on the destiny of Christ, expressed through the gestures and relative positions of the four protagonists, as well as in the intricate symbolism of the surrounding rocks and vegetation.[44]

The rocks themselves are rendered with astounding geological accuracy. Leonardo depicted a complex geological formation involving soft, weathered sandstone dissected by a layer of harder rock known to geologists as diabase. Numerous fine details in the rocks' textures and weathering patterns show the artist's profound knowledge, unmatched in his time, of such geological formations.[45] And finally—in a dramatic departure from the traditional decorative use of plants in the quattrocento—the plants growing in the surroundings of the rocky grotto are rendered not only in exquisite botanical detail but also in their proper habitat, with complete seasonal and ecological accuracy.[46]

Observations of similar innovations can be made in *The Last Supper*, the *Mona Lisa*, or the *Madonna and Child with Saint Anne*. It is no wonder that each of these masterpieces caused great commotion among Leonardo's contemporaries, generating animated discussions and numerous copies, which expanded the master's *discorso mentale* throughout Europe's artistic and intellectual circles.

IL CAVALLO

In the "Paragone," Leonardo introduces one of his lengthy arguments about the superiority of painting over sculpture with the following self-assured words:

> As I apply myself in sculpture no less than in painting, and practice both in the same degree, it seems to me that without being suspected of unfairness I can judge which of the two is of greater ingenuity and of greater difficulty and perfection.[47]

In a similar vein, Vasari refers to Leonardo as "Florentine painter and sculptor" in the title of his biography. And yet, we have no known sculpture from Leonardo's hand. His reputation as a sculptor rests on a single piece of work: a monumental bronze horse that was never cast, but which occupied Leonardo intensely for over ten years.

When he was in his late thirties and employed as "painter and engineer" at the court of Ludovico Sforza in Milan, Leonardo received a commission for an equestrian statue honoring the duke's father. The city's tremendous wealth at the time encouraged grandiose schemes, and accordingly Ludovico wanted the equestrian monument to be *grandissimo*, perhaps three or four times life-size. A bronze sculpture of that size had never been attempted before. The unprecedented challenges of the project fascinated Leonardo, and even though he was generally not fond of sculpture, he eagerly accepted the commission. It was a project that would draw on his scientific interests in anatomy, proportion, and the animal body in motion as well as his engineering skills and artistic talent. Beautifully told by Serge Bramly in his biography *Leonardo: Discovering the Life of Leonardo da Vinci*, the episode is closely linked to the fluctuating fortunes of the Sforza dynasty.[48]

At first, Leonardo considered a horse rearing over a vanquished enemy. The forceful vitality of that image appealed to him, but the structural problems turned out to be forbidding even for his genius. How could he create a horse weighing many tons that could stand on two legs? Even if he created additional support by making one of the forelegs rest on the vanquished enemy, how could he cast and balance the entire group? After a long and careful examination of these staggering technical difficulties, Leonardo abandoned the idea of a rearing horse and eventually settled on the classical pose of an antique equestrian statue, known as the Regisole, which he had greatly admired in Pavia.[49] He had been especially impressed by the statue's natural grace. "The movement is more praiseworthy than anything else," he jotted down in his notebook. "The trot almost has the quality of a free horse."[50]

While he pondered various poses of the bronze horse and the associated engineering problems, Leonardo seemed to have completely forgotten its rider. The statue of Duke Francesco, clad in armor, was to be cast separately and added later, but over the years Leonardo became so absorbed by the physical beauty, proportions, and movements of the horse that he referred to the monument simply as *il cavallo*.

Once he settled on the final pose of the horse, Leonardo repeatedly visited the princely stables of Ludovico as well as those of other wealthy Milanese noblemen in search of models for his *cavallo*. He identified several superb thoroughbreds, measured them meticulously to determine their proportions, and drew them from life in numerous positions. In typical fashion, he got carried away with the intellectual aspects of the undertaking, expanded it into a major research project, and ended up with a full treatise on the anatomy of the horse.[51] In addition, he produced a wealth of artistic studies of horses, now assembled in a special volume of the Royal Collection at Windsor Castle. In the opinion of art critic Martin Kemp, "No one has ever captured more convincingly the rippling beauty of a finely bred and groomed horse."[52]

Finally, after four years of preparatory studies, Leonardo built a full-scale model of the sculpture out of clay. At a height of slightly over twenty-three feet, it towered over the most famous equestrian statues of the time—that of Marcus Aurelius on the Capitol in Rome, Donatello's *Gattamelata* in Padua, and Verrocchio's *Colleoni* in Venice. Not surprisingly, the colossal model generated enormous excitement when it was displayed in front of the Sforza castle on the occasion of the marriage of Ludovico's niece Bianca Maria to the emperor Maximilian. "The vehement, life-like action of this horse, as if panting, is amazing," wrote Paolo Giovio, "not less so the sculptor's skill and his consummate knowledge of nature." Vasari claimed that those who saw the clay model felt that they had never seen a more magnificent piece of work. The court poets composed Latin epigrams in praise of the *gran cavallo*, and Leonardo's fame as a sculptor soon spread throughout Italy.

While completing the model, Leonardo thought deeply about the tremendous challenge of casting such a large piece. He collected all his notes on the subject in seventeen folios of a book (now bound at the end of the Codex Madrid II), beginning with the words: "Here a record shall be kept of everything related to the bronze horse presently under construction."[53]

The traditional method of casting was to divide the work into several smaller pieces to be cast separately, but Leonardo concluded that it would not be possible to make all the pieces of uniform thickness. As a result, he would not be able to estimate their weight and establish in advance the overall balance of the sculpture. Having investigated all aspects of the problem with his usual attention to meticulous details, he decided to cast the horse in one piece, something that had never been attempted before. His voluminous notes have allowed art historians to reconstruct Leonardo's method in detail.[54] It involved digging a huge pit to bury the mold upside down, so that the molten metal could run in through the animal's belly while the air escaped upward through the feet.

Leonardo left very detailed and beautiful drawings of the iron framework he had designed for the horse's head and neck, held in place by an ingenious set of hooks and wires. Other drawings show the wooden frame he intended to build for transporting the giant mold, as well as the elaborate machinery for maneuvering it. His descriptions cover every conceivable aspect of the casting process—from recipes for alloys and methods for controlling the temperature in the furnaces to dress rehearsals with small-scale models.

By early 1494, everything was ready for the casting. The materials had been acquired, and a start was probably made on digging the pit and building four specially designed furnaces around it. But then political necessity intervened. During the previous two years, several Italian political leaders had died, European alliances had shifted, and now Charles VIII, the new king of France, was about to attack Milan. Under this imminent threat, Ludovico decided to use Leonardo's precious seventy-two tons of bronze for new cannon instead of the *gran cavallo*. Leonardo remained optimistic that he would be able to proceed eventually, and continued to work on his project. But Ludovico ran out of money. It became clear that the glorious monument would never be cast. About a year later, Leonardo attached a simple note to a letter he had written to the duke: "About the horse I will say nothing, for I know the times."[55]

Leonardo's molds were never used, and his giant clay model eventually crumbled and decayed. His fame as a sculptor, however, lived on, as did his novel method of casting. Two hundred years later, it was used in France to make an enormous equestrian statue of Louis XIV, almost as tall as the *gran cavallo*. "Even the stance of the horse was the same," Bramly tells us, "and by remarkable coincidence, the same bad luck attended the statue: it was destroyed during the Revolution, so we cannot see it. But the fact that it was cast at all shows that [Leonardo's] method was sound."[56]

LEONARDO THE DESIGNER

Upon reflecting on the great diversity of Leonardo's interests and pursuits, virtually all those that cannot be seen strictly as "art" or "science" may be subsumed under the broad category of "design." The notion of design as a distinct discipline emerged only in the twentieth century: As a result, viewing Leonardo as a designer means applying a modern category that did not exist in his time.[57] Nevertheless, it seems intriguing to examine his wide-ranging pursuits from our contemporary perspective.

Design, then and now, has always been an integral part of a larger process of giving form to objects.[58] At its outset, the design process is purely conceptual, involving the visualization of images, the arrangement of elements into a pattern in response to specific needs, and the drawing of a series of sketches representing the designer's ideas. All these are activities that fascinated Leonardo and in which he excelled.

As the design process matures and moves closer to the implementation phase, its dependence on other disciplines increases. Hence, we classify different types of design according to the domains in which they operate. Today's design disciplines include those associated with civil, military, and mechanical engineering; architectural design; landscape and garden design; urban design; fashion and costume design; stage and theatrical design; and graphic design. Leonardo da Vinci was active in all these "design disciplines" throughout his life.

Good designers have the ability to think systemically and to synthesize. They excel at visualizing things, at organizing known elements into new configurations, at creating new relationships; and they are skillful in conveying these mental processes in the form of drawings almost as rapidly as they occur. Leonardo, of course, possessed all these abilities to a very high degree. In addition, he had an uncanny knack of perceiving and solving technical problems—another key characteristic of a good designer—so much so, in fact, that it was almost second nature to him.

Many of the machines and mechanical devices he drew were not original. But when he took them from sketches of earlier inventors, he would invariably modify and improve their design, often beyond recognition. When he worked on the large cartoon of *The Battle of Anghiari*, he constructed an ingenious scaffolding, according to Vasari, "which he could raise or lower by drawing it together or extending it." While he spent long hours in the Sforza stables drawing thoroughbred horses from life, he also designed and sketched a model stable featuring automated supply lines of fodder and water as well as runoffs for liquid manure, which would provide the basis for the Medici stables twenty-five years later.[59] Whatever he was engaged in, technical innovations were never far from Leonardo's mind.

FROM ENGINEERING TO SCIENCE

It was during his employment as "painter and engineer" at the Sforza court that Leonardo's technical inventiveness came into full bloom. The duties of an artist at a Renaissance court included, besides painting portraits and designing pageants and festivities, a variety of small engineering jobs that demanded unusual ingenuity and skills in the handling of materials.[60] Leonardo's many creative talents were perfectly suited for this. He invented a large number of astonishing devices during this time, which brought him considerable fame as an engineer-magician.

Many of these inventions were extraordinary for the period.[61] Among them were doors that opened and closed automatically by means of counterweights; a table lamp with variable intensity; folding furniture; an octagonal mirror that generated an infinite number of multiple images; and an ingenious spit, in which "the roast will turn slow or fast, depending upon whether the fire is moderate or strong."[62] Other inventions of a more industrial nature included a press for making olive oil, and a variety of textile machines for spinning, weaving, twisting hemp, trimming felt, and making needles.[63] Leonardo remained an avid inventor throughout his life. The total number of inventions attributed to him has been estimated at three hundred.[64]

But this combination of artist-engineer was not unusual in the Renaissance. Leonardo's teacher Verrocchio, for example, was a renowned goldsmith, sculptor, and painter as well as a reputable engineer. The great Renaissance architect Brunelleschi was trained as a goldsmith and first gained notice in Florence as a sculptor. Later on, when he was famous as an architect, he was also acclaimed for his inventive genius as an engineer, both civil and military. Brunelleschi died six years before Leonardo was born. The young Leonardo admired him greatly and declared his indebtedness to the great architect by drawing several of Brunelleschi's renowned lifting devices and architectural plans.[65]

What made Leonardo unique as a designer and engineer, however, was that many of the novel designs he presented in his Notebooks involved technological advances that would not be realized until several centuries later.[66] And second, he was the only man among the famous Renaissance engineers who made the transition from engineering to science. Like painting, engineering became a "mental discourse" for him. To know *how* something worked was not enough for Leonardo; he also needed to know *why*. Thus an inevitable process was set in motion, which led him from technology and engineering to pure science. As art historian Kenneth Clark notes, we can see the process at work in Leonardo's manuscripts:

> First, there are questions about the construction of certain machines, then . . . questions about the first principles of dynamics; finally, questions which had never been asked before about winds, clouds, the age of the earth, generation, the human heart. Mere curiosity has become profound scientific research, independent of the technical interests which had preceded it.[67]

ARCHITECTURAL DESIGN

Leonardo was active in the field of architecture throughout his life, but his name is not associated with any church or other building, nor is he mentioned in any architectural contract. Yet he was praised as an "excellent architect" by his contemporaries, and art historians such as Ludwig Heydenreich and Carlo Pedretti feel that he deserved this reputation.[68]

In architecture, as in many other fields, Leonardo's main interest was in design. His Notebooks are full of architectural drawings; he produced numerous designs for villas, palaces, and cathedrals, and he was often consulted as an expert on architectural problems.[69] However, his drawings are not of the kind that a patron would expect from a professional architect. They are never precise proposals or detailed plans, and, as Daniel Arasse observes, they are remarkably free of "any studies of the details of architectural vocabulary (columns, capitals, frames, cornices, moldings, and so on). It is the syntax, the logical linking and the reciprocal organization of the parts of the building that interest Leonardo."[70]

In other words, the problems Leonardo addresses are theoretical problems of architectural design. The questions he asks are the same questions he explores throughout his science of organic forms—questions about patterns, spatial organization, rhythm, and flow. The notes accompanying his drawings (written in his customary mirror writing, and hence intended for himself) can be seen as fragments of a treatise on architecture that Leonardo, according to Heydenreich, may have intended to compose.[71]

As a result of his unique systemic approach to architecture, Leonardo's architectural design is characterized by a remarkable indifference to classical forms and a high degree of originality. "The solutions which he imagines," writes Arasse, "are invariably (brilliantly) unconventional—that is to say, they are not 'classical,' being simultaneously Gothic in some respects and already Mannerist in others."[72]

Leonardo's originality revealed itself in his seemingly effortless integration of architecture and complex geometry. This is especially apparent in his many designs of centralized, radially symmetric churches and "temples" (see Fig. 2-5). Although churches with such central plans were a favorite design of Alberti, Brunelleschi, and other Renaissance architects, the playful clusters of geometric patterns—almost reminiscent of the fractals of today's complexity theory—are unique to Leonardo. "The mathematical integration of the parts," observes Martin Kemp, "somehow achieves a compelling sense of organic unity in the exterior perspective of the building in a way which is uniquely his own. Equally impressive and characteristic is the spatial

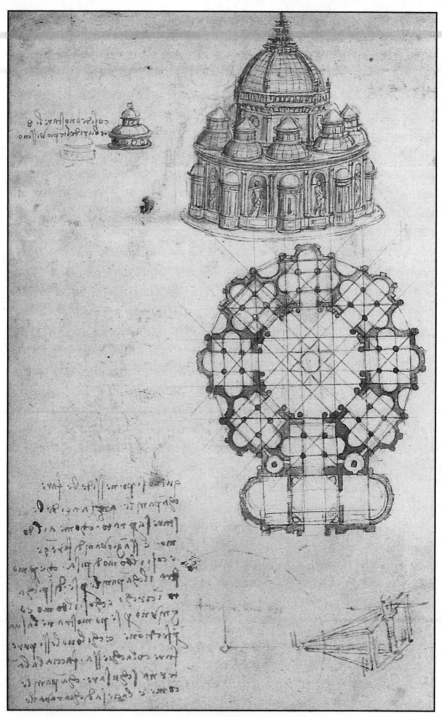

Figure 2-5: Design for Centralized "Temple," c. 1488,
Ms. Ashburnham I, folio 5v

vision which allows him to display his design as a fully three-dimensional concept, like a piece of sculpture, rather than as a compound of plan and flat elevations."[73]

In view of Leonardo's central focus on understanding nature's forms, both in the macro- and the microcosm, it is not surprising that he emphasized similarities between architectural structures and structures in nature, especially in human anatomy. In fact, this linking of architecture and anatomy goes back to antiquity and was common among Renaissance architects, who recognized the analogy between a good architect and a good doctor.[74] As Leonardo explained,

> Doctors, teachers, and those who nurse the sick should understand what man is, what is life, what is health, and in what manner a parity and concordance of the elements maintains it, while a discordance of these elements ruins and destroys it. . . . The same is also needed for the ailing cathedral, that is, a doctor-architect who understands well what a building is and from what rules the correct way of building derives.[75]

However, Leonardo went beyond the common analogies, for example, comparing the dome of a church to the human cranium, or the arches in its vaulting to the rib cage. Just as he was keenly interested in the body's metabolic processes—the ebb and flow of respiration, and the transport of nutrients and waste products in the blood—he also paid special attention to the "metabolism" of a building, studying how stairs and doors facilitate movement through the building.[76] A sheet from the Windsor Collection showing a diagram of human blood vessels next to a series of sketches of stairs makes it clear that Leonardo consciously applied the metaphor of metabolic processes in his architectural designs.[77]

Leonardo's special attention to how movements would flow through his buildings was not restricted to the interiors, but included the surrounding grounds as well, by means of doorways, loggias, and balconies. In fact, in most of his designs of villas and palaces, he considered the garden to be an integral part of the house. These designs reflect his continual efforts to integrate architecture and nature. The emergence and evolution of the Renaissance garden, and Leonardo's original contributions to landscape and garden design, are discussed in great detail by botanist William Emboden in his beautiful volume *Leonardo da Vinci on Plants and Gardens*.[78]

A further extension of Leonardo's organic view of buildings and his special focus on their "metabolism" is apparent in his pioneering contributions to urban design. When he witnessed the plague in Milan shortly after his arrival in the city in 1482, he realized that its devastating effects were largely due to Milan's appalling sanitary conditions. In typical fashion, he responded with a proposal for rebuilding the city in a way that would provide decent housing for people and shelters for animals, and would allow the streets to be cleaned regularly by flushing them with water. "One needs a fast flowing river to avoid the corrupt air produced by stagnation," Leonardo reasoned, "and this will also be useful for regularly cleansing the city when opening the sluices."[79]

Leonardo's design of the ideal city was radical for the time. He suggested dividing the population into ten townships along the river, each with approximately thirty thousand inhabitants. In this way, he wrote, "you will disperse such great agglomeration of people, packed like a herd of goats, on each other's backs, who fill every corner with their stench and sow the seeds of pestilence and death."[80]

In each township there would be two levels—an upper level for pedestrians and a lower level for vehicles—with stairs connecting them. The upper level would have arcaded walkways and beautiful houses with terraced gardens. At the lower level would be shops and storage areas for goods, as well as roads and canals for delivering the goods with carts and boats. In addition, Leonardo's design included underground canals to carry away sewage and "fetid substances."[81]

It is clear from Leonardo's notes that he saw the city as a kind of living organism in which people, material goods, food, water, and waste needed to move and flow with ease for the city to remain healthy. Ludovico, unfortunately, did not implement any of Leonardo's novel ideas. Had he done so, the history of European cities might have been quite different. As physician Sherwin Nuland points out, "Leonardo had envisioned a city based on principles of sanitation and public health that would not be appreciated for centuries."[82]

Two years before he died, Leonardo had another opportunity to reflect on urban design when he was asked by the king of France to draw up plans for a new capital and royal residence.[83] Once more, Leonardo designed a city crisscrossed with canals, to be used not only for the water supply of splendid fountains but also for irrigation, transportation, and for cleaning the city and removing waste. Again, Leonardo insisted on the importance of water circulation for the health of the urban organism. This time, work on the huge project was actually begun, but it was abandoned a few years later when an epidemic decimated the workforce.

Leonardo's idea of urban health, based on the view of the city as a living system, was reconceived very recently, in the 1980s, when the World Health Organization initiated its Healthy Cities Project in Europe.[84] Today, the Healthy Cities movement is active in over one thousand cities around the world, most likely without participants being aware that the principles on which it is based were set forth by Leonardo da Vinci more than five centuries ago.

THE ARTIST AS MAGICIAN

One of the essential duties of the courtly artist in the Renaissance was to design the settings and scenery for court festivities—pageants and theatrical performances—with all the accessory decorations, costumes, and ephemeral architecture. Through these spectacles, the artist created for the court the images of magnificence, wealth, and power that its ruler wanted to project. The Sforza court in Milan was famous for the ostentatious affluence of its pageants, which took place at annual religious festivals as well as at a series of spectacular royal weddings. Leonardo was well aware of the importance of his role in creating dazzling spectacles for such events. He dedicated considerable time and energy to these tasks and excelled in them no less than in his other artistic pursuits. Indeed, as Arasse points out, during his lifetime "Leonardo [owed] much of his fame to his unrivaled talents as artist of the ephemeral."[85]

Theatrical performances in particular were an ideal vehicle for Leonardo to show his diversity and brilliance as a designer. For many plays at court he acted as producer, stage and costume designer, and makeup artist as well as inventor of stage machinery.[86] He carefully studied these theatrical arts and went on to create many innovations. For example, it was Leonardo who invented the first revolving stage in the history of the theater; he was also the first to raise the curtain, rather than have it fall at the start of the performance, as had been the custom.[87]

For the most elaborate performances, Leonardo combined his skills of painting, costume design, musical composition, and engineering to create a complete spectacle, with moving scenery and "special effects" produced by his stage machines. To his contemporaries, these performances were awe-inspiring, bordering on magic. For example, in the production of Baldassare Taccone's *Danaë*, Leonardo created dazzling illusions of Zeus's transformation into golden rain, and of Danaë's metamorphosis into a star. During the latter "the audience could see a star . . . rising up slowly towards heaven, with sounds so powerful that it seemed the palace would fall down."[88] When he staged the play *Orfeo* by Angelo Poliziano, Leonardo invented a system of gearwheels and counterweights to create a mountain that would suddenly split open, revealing Pluto on his throne, rising from the depths of the under-world, accompanied by terrifying sounds and illuminated by "infernal" lights.[89] These spectacular performances firmly established Leonardo's fame as a brilliant engineer and peerless magician of the stage.

INTERWOVEN STRANDS

The tapestries and other decorative elements designed for the courtly pageants and "masques" usually included elaborate emblems and allegories, rich in symbolism and wordplay, which served to glorify the ruling powers. Leonardo produced many of these allegorical drawings, with complex symbolic messages, many of which have been impossible for modern scholars to interpret. He also became fascinated with and used a more abstract kind of emblem featuring tangled curves in the form of knots and scrolls. These knot designs, which were very popular in the late fifteenth century, were known as *fantasie dei vinci*, after the reeds *(vinci)* used in basketry. Exploiting the fortuitous connection with his name, Leonardo used such interlaced *vinci* motifs as his signature designs in numerous sketches.[90]

During his last two years at the Sforza court, Leonardo created the ultimate emblem for Prince Ludovico—a vast and complex *fantasia dei vinci* that covered the walls and vaulted ceiling of an entire room. Known as the Sala delle Asse (Room of the Wooden Boards), this is a large square room in the north tower of the Sforza Castle, in which four lunettes on each wall combine to generate an elaborate vaulting. Leonardo's highly inventive decoration shows a grove of mulberry trees rooted in rocky subsoil, their trunks rising up to the ceiling like columns supporting the actual vaulting, their branches crisscrossing the vault in a Gothic rib structure of elegantly intertwined curves.[91] The smaller twigs and leaves form a luxuriant tangled labyrinth of greenery spreading around the walls and across the ceiling. The entire composition is held together by a single endless golden ribbon winding in and out of the branches, in the complex arabesques of traditional knot designs.

The painting in the Sala delle Asse is remarkable on several levels. With his extensive knowledge of plants, Leonardo gave the branches and leaves a surprisingly realistic appearance of exuberant growth, and he gracefully and beautifully integrated these natural growth patterns into the existing architectural structure and into the geometry of the formal decoration (see Fig. 2-6). In addition, Leonardo wove multiple meanings into his leafy labyrinth that went far beyond the obligatory glorification of the Prince.[92] The dedication of the room to Ludovico's magnificence is obvious. Inscriptions on four prominently placed tablets praise his politics, and a shield bearing the joint coats of arms of Ludovico and his wife, Beatrice d'Este, adorns the center of the vault. The intertwining branches were meant to commemorate their union.

But there are more subtle layers of meaning to Leonardo's design. The mulberry tree itself is rich in symbolism. The use of a stylized tree with leaves and roots was one of the Sforza emblems. The mulberry is an allusion to the prince's well-known appellation *il Moro* ("the Moor"), which also means "mulberry." The mulberry was also considered a wise and cautious tree, since it flowers slowly and ripens quickly, and hence

*Figure 2-6: Detail from the Sala
delle Asse, 1498–99, Castello Sforzesco, Milan*

was known as a symbol of wise government. In addition, the mulberry was connected with silk production, a major industry in Milan which Ludovico strongly encouraged. This link to industry is reinforced by the golden ribbon, which not only evokes the elegance of the Sforza court but is also a reminder of the manufacture of gold thread, another Milanese specialty.

At an even deeper level, Leonardo's decoration conveys in symbolic form his conviction that human industry should integrate itself harmoniously into nature's living forms. Indeed, it may not be too far-fetched to see the *vinci* decoration of the Sala delle Asse as a symbol of Leonardo's science. The individual trunks, or columns, on which it rests, might be seen as the treatises he planned to write on various subjects, grounded in the soil of traditional knowledge, but intended to break through the rocks of the Aristotelian worldview and take human knowledge to new heights. As the contents of each treatise unfolded, they would interlink with each other to form a harmonious whole. The similarities of patterns and processes that interconnect different facets of nature provide the golden thread that integrates the multiple branches of Leonardo's science into a unified vision of the world.

One hundred years after Leonardo, the French philosopher René Descartes compared science (or "natural philosophy," as it was then called) to a tree. "The roots are metaphysics," he wrote, "the trunk is physics, and the branches are all the other sciences."[93] In Descartes' metaphor, physics, itself grounded in metaphysics, was the single foundation of all the sciences, the discipline that provides the most fundamental description of reality. Leonardo's science, by contrast, cannot be reduced to a single foundation, as we have seen. Its strength does not derive from a single trunk, but from the complex interconnectedness of the branches of many trees. For Leonardo, recognizing the numerous patterns of relationships in nature was the hallmark of a universal science. Today, we, too, sense a greater need for such universal, or systemic, knowledge, which is one of the reasons why Leonardo's unified vision of the world is so relevant to our time.

In the following chapters I shall follow Leonardo's golden ribbon along various branches of his science of living forms. But before beginning that journey, it is important to know more about when and where those branches grew and foliated in his own life.

THREE

The Florentine

In view of the enormous fame Leonardo enjoyed during his lifetime and the voluminous notes he left behind, it is astonishing that reliable biographical information about his life is very scant. In his Notebooks, he rarely commented on external events; he rarely dated his entries or drawings; and there are very few exact references to specific events in his life in official documents or the letters of his time.

Thus it is not surprising that succeeding generations of biographers and commentators relied to a degree on legends and myths about this great genius of the Renaissance. It was not until the late nineteenth century, when the Notebooks were finally transcribed and published, that the full extent of Leonardo's intellect began to emerge, and only in the twentieth century that biographers and art historians finally were able, with a great deal of detective work, to separate fact from fiction and produce accurate biographies.[1]

These detailed accounts make it clear that Leonardo's life was driven by his tremendous scientific curiosity. He always sought to find stable situations with regular incomes that allowed him to engage in his intellectual pursuits relatively undisturbed, rather than relying on infrequent commissions for works of art. Leonardo was very successful in this endeavor, living quite comfortably for most of his life. He was employed as court artist and engineer by various rulers in Milan, Rome, and in France, and he did not hesitate to change his allegiances when the political fortunes of his patrons shifted—as long as the new ruler again offered him a stable income and enough freedom to continue his scientific investigations.

Leonardo's desire for stable circumstances, in which he could calmly practice his art and science as well as carry out the many duties expected from him at court, stands in strong contrast to the turbulent times in which he lived. Italy in the fifteenth century was a kaleidoscope of over a dozen independent states, which formed ever-shifting alliances in a constant struggle for economic and political power that was always on the verge of degenerating into war. The principal powers of the time were the duchies of Milan and Savoy and the republic of Venice in the north, the republic of Florence and the territories of the papacy in the center of the peninsula, and the kingdoms of Naples and Sicily in the south. In addition, there were a number of smaller states—Genoa, Mantua, Ferrara, and Siena.

Leonardo had to move many times in the face of impending war, foreign occupations, and other changes of political power. Thus the trajectory of his life led him from Florence to Milan, from Milan to Venice, back to Florence, back again to Milan, then to Rome, and finally to Amboise in France. In addition, he made many short journeys within Italy, including several trips from Florence to Rome and to various places in Tuscany and Romagna, and from Milan to Pavia, Lake Como, and Genoa. About the many sudden changes and forced movements in his life, there is hardly a word in Leonardo's Notebooks. Considering that travel by horse and mules took considerable time in those days, it is evident that he spent a significant portion of his life on the road, which makes his vast scientific and artistic output even more impressive.

In spite of all these peregrinations, Leonardo's art and culture remained rooted in Florence. He spoke a distinctive, eloquent Tuscan that was greatly admired at the Sforza court in Milan, and throughout his life he was known as "Leonardo da Vinci, the Florentine." Before he acquired his Florentine culture, however, Leonardo had several formative childhood experiences in the Tuscan countryside that exerted lasting influences on his character and intellect.

CHILDHOOD IN VINCI

Leonardo was born on April 15, 1452, in Vinci, a charming Tuscan village on the slopes of Montalbano, some twenty miles west of Florence. His father, Ser Piero da Vinci, was a young and ambitious notary,[2] his mother a peasant girl named Caterina. Leonardo was an illegitimate child, which severely limited his career options later on. Soon after his birth, his mother was married off to a local peasant, while his father married a young woman from the Florentine bourgeoisie, probably in order to further his career in Florence, where he gradually built up a clientele. The boy was raised by his elderly grandparents and his uncle Francesco, who managed their farm in Vinci.

Francesco da Vinci, only sixteen years older than Leonardo, was very fond of his nephew and soon became a father figure to him. He was a gentle and contemplative man who loved nature and knew it well. He would have spent many hours with the boy, walking through the vineyards and olive groves that surrounded Vinci (as they do today), observing the birds, lizards, insects, and other small creatures that inhabited the countryside, teaching him the names and qualities of the flowers and medicinal plants that grew in the region.

Doubtless it was Francesco who instilled in the young Leonardo his deep respect for life, his boundless curiosity, and the patience required for intimate observation of nature. Leonardo also began to draw early on in his childhood. In his Notebooks he listed "many flowers portrayed from nature" among the works he had produced in his youth,[3] and his earliest extant drawing, done at age twenty-one, is a view of the

Tuscan countryside of his childhood, tilled fields framed by the foothills and rocks of Montalbano.[4]

It is striking that in this early drawing as well as in that of a ravine with waterbirds (Fig. 3-1) that he made a few years later, Leonardo already pictured the dramatic rock formations that would form the backgrounds of most of his paintings. It seems that his lifelong fascination with pinnacles of rocks, carved out by water and eventually turning into gravel and fertile soil, originated in his childhood experience of the mountain streams and rocky outcroppings that are typical of parts of the countryside around Vinci.

As a young boy, Leonardo explored these mysterious rock formations, waterfalls, and caves. Over the years, their memory no doubt intensified as he embraced the ancient analogy of macro- and microcosm and began to view the rocks, soil, and water as the bones, flesh, and blood of the living Earth. Thus the rock formations of his childhood became Leonardo's personal mythical language that would forever appear in his paintings.

In Vinci, Leonardo attended one of the customary *scuole d'abaco* ("abacus schools"), which taught children reading, writing, and a rudimentary knowledge of arithmetic adapted to the needs of merchants.[5] Students who prepared for university then moved on to a *scuola di lettere* ("school of letters"), where they were taught the humanities based on the study of the great Latin authors. Such an education included rhetoric, poetry, history, and moral philosophy.

Being an illegitimate child, Leonardo was barred from attending university, and hence was not sent to a *scuola di lettere*. Instead he began his apprenticeship in the arts. This had a decisive influence on his further education and intellectual development. Being "unlettered" meant that he knew almost no Latin and was therefore unable to read the scholarly books of his time, except for the few texts that had been translated into the vernacular. It also meant that he was not familiar with the rules of rhetoric observed in philosophical disputations.

In his later life, Leonardo constantly strove to overcome this handicap by educating himself in numerous disciplines, consulting scholars wherever he could and assembling a considerable personal library. On the other hand, he also realized that not being constrained by the rules of classical rhetoric was an advantage because it made it easier for him

Figure 3-1: Ravine with waterbirds, c. 1483, Windsor Collection, Landscapes, Plants, and Water Studies, folio 3r

to learn directly from nature, especially when his observations contra-dicted conventional ideas. "I am fully aware that, not being a man of letters, certain presumptuous persons will think that they may with reason discredit me," he wrote in his own defense as he approached forty. "Foolish folk! . . . They don't know that my matters are worth more because they are derived from experience, rather than from the words of others, and she is the mistress of those who have written well."[6]

Leonardo showed great artistic talent early in his youth; his synthe-sis of art and science was also foreshadowed early on. This is vividly il-lustrated in a story related by Vasari. When Piero da Vinci was asked by a peasant to have a "buckler" (a small wooden shield) decorated with a painting in Florence, he did not give the shield to a Florentine artist but instead asked his son to paint something on it. Leonardo decided to paint a terrifying monster.

"To do what he wanted," writes Vasari, "Leonardo carried into a room of his own, which no one ever entered except himself, a number of lizards, crickets, serpents, butterflies, locusts, bats, and various strange creatures of this nature. From all these he took and assembled different parts to create a fearsome and horrible monster. . . . He de-picted the creature emerging from a dark cleft of a rock, belching forth venom from its open throat, fire from its eyes, and smoke from its nos-trils in so macabre a fashion that the effect was altogether monstrous and horrible. Leonardo took so long over the work that the stench of the dead animals in his room became unbearable, although he himself failed to notice because of his great love of painting."

When Ser Piero came to see the finished painting, "Leonardo went back into the room, put the buckler on an easel in the light, and shaded the window. Then he asked Piero to come in and see it. When his eyes fell on it, Piero was completely taken by surprise and gave a sudden start, not realizing that he was looking at the buckler and that the form he saw was, in fact, painted on it. As he backed away, Leonardo stopped him and said: 'This work certainly serves its purpose. It has produced the right reaction, so now you can take it away.'"

The story illustrates several of the qualities that became essential elements of Leonardo's genius. The painting is an expression of the boy's *fantasia*, but it is based on his careful observation of natural forms. The result is a picture that is both fantastic and strikingly real, and this effect is greatly enhanced by the artist's flair for the theatrical when he presents his work. Moreover, Vasari's description of the youth working for long hours, undisturbed by the stench of rotting corpses, eerily anticipates the anatomical dissections Leonardo would vividly describe some forty years later.[7]

APPRENTICESHIP IN FLORENCE

At the age of twelve, Leonardo's life changed dramatically. His grandfather died, and his uncle Francesco got married. As a result, Leonardo left Vinci to live with his father in Florence. A few years later he began his apprenticeship with the renowned artist and craftsman Verrocchio. Ser Piero, in the meantime, had remarried after his first wife died in childbirth. The exact sequence of Leonardo's movements at this time of his life is uncertain. He may have stayed in the country with his grandmother a couple of years longer, or he may have joined Verrocchio's workshop at the age of twelve. Most historians believe, however, that he began his apprenticeship at about age fifteen.

Florence in the 1460s had no more than 150,000 inhabitants, but in its economic power and cultural importance it was on a par with Europe's great capitals.[8] It had trading posts in the major regions of the known world, and its wealth attracted scores of artists and intellectuals, who made it the focal point of the emerging humanist movement. The Florentines were proud of their city's importance, its liberty and republican government, the beauty of its monuments, and especially of the fact that Florence had left its chaotic medieval past behind and embodied the spirit of a new era.

Throughout the 1300s, Florence had been the scene of many deadly feuds; succeeding factions had fought openly in the streets, and the wealthy families had built their houses like citadels, often fortified with imposing towers. By the time Leonardo arrived in the city, most of these menacing fortresses had disappeared. Narrow and twisting medieval streets had been widened and straightened; the unhealthiest districts had been cleaned up, and the wealthy Florentine bourgeoisie were busy building magnificent *palazzi*, using the local sandstone known as *pietra serena* and the severe symmetries of the new Renaissance architecture to give their city a uniform air of noble elegance.

To the adolescent Leonardo, arriving in Florence from a farm and a small village of a few dozen houses, this lively, enterprising, and beautiful city must have seemed like something out of a fairy tale. Brunelleschi's magnificent dome, crowning the shining marble of Santa Maria del Fiore, the cathedral of Florence, was newly finished and already being admired as a wonder of the modern world. The river Arno was spanned by four bridges. In the city's center, Leonardo would have frequently passed by the proud and stately palace of the Medici family. Near the Ponte Vecchio, one of the city's great bridges, he would have seen the finely proportioned Palazzo Ruccellai, both built just before his birth. On the other side of the Arno, construction had begun on the imposing Palazzo Pitti. Two dozen more palaces would be built during the sixteen years Leonardo spent in Florence. This massive beautification of the city was supported by a huge number of workshops in which artists and artisans produced the required materials, works of art, and splendid decorations. During Leonardo's apprenticeship, Florence could boast of 54 workshops for working marble, 40 goldsmiths, and 84 workshops for woodworking in addition to 83 for silk and 270 for wool.[9]

Leonardo's apprenticeship came about as a result of the connections his father had. When Leonardo came to live with Ser Piero, he brought with him the drawings he had made in Vinci. "One day," Vasari tells us, "Piero took some of Leonardo's drawings to Andrea del Verrocchio (who was a close friend of his) and earnestly begged him to say whether it would be profitable for the boy to study drawing.[10] Andrea was amazed to see what extraordinary beginnings Leonardo had made and he urged Piero to make him study the subject. So Piero arranged for Leonardo to enter Andrea's workshop." Ser Piero had not shown much concern for his son's early education, but with the choice of Verrocchio he redeemed himself. Of all the workshops in Florence, Verrocchio's was the most prestigious, the best connected, and for Leonardo the ideal place to nurture his talents.

Andrea del Verrocchio, who was about the same age as Leonardo's uncle Francesco, was a brilliant teacher. Originally trained as a goldsmith, he was a skilled craftsman, an accomplished painter, and a noted sculptor. He also had considerable engineering skills. He had excellent connections to the Medici family and a solid reputation, and hence received a steady stream of commissions. It was well known in Florence that his workshop could handle every kind of request.

Verrocchio's workshop, like those of the many other Florentine artists and artisans, was quite different from the painters' studios of subsequent centuries. In his biography of Leonardo, Serge Bramly gives us a vivid description.

> This was a *bottega*, a shop—just like that of the shoemaker, butcher, or tailor—a set of ground-floor premises opening directly onto the street . . . an awning was pulled down to act as a door or shutter. The living quarters would be at the back or upstairs. Artists' materials would be hanging on the walls, alongside sketches, plans, or models of work in progress, while ranged around the room would be a collection of sculptors' turntables, workbenches, and easels; a grindstone might stand alongside a firing kiln. Several people, including the young apprentices and assistants (who generally lived under the same roof as the master and ate at his table), would be working away at different tasks.[11]

The *bottega* of a master like Verrocchio would produce not only paintings and sculptures but also a vast variety of objects—pieces of armor, church bells, candelabras, decorated wooden chests, coats of arms, models for architectural projects, and banners for festivities as well as sets and scenery for theatrical performances. The works leaving the *bottega* (even those of the highest quality) were rarely signed and usually produced by the master with a team of assistants.

Leonardo spent the next twelve years in this creative environment, during which he diligently followed the rigorous course of a traditional apprenticeship.[12] He would have drawn on tablets and familiarized himself with the artists' materials, which could not be bought readymade but had to be prepared in the workshop. Pigments had to be freshly ground and mixed every day; he would have learned to make paintbrushes, prepare glazes, apply gold to backgrounds, and finally, after several years, to paint. In addition, he would have absorbed considerable technical knowledge by watching the master work on a variety of projects. Over the years, as he honed his skills by imitating his elders, he and the other apprentices would have increasingly participated in the *bottega*'s production until he was finally designated a master craftsman and accepted into the appropriate association, or guild, of craftsmen.

In Verrocchio's workshop, Leonardo was introduced not only to a wide variety of artistic and technical skills, but also to many exciting new ideas. The *bottega* was a place where lively discussions of the latest events took place daily. Music was played in the evenings; the master's friends and fellow artists dropped by to exchange plans, sketches, and technical innovations; traveling writers and philosophers visited when they passed through the city. Many of the leading artists of the time were drawn to Verrocchio's *bottega*. Botticelli, Perugino, and Ghirlandaio all spent time there after they were already accomplished masters to learn novel techniques and discuss new ideas.

The Florentine *bottega* of the fifteenth century fostered a unique synthesis of art, technology, and science, which found its highest expression in Leonardo's mature work. As historian of science Domenico Laurenza points out, this synthesis lasted for just a hundred years: by the end of the sixteenth century, it had dissolved.[13] For Leonardo's own artistic and intellectual development, the years he spent in Verrocchio's workshop were decisive. His way of working and his entire approach to art and science were shaped significantly by his long immersion in that workshop culture.

One important influence on Leonardo's future work habits was the use of a *libro di bottega* ("workbook"), which all apprentices had to keep.[14] It was a journal in which they recorded technical instructions or procedures, personal reflections, solutions to problems, and drawings and diagrams of their ideas. Continuously updated, annotated, and corrected, the *libro di bottega* provided a daily record of the activities in the workshop. Its composite character of accumulated notes and drawings, without any particular organization, is recognizable in many pages of Leonardo's Notebooks.

Shortly after Leonardo began his apprenticeship, Verrocchio received a commission for his biggest and most spectacular engineering project yet—the construction of a gilded copper ball, 2.5 meters in diameter, or roughly seven feet, to be placed together with a cross on top of the marble lantern of Brunelleschi's dome. The famous architect had died before being able to crown his masterpiece, but had left detailed plans for the lantern and copper ball, which Verrocchio was charged to execute. The project took three years, and the young Leonardo was able to observe every stage of it, and likely contributed to it as well.[15]

It was a complex project, involving securing the lantern to withstand strong winds; precisely casting, shearing, and welding the copper ball's many sections; and finally, hoisting the heavy ball and cross to the top of the lantern by using special hoisting devices, designed by Brunelleschi himself. The welding alone was a major feat of science and engineering, because there were no welding torches in the fifteenth century. Small welds could be executed at the forge, but the copper ball was so big that the only way to weld it with a hot flame at precise points was to use concave mirrors to "burn" a weld (a technique that had been known since antiquity). Manufacturing such concave mirrors required considerable knowledge of geometrical optics and very precise grinding equipment. This explains Leonardo's frequent studies of the geometry of "fire mirrors," as he called them, in his early drawings.[16] They later led him to formulate sophisticated theories of optics and perspective.

The project was finally completed in 1471. Contemporary chroniclers recorded that on May 27 of that year a large crowd gathered in front of the Duomo to watch the hoisting of the great gilded ball, perfectly smooth and shining, to the top of the marble lantern, where, after a fanfare of trumpets, it was secured to the plinth to the sounds of the "Te Deum." It was a spectacle that Leonardo never forgot. Forty-five years later, when he was over sixty and working on the design of a large parabolic mirror in Rome, he wrote in his Notebook as a reminder to himself, "Remember how we welded together the ball of Santa Maria del Fiore!"[17]

Toward the end of Leonardo's apprenticeship, Verrocchio was working on a picture of the *Baptism of Christ* (Fig. 3-2). Since the youth had shown great promise, the master let him paint parts of the background and one of the two angels. These portions of the painting, the first record we have of Leonardo as a painter, already show features of his distinctive style. In the background, we see wide, romantic hills,

Figure 3-2: Andrea del Verrocchio and Leonardo da Vinci,
Baptism of Christ, *c. 1476, Uffizi Gallery, Florence*

rocky cliffs, and water flowing from a pool in the far distance all the
way to the foreground, where it forms small waves rippling around the
legs of Christ. Close inspection of this flow of water in the original
painting, now in the Uffizi Gallery, reveals several tiny waterfalls and
turbulences of the kind that fascinated Leonardo throughout his life.

Equally striking is the originality of Leonardo's angel. Its grace and beauty are far superior to those of Verrocchio's, which the master could not fail to notice. "This was the reason," reports Vasari, "why Andrea would never touch colors again; he was so ashamed that a boy understood their use better than he did." Indeed, it seems that from that time on, Verrocchio concentrated on sculpture, and left the execution of paintings to his senior assistants.[18]

YOUNG MASTER PAINTER AND INVENTOR

At the age of twenty, Leonardo was recognized as a master painter, and in 1472 he was admitted to the guild of painters known as Compagnia di San Luca. Curiously, the company was included in the guild of physicians and apothecaries, which was based at the hospital of Santa Maria Nuova. For Leonardo, this was the beginning of a long association with the hospital. For many years he used the guild as a bank for his savings, and it was at Santa Maria Nuova that he found his first opportunities to perform anatomical dissections.

The young Leonardo was already familiar with the dissection of muscles; close to Verrocchio's workshop was the *bottega* of the brothers Pollaiolo, whose paintings were known for their vivid rendering of muscular bodies. They had derived their knowledge of muscles from frequent dissections, which Leonardo must have watched closely during his apprenticeship. A few years later, he used his acute knowledge of the musculature of the neck and shoulder to give the figure of the ascetic *Saint Jerome* a powerful expression of pain and sorrow.

After his acceptance into the painters' guild, Leonardo remained in Verrocchio's workshop for another five years, but he was now employed as a collaborator of the master rather than an assistant. This was not unusual; the large number of commissions received by Verrocchio encouraged his apprentices to continue working with him after they had become masters.

There was probably another good reason for Leonardo to stay on. During his apprenticeship, he had become familiar with a wide variety of mechanical and optical devices, and he was now increasingly experimenting with improvements of existing machines as well as the invention of new ones. In the *bottega*, his curious and creative mind would have found endless challenges as new commissions kept coming in. He also had at his disposal all the necessary instruments, equipment, and raw materials for his mechanical and optical experiments. As he embarked on his dual career of painter and inventor, Verrocchio's *bottega* continued to be an ideal working environment.

In addition to his designs of concave mirrors, Leonardo's early optical inventions included new ways of controlling light, most likely in connection with stage design. "How to make a great light," he writes next to a sketch of light going through a convex lens; elsewhere he draws "a lamp that makes a beautiful and great light" (a candle in a box equipped with a lens).[19] On a sheet of the Codex Atlanticus from that period there is a sketch of a machine "for generating a big voice," and on other sheets drawings of various lanterns, one of them with the notation "put above the stars"—all of them evidently meant for theatrical settings.[20]

Other inventions he created from that time involved fire and hot air.[21] In addition to the self-regulating spit mentioned earlier, Leonardo invented a method of creating a vacuum to raise water by means of a fire burning in a closed bucket, based on the observation that a burning flame consumes air. During these early years he also developed his first versions of a diving apparatus. During a visit to Vinci he designed an olive press with more efficient leverage than the presses used at the time. While he was engaged in these multiple projects of invention, design, and engineering, Leonardo also painted his *Annunciation*, two *Madonnas*, and the portrait of *Ginevra de' Benci*.

In 1477, Leonardo left Verrocchio's workshop to establish himself as an independent artist. But he did not seem to devote much energy to this enterprise. A few months later, perhaps through the influence of his father, he received a prestigious commission for an altarpiece in the chapel of San Bernardo in the Palazzo Vecchio.[22] He was paid a sizable advance but never delivered a finished painting. Around this time, he wrote in his Notebook, "Have begun two Virgin Marys" without giving any further details.[23]

In fact, very little is known about Leonardo's activities between the years 1477 and 1481. Some historians assume that, after many years of rigid discipline in the *bottega*, Leonardo—now a dashing, athletic

young man of twenty-five—simply joined the extravagant life of the
well-to-do Florentine youth. "Presumably," writes art historian and
critic Kenneth Clark, "Leonardo, like other young men with great
gifts, spent a large part of his youth . . . dressing up, taming horses,
learning the lute [and] enjoying the *hors d'oeuvres* of life."[24]

If true, it was not a time without frustrations, however. For unknown reasons, the Medici never extended to Leonardo their vast patronage of the arts. Although Verrocchio was on excellent terms with
the family, enjoyed their support, and would not have failed to recom-
mend Leonardo to Lorenzo de' Medici, Lorenzo did not offer Leonardo
a single full-scale commission.[25]

A family of bankers and merchants, the Medici were the undis-
puted rulers of Florence for two centuries, despite the fact that they
never held public office. With their enormous wealth and their passionate patronage of the arts, literature, and learning, they influenced
every facet of Tuscan public life and culture. They also counted among
their family members several cardinals, three popes, and two queens of
France. In the words of Serge Bramly, "The Medici behaved less and
less like businessmen and more and more like princes, becoming the
avowed masters of a city that remained a republic in name only."[26]

Lorenzo de' Medici, also known as *il Magnifico*, at the young age of
twenty followed in the footsteps of his father as the ruler of Florence.
Lorenzo was just three years older than Leonardo, and the two had
much in common, including a love for horses, music, and learning.
However, there was also much in their characters and tastes that kept
them apart.[27] Lorenzo was not a handsome man and dressed with delib-
erate simplicity. Leonardo, on the other hand, was strikingly beautiful
and flamboyant in his gestures and behavior. Lorenzo had received a
classical education and had a genuine love for formal learning. He surrounded himself with writers. Leonardo, by contrast, was self-taught;
he knew no Latin or Greek and despised what he must have perceived
as literary pretension at the Medici "court." These contrasts were apparently so strong that they stood in the way of any mutual sympathy
forming between them. Nevertheless, Lorenzo's low esteem of Leonardo
as an artist is surprising.

Prudent and cunning, Lorenzo de' Medici could be brutal as well
as magnanimous. When he came to power, he consolidated his control

of the government, restructured the family banks and trading houses, made new alliances, and dissolved old ones. He also inaugurated lavish festivals and spectacles for the city to assure his popularity.

However, Lorenzo's political maneuvers inevitably generated opposition.[28] He had allied himself with the city-state of Venice against Rome and Naples, whereupon Pope Sixtus IV transferred the management of Vatican finances from the Medici to the rival Pazzi family. Lorenzo quickly retaliated by accusing one of the Pazzi of treason, and arresting him. The Pazzi family, in turn, planned revenge with the support of the pope, and in April of 1478, Lorenzo and his brother Giuliano were attacked while attending mass in the cathedral. Giuliano was killed; Lorenzo was seriously wounded but managed to escape. But the Pazzi conspiracy did not succeed in triggering a revolt against the Medici, as the pope had intended. Because of Lorenzo's popularity, the citizens of Florence soon hunted down the criminals, including a member of the Pazzi family, an archbishop, and several priests. All were hanged within hours of the attempted uprising.

The turbulent time of the Pazzi conspiracy brought a sudden end to the city's extravagant festivals, and perhaps this helped Leonardo to concentrate again on his work. The year 1478 is the date of his earliest drawings of machines in the Codex Atlanticus, most of them renderings of devices invented by Brunelleschi for the construction of the dome of Santa Maria del Fiore.[29] The Pazzi conspiracy may also have turned Leonardo's mind to the science and engineering of war. In the following years he recorded numerous military inventions, including multibarreled guns, assault bridges for attacking ramparts, and mechanisms for overturning ladders used for scaling fortified walls. Many of these creations were derived from the work of previous inventors, although they were invariably modified, and significantly improved.[30]

When the Vatican's support of the Pazzi conspiracy became apparent, Florence declared war on the pope. But Lorenzo resolved the crisis with a daring move. He traveled to Naples and negotiated a peace agreement with King Ferrante, thus depriving the pope of his strongest ally. Shortly thereafter, Florence and Rome were reconciled again, and in 1481—three years after conspiring to kill him—Pope Sixtus IV asked Lorenzo to lend him his best painters to decorate the Sistine Chapel, which he had just built and which had been named after him. It was a tremendous opportunity for Florentine painters, and Leonardo must have been very keen to participate. Once again, however, he was conspicuously ignored by Lorenzo, who sent several of Leonardo's former companions to Rome, including Botticelli, Ghirlandaio, and Perugino.

The humiliation may have been the lowest point in Leonardo's career. Over the years, he had been repeatedly snubbed by the Medici and passed over in favor of lesser artists. Now he was deprived of the chance to seek glory in Rome, which he certainly deserved. But Leonardo put aside his feelings of disappointment and despair, and marshaled his powers of concentration to paint his first masterpiece.

In March 1481 the monks of the Augustinian monastery of San Donato (whose legal affairs were handled by Ser Piero) commissioned Leonardo to create a large altarpiece representing the *Adoration of the Magi*. The artist made numerous preparatory drawings and worked on the project intensely for a year.[31] His first approach was a masterful exercise in linear perspective, showing a courtyard with two flights of stairs and elaborate arcades. "This carefully measured courtyard," writes Kenneth Clark, "has been invaded by an extraordinary retinue of ghosts; wild horses rear and toss their heads, agitated figures dart up the staircase and in and out of the arcades; and a camel, appearing for the first and last time in Leonardo's work, adds its exotic bulk to the dreamlike confusion of forms."[32]

In the final painting, Leonardo abandoned the use of perspective in favor of a dynamic configuration created by the highly emotional gestures of an agitated throng of figures surrounding the Virgin and Child. In the background of the painting, a group of clashing horsemen represents the moral blindness of violence, in contrast to the Epiphany's glorious message of peace on earth, foreshadowing Leonardo's forceful condemnation of war in *The Battle of Anghiari* two decades later.[33] Indeed, the entire painting is full of visual themes that would recur in the artist's later work.[34] Art historian Jane Roberts describes Leonardo's *Adoration* as "the first mature and independent statement of his genius."[35] At the same time, it is a radical departure from traditional representations of the subject as a calm ceremonial gathering. As Daniel Arasse explains, "To paint the moment when the presence of the Son of God was publicly recognized as such, [Leonardo] depicted the tumult of a universal dazzlement—reflecting in this the meaning that Saint Augustine and the monks of his order who had commissioned the painting gave to the Epiphany."[36]

Early in the following year, while Leonardo was still working on his *Adoration of the Magi*, Lorenzo de' Medici decided to make a diplomatic gesture to Ludovico Sforza, his most powerful ally, in the form of a gift. As the Anonimo Gaddiano reports, "It is said that when Leonardo was thirty years old, the *Magnifico* sent him to present a lyre to the Duke of Milan, with a certain Atalante Migliorotti, for he played upon this instrument exceptionally well."[37] Sending Leonardo to the Sforza court in Milan as a musician rather than as a painter may have seemed like another indignity. However, Leonardo did not hesitate. He must have felt that it was time for a fresh start; without Lorenzo's support, his avenues to further commissions were limited in Florence. So he put down his brushes, packed his belongings, and, with his masterpiece unfinished, left the city that had nurtured his art.

MILAN

Milan in the 1480s was a vibrant trading center of tremendous wealth that exported armaments, wool, and silk. It was comparable to Florence in size, but very different in its architecture and culture. Its Latin name, Mediolanum, was probably derived from its location in the middle of the Plain of Lombardy *(in medio plano)*. It was definitely a northern city. Most of its palaces and churches were built in the Romanesque or Gothic style. Unlike Florence, Milan had no elegant town plan. The city's medieval houses huddled together, creating a labyrinth of narrow, bustling streets.

The duchy of Milan had been ruled by the Sforza family since 1450. Like the Medici, the Sforzas were cunning and ruthless, but their family tended to be full of warriors rather than bankers. Ludovico Sforza, only a few months older than Leonardo, was one of the wealthiest and most powerful Renaissance princes.[38] Nicknamed *il Moro* ("the Moor") because of his dark hair and skin, he was also a subtle diplomat whose alliance with the king of France was a potent ingredient in the volatile mixture of Italian politics. With his wife, Beatrice d'Este,

Ludovico held an elegant court and spent immense sums of money to further the arts and sciences.

When Leonardo arrived in Milan, the city had no renowned painters or sculptors, although the Sforza court was filled with doctors, mathematicians, and engineers. Its culture was linked to that of the great universities of northern Italy, whose emphasis was on the study of the physical world rather than on moral philosophy, as had been the case in Florence.[39] While the Medici spent their time composing verses in Tuscan and Latin,[40] Ludovico organized scientific debates among learned professors. In this stimulating intellectual environment, Leonardo soon transcended his Florentine workshop culture and turned toward a more analytic and theoretical approach to the understanding of nature.

Because he arrived at the Sforza court as a musician, he and Atalante (who was his student on the *lira*, according to the Anonimo Gaddiano) probably played frequently to entertain the court. But Leonardo had no intention of pursuing a musical career. Realizing that the power of the Sforzas came from their military might, and that Milan's dominant position in trade required a well-functioning city infrastructure, he wrote a carefully composed letter to the Moor, in which he offered his services as a military and civil engineer, and also mentioned his skills as an architect, sculptor, and painter. Leonardo began his letter with a telling reference to his "secrets," revealing a taste for secrecy that became a characteristic trait of his personality as he became older.[41] "Most illustrious Lord," he wrote, "having now sufficiently seen and considered the works of all those who claim to be masters and artificers of instruments of war . . . I shall endeavor, without prejudice to anyone else, to reveal my secrets to your Excellency, and then offer to execute, at your pleasure and at the appropriate time, all the items briefly noted below."

He then proceeded to list under nine headings the different instruments of war he had designed and was prepared to build: "I have models for strong but very light bridges, extremely easy to carry . . . an endless variety of battering rams and scaling ladders . . . methods of destroying any citadel or fortress that is not built of rock . . . mortars that are very practical and easy to transport, with which I can fling showers of small stones, and their smoke will cause great terror to the enemy . . . secret winding underground passages, dug without noise . . . covered wagons, safe and unassailable, which will penetrate enemy ranks with their artillery . . . bombards, mortars, and light artillery of beautiful and practical forms . . . engines to hurl large rocks, fire-throwing catapults, and other unusual instruments of marvelous efficiency."

"In short," he concluded his list, "whatever the situation, I can invent an infinite variety of machines for both attack and defense." Then he added, almost as an afterthought, "In peacetime, I think I can give perfect satisfaction and be the equal of any man in architecture, in the design of public and private buildings, and in conducting water from one place to another. Furthermore, I can carry out sculpture in marble, bronze, or clay; and likewise in painting I can do any kind of work as well as any man. . . ." And finally, he ended with an enticing prospect: "Moreover, the bronze horse could be made that will be to the immortal glory and eternal honor of the Prince your father of blessed memory, and the illustrious house of Sforza."[42]

This astonishing letter, in which Leonardo refers to himself as an artist in only six out of thirty-four lines, shows how quickly he was able to assimilate the spirit of this northern city, presenting his many talents in the order in which he thought they would be most valued by Ludovico. The letter may sound boastful, but all of Leonardo's offers were serious and well thought out. He had undoubtedly studied the work of the leading military engineers of his time, as he said in the letter; there are about twenty-five sheets of drawings of military machines, dating from his time in Florence, in the Codex Atlanticus; and there are over forty in a slightly later style.[43] By juxtaposing this letter, item by item, with existing drawings, Leonardo scholar Kenneth Keele has demonstrated the validity of every claim Leonardo made.[44] Indeed, in his later life, Leonardo was employed in all the capacities he laid out in the letter to *il Moro*.

He did not receive an immediate response to his letter from the court, let alone an offer of employment. So Leonardo turned once more to painting—the profession in which he was an accomplished and acknowledged master. He began a collaboration with the brothers Ambrogio and Evangelista Predis, the former a successful portrait painter and the latter a woodcarver.[45] The Predis brothers were clearly the lesser artists, but they were well connected in Milan and gladly welcomed Leonardo to their *bottega*. Indeed, Ambrogio was soon able to negotiate a lucrative contract for the three of them.

In April 1483, the Confraternity of the Immaculate Conception commissioned Leonardo and the Predis brothers to paint and decorate a large altarpiece in the church of San Francesco Grande with the central panel "to be painted in oil by Master Leonardo, the Florentine." The contract specified not only the size and composition of the painting (the Virgin Mary flanked by two prophets, with God the Father appearing overhead, surrounded by angels), but also the traditional colors of gold, blue, and green, the angels' golden halos, and so on.

Leonardo worked on the painting for about three years. The result was his second masterpiece, the *Virgin of the Rocks*, now in the Louvre (see Fig. 2-4 on p. 47). The finished work bore little resemblance to what the confraternity had ordered.[46] In fact, the priors were so upset that they brought a lawsuit before the duke, which dragged on for over twenty years.[47] Leonardo eventually painted a second version, which now hangs in the National Gallery in London. This could not have pleased the priors much better, as he made only minor changes in the painting's composition.

Art historians believe that Leonardo may have let Ambrogio Predis paint large parts of the London version. This seems to be confirmed by recent analyses of the rocks and plants in the painting's background. Scientists have noted that both the geological and botanical details in the London version are significantly inferior to those in the painting in the Louvre. It is highly unlikely that they were painted by Leonardo.[48]

The confraternity may have had good reasons to be dissatisfied with the *Virgin of the Rocks*, but in the *botteghe* and intellectual circles of Milan, Leonardo's masterpiece caused a sensation. The artist's low tones of olive green and gray were in stark contrast to the bright colors of the quattrocento, and the Milanese could not have failed to notice the subtle gradations of light and shade, nor the powerful effect of the surrounding grotto. As Kenneth Clark describes it, "Like deep notes in the accompaniment of a serious theme, the rocks in the background sustain the composition and give it the resonance of a cathedral."[49]

SYSTEMATIC STUDIES

In 1484, while Leonardo was working on *Virgin of the Rocks*, Milan was hit by the plague. The epidemic raged on for a full two years and would kill close to one-third of the population. Leonardo, recognizing the critical role of poor sanitation in the spread of the disease, responded with a proposal for a new city design that was far ahead of its time, as I discussed earlier.[50] But it was ignored by the Sforzas. This renewed failure to get the court's attention with his ideas brought Leonardo face-to-face with the huge handicap of his upbringing: his lack of a formal education. He was attempting to be accepted as an intellectual in a culture that was in close contact with the leading universities, a culture dominated by the written word, in which Latin was used almost exclusively. Being an "unlettered man," Leonardo was not only ignorant of Latin but, even in his native Tuscan, did not have the abstract vocabulary necessary for precise and elegant formulations of his theories.

Leonardo tackled this seemingly insurmountable problem in his methodical, sustained, and uncompromising way. "In his mid-thirties and practically without any knowledge of Latin," writes historian of science Domenico Laurenza, "he embarks on an intense and in some ways obsessive program of self-education. The years between 1483 and 1489 are dedicated largely to this obstinate attempt of cultural emancipation."[51]

Leonardo began his extensive program of self-education with a systematic attempt to enlarge his vocabulary. This was the time when Italian as a literary language was just beginning to emerge from Florentine Tuscan. Dante, Petrarch, and Boccaccio had all written in Tuscan, but the orthography had not yet been codified; grammars and dictionaries had not been published. The new vernacular was beginning to replace Latin as a written language, especially in texts about art and technology, and in the process it became enriched by a vast assimilation of Latin words. Leonardo was familiar with compilations of these *vocaboli latini* (new Italian words derived from Latin), and he laboriously copied them into his Notebooks.[52] In his earliest manuscript, the Codex Trivulzianus, page after page is filled with lists of such words. In fact, Leonardo referred to this Notebook as "my book of words."[53]

As he turned to the written word, Leonardo also began to build up a personal library. In Florence he had read some literature and poetry, but had not studied scientific texts. He had acquired a rudimentary scientific education by studying the drawings of architects and engineers, and by having discussions with various experts in the *bottega*.[54] When he left Florence, he made a list of the things he wanted to take with him to Milan.[55] This list did not contain a single book.

A few months after his arrival in Milan, Leonardo listed five books in his possession; by 1490 he had added 35 new titles, and from then on the number of books in his library increased steadily, reaching 116 at its peak in 1505. In addition to the volumes he owned, Leonardo regularly borrowed books, so that his full personal library would have included about 200 books—a substantial library even for a Renaissance scholar.[56]

The subject matter of these books was diverse.[57] Over half of them dealt with scientific and philosophical matters. They included books on mathematics, astronomy, anatomy and medicine, natural history, geography, and geology as well as architecture and military science. Another 30 or 40 were literary books. A dozen or so contained religious stories, which Leonardo would have consulted when he painted religious subjects.

These books provide ample evidence that Leonardo, during the last two decades of the fifteenth century, not only honed his language skills but was well versed in the major fields of knowledge of his time. As with everything he tackled, he would investigate several areas simultaneously while being involved in various artistic projects. He always looked for patterns that would interconnect observations from different disciplines; his mind seemed to work best when it was occupied with multiple projects.

The beginning of Leonardo's systematic studies in 1484, not surprisingly, coincides with the first entries in his Notebooks. Once he embarked on his interdisciplinary program of research, he regularly recorded all new ideas and observations. Now in his mid-thirties, it was the time when he deepened his theoretical investigations beyond his needs as an artist and inventor. For example, when he studied the nature of light and shadow, he did so at first to develop his theory of painting. But eventually he went much farther. As Kenneth Clark observed,

> He drew [a] long series of diagrams showing the effect of light falling on spheres and cylinders, crossing, reflecting, intersecting with endless variety. . . . The calculations are so complex and abstruse that we feel in them, almost for the first time, Leonardo's tendency to pursue research for its own sake, rather than as an aid to his art.[58]

While he carried out his investigations of light falling on solid objects, Leonardo also became interested in the physiology of vision, and then went on to study the other senses. His earliest anatomical drawings, based on dissections dating from the late 1480s, are beautiful images of human skulls, all of which reveal the optic nerve and the path of vision.[59] These are no longer drawings merely for the benefit of the painter; they are also, and perhaps more important, the first scientific diagrams of Leonardo's anatomical research.

In his drawings of machines of that period, too, one can see a definite movement toward exploring deeper theoretical problems. (As Domenico Laurenza has pointed out, Leonardo seems to have revised his early technical drawings around 1490 by adding various theoretical comments.)[60] What one sees in all these examples—from optics to anatomy and engineering—is the emergence of Leonardo the scientist.

GRADUAL ACCEPTANCE AT COURT

After the devastation of the plague, Milan's citizens emerged with a new optimism and sense of excitement encouraged by the lavish spending of the aristocracy. In large parts of the city, houses were remodeled, new squares and avenues were built, and in 1487 a competition was held to design a *tiburio* (a central tower above the cross of the transepts) for the huge Gothic cathedral, which attracted architects from all over

Italy. Caught up in the general enthusiasm, Leonardo became deeply interested in architecture during those years and participated in the competition for the *tiburio*, together with Donato Bramante, Francesco di Giorgio, and other renowned architects.

The project was quite difficult, since the high Gothic tower would have to be balanced on four slim pillars, and the existing parts of the cathedral already had structural problems. Leonardo examined all aspects of the cathedral and sketched a variety of solutions before settling on a design and producing a wooden model.[61] When he submitted his design to the authorities, he sent along an introductory letter, which began with his comparison of the cathedral to a sick organism; himself, the architect, he compared to a skilled doctor.[62]

The judges of the competition deliberated for a long time before finally awarding the contract to two Lombard architects in 1490, with the instruction that they produce a model that would be a harmonious blend of the best parts of all the submitted designs. For Leonardo, this turned out to be a very felicitous outcome. It allowed him to discuss his ideas about the *tiburio*, as well as his views on architecture in general, with the other competitors, especially with Bramante and Francesco di Giorgio, the two most famous architects in the group. Both of them would eventually become close friends of Leonardo, would exchange many ideas with him, and would greatly further his career during those years when he began to develop his theories.

His friendship with Bramante, in particular, was very advantageous for Leonardo. Born near Urbino, Bramante had come to Milan a few years earlier and had already gained the respect of the Sforzas when they met. The two artists had much in common.[63] Both were accomplished painters, were interested in mathematics and engineering, liked to improvise on the lute, and admired the famous architect and intellectual Alberti. Both also came from central Italy and were seeking to establish themselves in this northern city. Bramante, who later would design Saint Peter's in Rome, was said to be completely free of professional jealousy and likely opened many doors at court for his new friend. Historians of art also believe that Leonardo, with his thorough grasp of the principles of architectural design, had a significant influence on Bramante's work.[64]

In 1488, six years after he first arrived in Milan, Leonardo finally had his breakthrough at the Sforza court. In the wake of the reputation he had gained with the *Virgin of the Rocks*, and perhaps aided by a recommendation from Bramante, he was asked by Ludovico to paint a portrait of the Moor's mistress, the young and lovely Cecilia Gallerani. Leonardo painted her holding an ermine, a symbol of purity and moderation which, because of its Greek name, *gale*, was also a veiled allusion to her name, Gallerani. *Lady with an Ermine*, as it is called today, was a highly original portrait in which Leonardo invented a new pose, with the model looking over her shoulder with an air of surprise and subdued delight, caused, perhaps, by the unexpected arrival of her lover.[65] Her gesture is graceful and elegant, and is echoed in the animal's twisting movement.

Ludovico was very pleased with the portrait. Soon after its completion, he asked Leonardo to create a "masque" for a magnificent gala, *la festa del paradiso*, in celebration of the wedding of the duke's nephew, Gian Galeazzo, to Isabella of Aragon. At the same time, the Moor fulfilled one of Leonardo's greatest dreams by awarding him the commission for *il cavallo*—the giant equestrian statue in honor of Ludovico's father.[66]

Leonardo's "Masque of the Planets" was the climax of the theatrical performance that took place at the grandiose feast in January 1490. On a giant revolving stage, the signs of the zodiac, illuminated by torches, could be seen behind colored glass, and the seven planets, represented by costumed actors, circled through the heavens accompanied by "marvelous melodies and soft harmonious songs."[67] The Masque was a huge success and made Leonardo famous throughout Italy, even more so than his paintings had done. From that point on he was in great demand at the Sforza court as a brilliant magician of the stage, and was referred to in official documents as painter and "ducal engineer." At the age of thirty-eight, Leonardo had achieved, at last, the position he had desired when he wrote his memorable letter to the Moor years before.

FOUR

A Well-Employed Life

Beginning in 1490, the whole of Italy experienced several years of peace and political stability, during which its city-states accumulated great wealth. In Milan, palaces were renovated, streets paved, and gardens laid out. There were pageants, costumed tournaments, and a succession of performances in a new theater Ludovico had given the city.

Leonardo had become the Moor's favorite court artist. He was given a large space for his workshop and living quarters in the Corte Vecchia, the old ducal palace next to the cathedral, where Ludovico housed important guests. He seemed to have had an entire wing at his disposal, where he designed sets and costumes for festivities, invented mechanical devices, carried out scientific experiments, prepared the molds for the *gran cavallo* he was creating, and tested his first flying machines. To satisfy the constant demands of the court, he employed several apprentices, assistants, and contracted workers in addition to maintaining a small household of domestic staff.[1] The *bottega di Leonardo* was a very busy place indeed.

For Leonardo himself, the 1490s were a period of intense creative activity. With two major projects—the equestrian statue and *The Last Supper*—his artistic career was at its peak, he was consulted repeatedly as an expert on architectural design, and he embarked on extensive and systematic research in mathematics, optics, mechanics, and the theory of human flight.

NEW FOCUS ON MATHEMATICS

This phase of intense research was triggered by Leonardo's introduction to the library of Pavia in the summer of 1490. Ludovico had sent him to Pavia, which belonged to the duchy of Milan, to inspect the work on the city's cathedral together with the architect Francesco di Giorgio. For Leonardo, the journey was intellectually stimulating and personally rewarding in several ways. During the weeks they spent together, he formed a close friendship with Francesco, who was highly regarded as an architect and engineer and whose treatise on civil and military engineering would greatly influence Leonardo in the coming years.[2]

Even more important for Leonardo, however, was his discovery of the magnificent library in the city's Visconti Castle. Pavia was the seat of one of Europe's oldest universities and had become a major artistic and intellectual center. The great hall of its library, its walls lined with shelves of manuscripts, was famous among scholars all over Italy.[3] Leonardo was overwhelmed at the sight of this immense intellectual treasure. Indeed, he did not return to Milan with Francesco when their work was completed, but stayed in Pavia for another six months to further explore the library.

While he was immersed in this research, he met Fazio Cardano, a professor of mathematics at the University of Pavia who was a specialist in the "science of perspective," which in the Renaissance included geometry and geometrical optics.[4] Leonardo's discussions with Cardano and his studies in the library ignited a passion for mathematics, especially geometry, and fueled his subsequent research. Immediately after his return to Milan, he began two new Notebooks, now known as Manuscripts A and C, in which he applied his new knowledge of geometry to a systematic study of perspective and optics as well as to elementary problems involving weights, force, and movement— the branches of mechanics known today as statics, dynamics, and kinematics.

Leonardo's research in statics and dynamics was concerned not only with the workings of machines but also, and even more important, with understanding the human body and its movements. For example, he investigated the body's ability to generate various amounts of force in different positions. One of his key aims was to find out how a human pilot might generate enough force to lift a flying machine off the ground by flapping its mechanical wings.[5]

In his studies of machines during that period, Leonardo began to separate individual mechanisms—levers, gears, bearings, couplings, etc.—from the machines in which they were embedded. This conceptual separation did not arise again in engineering until the eighteenth century.[6] In fact, Leonardo planned (and may even have written) a treatise on *Elements of Machines*, perhaps influenced by his discussions with Fazio Cardano of Euclid's celebrated *Elements of Geometry* in Pavia.

Amazingly, in the midst of those years of intensive research, and while his workshop was fully occupied with a stream of orders from the Sforza court, Leonardo also continued his literary self-education. In 1493 he began to study Latin. In a special little Notebook, Manuscript H, he copied passages from a popular book of Latin grammar as well as Latin words from a contemporary vocabulary. It is very touching to see passages in which Leonardo, over forty years old and at the height of his powers and fame, wrote out the same basic conjugations—*amo, amas, amat* . . . —schoolboys have to memorize at age thirteen.

FRIENDSHIP AND BETRAYAL

In the midst of his studies and experimentation, and his final preparations for the casting of the giant bronze horse, Leonardo received the commission from Ludovico to paint *The Last Supper*—the masterpiece that most would argue stands at the climax of his career as a painter. It was to be a large fresco in the refectory of the Dominican convent of Santa Maria delle Grazie in Milan. The monastery was the Moor's favorite place of worship; the last meal Jesus shared with his disciples was a traditional subject for decorating convent refectories.

As always, Leonardo contemplated the subject carefully within its religious, artistic, and architectural context. He made numerous preparatory sketches and completed the painting within two or three years—a relatively short period considering that he had to divide his time between painting in the "Grazie" and working on *il cavallo* in the Corte Vecchia.

Leonardo's *Last Supper*, generally considered the first painting of the High Renaissance (the period of Italian art between, approximately, 1495 and 1520), is dramatically different from earlier representations of the subject. Indeed, it became famous throughout Europe immediately after its completion and was copied innumerable times. The first highly imaginative feature one notices is the way Leonardo integrated the fresco into the architecture of the refectory. Demonstrating his mastery of geometry, Leonardo contrived a series of visual paradoxes to create an elaborate illusion—a complex perspective that made the room of the Last Supper look like an extension of the refectory itself, in which the monks ate their meals.[7]

One consequence of this complex perspective is that from every viewing position in the room, the spectator is drawn into the drama of the picture's narrative with equal force. And dramatic it is. Whereas traditionally the Last Supper was pictured at the moment of communion, a moment of calm, individual meditation for each apostle, Leonardo chose the ominous moment when Jesus says, "One of you will betray me."

The words of Christ have stirred up the solemn company, creating powerful waves of emotion. However, the effect is far from chaotic. The apostles are clearly organized into four groups of three figures, with Judas forming one of the groups together with Peter and John. This is another striking compositional innovation. Traditionally, Judas was pictured sitting on the other side of the table, facing the apostles, with his back to the spectator. Leonardo had no need to identify the traitor by isolating him in this way. By giving the apostles carefully chosen expressive gestures, which together cover a wide range of emotions, the artist made sure that we immediately recognize Judas, as he shrinks back into the dark of John's shadow, nervously clutching his bag of silver. The depiction of the apostles as embodiments of individual emotional states and the integration of Judas into the dramatic narrative were so revolutionary that after Leonardo, no self-respecting artist could go back to the previous static configuration.

Throughout his career as a painter, Leonardo was famous for his ability to capture emotional subtleties—the "movements of the soul"—in facial expressions and eloquent gestures, and to weave them into complex compositional narratives. This exceptional ability was already apparent in his early *Madonnas* and reached its climax in *The Last Supper* and his other mature works.

The playwright and poet Giovanni Battista Giraldi, whose father knew Leonardo, provided a fascinating glimpse of the artist's methods in achieving this singular mastery. "When Leonardo wished to paint a figure," Giraldi wrote, "he first considered what social standing and what nature it was to represent; whether noble or plebeian, gay or severe, troubled or serene, old or young, irate or quiet, good or evil; and when he had made up his mind, he went to places where he knew that people of that kind assembled and observed their faces, their manners, dresses, and gestures; and when he found what fitted his purpose, he noted it in a little book which he was always carrying in his belt. After repeating this procedure many times, and being satisfied with the material thus collected for the figure which he wished to paint, he would proceed to give it shape."[8]

During this period, while Leonardo painted *The Last Supper* and meditated on the nature of human frailty and betrayal, his personal life was enriched by an encounter that would turn into a lasting friendship. In 1496 the Franciscan monk and well-known mathematician Luca

Pacioli came to teach in Milan. Fra Luca had established his reputation as a mathematician with a vast treatise, a kind of mathematical text-book, titled *Summa de aritmetica geometrica proportioni et proportionalità* (*Summary of Arithmetic, Geometry of Proportion, and Proportionality*). Written in Italian rather than in the customary scholarly Latin, it con-tained synopses of the works of many great mathematicians, past and present. Leonardo, who had been keenly interested in mathematics since his studies at the library of Pavia, was fascinated by Pacioli's trea-tise and immediately attracted to its author.

Fra Luca was a few years older than Leonardo and a fellow Tuscan, which may have helped them establish an easy rapport that soon turned into friendship. This friendship gave Leonardo a unique opportunity to deepen his mathematical studies. Pacioli not only helped him under-stand various portions of his own treatise, but guided him in a thor-ough study of the Latin edition of Euclid's *Elements*. With the help of his friend, Leonardo systematically worked through all thirteen vol-umes of Euclid's foundational exposition and filled two Notebooks with mathematical notes.[9]

Soon after they began their study sessions, Leonardo and Fra Luca decided to collaborate on a book, titled *De divina proportione*, to be writ-ten by Pacioli and illustrated by Leonardo. The book, presented to Ludovico as a lavish manuscript and eventually published in Venice, contains an extensive review of the role of proportion in architecture and anatomy—and in particular of the golden section, or "divine pro-portion"—as well as detailed discussions of the five regular polyhedra known as the Platonic solids.[10] It features over sixty illustrations by Leonardo, including superb drawings of the Platonic solids in both solid and skeletal forms, testimony to his exceptional ability to visual-ize abstract geometric forms. What further distinguishes this work is that it is the only collection of drawings by Leonardo published during his lifetime.[11]

While Leonardo drew the illustrations for Pacioli's book, he also continued work on *The Last Supper*. Progress was steady but slow, as the artist worked on in his typical thoughtful and meditative way. He spent considerable time roaming the streets of Milan looking for suit-able models for the faces of the apostles.[12] By 1497 the only part left to complete was the head of Judas.[13] At that point, the prior of the convent became so impatient with Leonardo's slowness that he complained to the duke, who summoned the artist to hear his reasons for the delay. According to Vasari, Leonardo explained to the Moor that he was working on *The Last Supper* at least two hours a day, but that most of this work took place in his mind. He went on, slyly, to say that, if he did not find an appropriate model for Judas, he would give the villain the features of the petulant prior. Ludovico was so amused by Leonardo's reply that he instructed the prior to be patient and let Leonardo finish his work undisturbed.

A few months later *The Last Supper* was completed. Unfortunately, it soon began to deteriorate. The painting is not a fresco, strictly speaking; it was not painted *al fresco* with water-based pigment on damp, fresh plaster. The fresco technique resulted in lasting murals but required fast execution, which was incompatible with Leonardo's way of painting. Instead, the artist experimented with a mixture of egg tempera and oil. Because the wall was damp, the painting soon began to suffer. Tragically, subsequent attempts to halt or reverse its deterioration have been unsuccessful. Over the centuries there have been countless restorations of *The Last Supper*, many involving questionable techniques and often without exact records being kept. As Kenneth Clark wrote in 1939, "It is hard to resist the conclusion that what we now see on the wall of the Grazie is largely the work of restorers."[14]

The last effort to restore Leonardo's masterpiece, completed in 2000 under the direction of Pinin Brambilla Barcilon, was by far the most elaborate and sophisticated, taking more than twenty years.[15] The restorer and her team removed almost all the traces of earlier restorations in order to expose as much of Leonardo's paint as could be found. Instead of concealing the damage, they reconstructed the original contours and filled the empty spaces between the existing fragments with watercolor of the same general hue. What the spectator now sees from a close distance are clear distinctions between the original paint and the empty spaces, while from farther back these distinctions disappear, giving way to the impression of seeing a faded version of the original painting.

In spite of the fact that very little is now left of Leonardo's original masterpiece, the restored work does show the eloquence and power of the protagonists' gestures, and even a hint of the luminosity that is so characteristic of Leonardo's paintings. "We still catch sigh, perhuman forms of the original," writes Kenneth Clark, "and drama of their interplay we can appreciate some of the qualities w made *The Last Supper* the keystone of European art."[16]

POLITICAL TURMOIL

When Leonardo finished *The Last Supper* in 1498, he did not know that his position at the Sforza court and his stay in Milan would come to an abrupt end two years later. His study and research program continued unabated. He kept up his mathematical studies with Fra Luca, worked on the theory of human flight, and experimented with various flying machines. In addition, he painted a portrait of Ludovico's new mistress, Lucrezia Crivelli,[17] and after the tragic death of the duke's wife Beatrice, Ludovico entrusted him with the decoration of the Sala delle Asse in her memory.[18]

In those last two years at the Sforza court, Leonardo also made several journeys within northern Italy. In 1498 he accompanied the Moor on a visit to Genoa, and on another occasion he made a trip to the Alps. There, he climbed the Monte Rosa,[19] Europe's second-highest mountain, a huge glacier-covered massif at the Swiss-Italian border with ten major peaks, most of them higher than 4,000 meters (13,000 feet). Even today, ascending any one of these peaks is very strenuous, although technically not difficult, involving five to ten hours of climbing up steep grades, and walking long stretches on glaciers. One has to be in good physical condition, accustomed to high altitude. In Leonardo's time, such an ascent must have been extraordinary.

Several of his contemporaries describe Leonardo as being very athletic in his youth;[20] clearly, he still had the necessary strength to climb mountains in his forties. In his notes he describes the deep blue of the sky "almost above the clouds," and the silvery threads of rivers in the valleys below. The view from that height, several hundred years before the age of industrial pollution, must have been spectacular indeed. He could see the "four rivers that water Europe"—the Rhine, the Rhône, the Danube, and the Po.[21]

While Leonardo enjoyed the clear view of the valleys and rivers from Monte Rosa, political clouds threatening the peace were gathering. In 1494 the king of France, Charles VIII, crossed the Alps at the head of a large army; Ludovico sacrificed the bronze retained for the casting of Leonardo's *gran cavallo* in order to defend Milan.[22] During the subsequent years, the French steadily advanced through Italy. In 1498, after Charles VIII died in an accident, the new French king, Louis XII, declared himself duke of Milan and prepared to conquer the city.

In the summer of 1499, Louis formed a secret alliance with Venice and invaded Lombardy to attack its capital, Milan, while the Venetians attacked from the east. Ludovico, in panic, fled to Innsbruck, Austria, with his family to seek the protection of his relative, Emperor Maximilian. In September, Milan capitulated without a shot being fired.[23] Leonardo, apparently quite oblivious to the political turmoil around him, calmly recorded some new observations on "movement and weight" in his Notebooks.[24]

In October, Louis XII entered Milan in triumph. Apparently, he offered Leonardo a position as military engineer. Louis was so enchanted by *The Last Supper* that he inquired whether it could be removed from the wall of the Grazie and taken to France.[25] Leonardo, however, turned down the king's offer, perhaps because he had witnessed widespread looting and killing by the French troops. When a detachment of archers used the clay model of his *cavallo* for target practice, he realized it was time for him to leave the city. He put his affairs in order, sent his savings to his bank at Santa Maria Nuova in Florence, and before the year was out, he and his friend Fra Luca left Milan.

RETURN TO FLORENCE

Luca Pacioli traveled directly to Florence; Leonardo made a long detour via Mantua and Venice and joined his friend a few months later. When he returned to Florence, where he would spend the next six years, Leonardo, now forty-eight, was at the beginning of what was then considered old age. However, his artistic and scientific creativity continued undiminished. Over the next fifteen years he would paint several more masterpieces and produce his most substantial scientific work.

He was now famous as an artist and engineer throughout Italy. And it was well known by his contemporaries that he dedicated much of his time to scientific and mathematical studies. The fact that hardly anyone knew what those studies were about only enhanced his image as an enigmatic genius.

Leonardo was in great demand as a consultant in architecture and military engineering as well as for lucrative commissions for paintings. Having been paid handsomely by Ludovico Sforza for the past decade, he had enough financial security that he did not have to curry favor with the powerful and wealthy, even though steady and lucrative employment was his preference. However, he continued to be utterly aloof from politics, and showed little loyalty to any state or political ruler.

Many of Leonardo's consulting assignments, especially those in military engineering, required him to travel to other cities in northern Italy, and his second period in Florence was punctuated by frequent journeys. But his travels seemed to inspire him to ever more intense work. In addition to examining military fortifications and producing numerous drawings with suggestions for improvements, he studied the flora and geological formations of the areas he visited, drew beautiful, detailed maps that showed distances and elevations, and visited renowned libraries to continue his theoretical studies.

Leonardo's maps from that period show geographical details with a degree of accuracy far beyond anything attempted by the cartographers of his time.[26] He used washes of different intensities to follow the contours of mountain chains, different shades representing different elevations, and he pictured the rivers, valleys, and settlements in such a realistic manner that one has the eerie feeling of looking at the landscape from an airplane (see Fig. 7-7 on p. 209). In most of his maps, Leonardo focused specifically on the network of rivers and lakes. In some views of stretches of the river Arno (Fig. 4-1), he uses blue wash of varying hues to produce a striking resemblance between the flow of the river's watercourses and the flow of blood in the body's veins (Fig. 4-2)—an exquisitely beautiful and moving testimony of how Leonardo saw water as the veins of the living Earth.

Leonardo also continued to create great artistic works (including the *Madonna and Child with the Yarnwinder*, various sketches for the *Madonna and Child with Saint Anne*, and two different compositions for

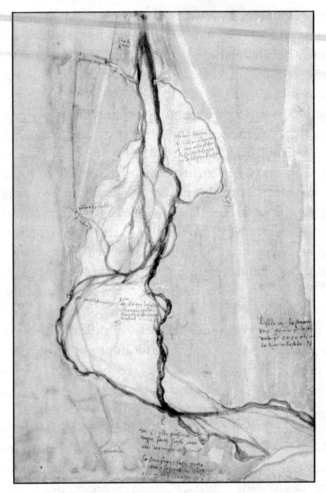

*Figure 4-1: The water veins of the Earth, river Arno,
c. 1504, Drawings and Miscellaneous Papers,
Vol. IV, folio 444r*

Leda and the Swan), many of which exerted considerable influence on contemporary painters, including Raphael and Michelangelo.[27] "Surprisingly," writes Martin Kemp, "this period is marked by an astonishing richness of artistic activity, in which more than a dozen significant compositions were conceived and taken to various stages of completion by Leonardo himself or his assistants."[28]

In February 1500, soon after leaving Milan, Leonardo spent a few weeks in Mantua at the invitation of Isabella d'Este, the elder sister of Ludovico's late wife Beatrice. Beautiful and sophisticated, Isabella was

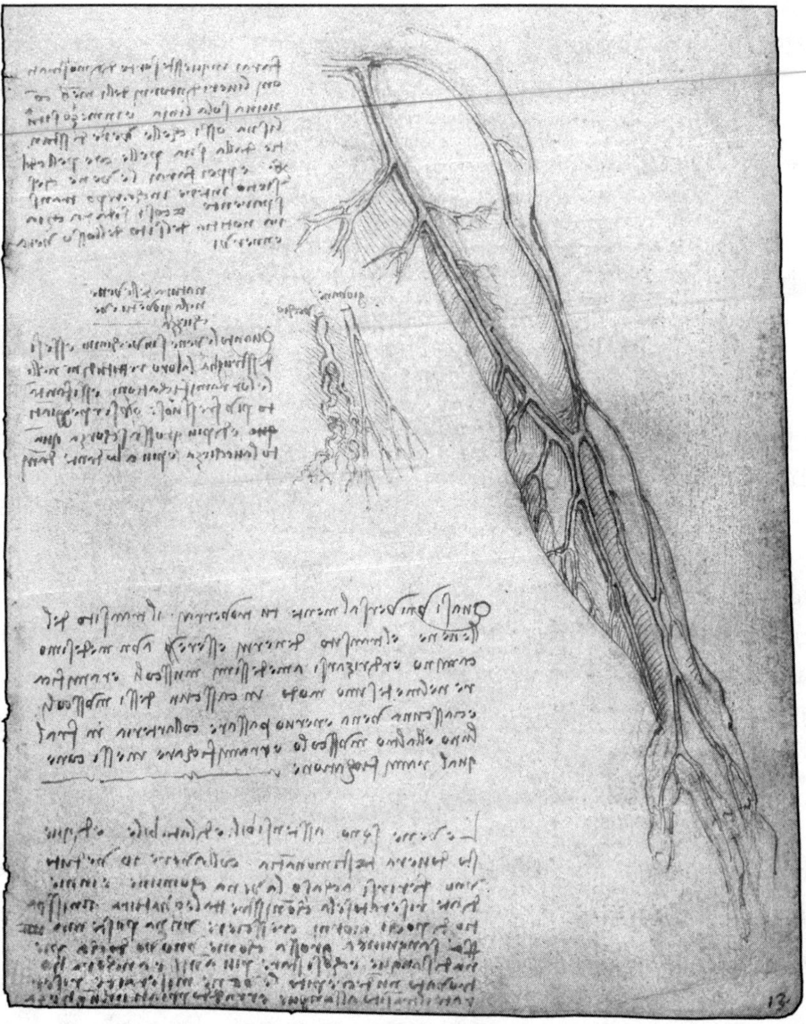

Figure 4-2: Blood veins in the left arm, c. 1507–8,
Anatomical Studies, folio 69r

a renowned art collector and generous patron of the arts, if temperamental and tyrannical.[29] She was mainly interested in paintings that praised her merits and would often dictate their composition, even the colors to be used. It was well known how she had harassed Giovanni Bellini, taking him to court to obtain exactly the picture she wanted, and how she had written no fewer than fifty-three imperious letters to Perugino, pressing him to finish an allegory she had designed.

Isabella had met Leonardo often at the Sforza court and had always beseeched him to paint her portrait. In Mantua, the artist seemed to obey. He drew her in profile in black and red chalk and probably also offered her a copy, implying that he would keep the original in order to transfer it to a panel and paint it later.[30] However, in spite of many subsequent entreaties by Isabella's emissaries, Leonardo never painted the full portrait. Apparently, he had no desire to subject himself to Isabella's whims. Beneath his exquisite courtesy and charm, he always remained fiercely independent when his artistic integrity was at stake.

From Mantua, Leonardo journeyed to Venice, where the Senate was in urgent need of a military engineer with his talents. The Venetians had just suffered a defeat in a naval battle against the Turks. And the Ottoman army was encamped in the Friuli region on the banks of the river Isonzo, threatening an invasion from the republic's northeastern borders. Leonardo went to Friuli, studied the topography of the land, and came back to the Senate with a plan to build a movable lock on the Isonzo. He argued that this could be used to dam up a large body of water, which could be released to drown the Turkish armies when they crossed the river.[31] Ingenious as the plan was, the Venetian Senate rejected it.

The Venetians were also concerned about a possible attack by the Turkish navy. Leonardo responded to this challenge with designs of diving apparatus, invisible from the surface, to be used in marine warfare—small submarines that could be sent out "to sink a fleet of ships"; divers equipped with airbags, goggles, and special devices to bore holes into the planks of ships; frogmen with flippers, and the like. The modern look of these designs is quite astonishing.[32] Leonardo was well aware of the conflict between his work as a military engineer and his pacifist nature.[33] "I do not describe my method for remaining under water for as long as I can remain without food," he wrote in the Codex Leicester. "This I do not publish or divulge because of the evil nature of men, who might practice assassinations at the bottom of the seas by breaking the ships in their lowest parts and sinking them together with the crews who are in them."[34]

Leonardo was also asked to examine the Venetian canal system for possible improvements. In the course of this work, he invented a beveled lock gate that played a part in the evolution of canal design.[35]

In view of all these interesting projects in civil and military engineering, it is surprising that Leonardo did not stay in Venice for more than a few weeks. Yet, by April 1500, he was back in his native Tuscany.

The most likely explanation for his quick return to Florence is that Luca Pacioli had, in the meantime, been awarded the chair of mathematics at the University of Florence. Leonardo must have seen it as an ideal opportunity for him to continue his studies with Fra Luca, and to meet leading Florentine intellectuals. Besides, he was also likely looking forward to being appreciated as an artist in the city that had nurtured his genius in his formative years.

Leonardo's expectations of a warm welcome in Florence were amply met. Soon after his arrival in the city, he was invited to paint an altarpiece for the Servite convent of the Santissima Annunziata. To make the commission more attractive, the friars provided spacious lodgings for Leonardo and his household in the convent's guest quarters.[36] Leonardo gladly accepted the commission and took up residence in the Annunziata, although he kept them waiting a long time before starting the commission. Instead of painting, he calmly pursued his mathematical studies with Pacioli and continued his experiments on weight, force, and movement.

"Finally," Vasari writes, "he did a cartoon showing Our Lady with Saint Anne and the infant Christ. This work not only won the astonished admiration of all the artists but, when finished, for two days it attracted to the room where it was exhibited a crowd of men and women, young and old, who flocked there, as if they were attending a great festival, to gaze in amazement at the marvels he had created." Leonardo could not have wished for a more enthusiastic reception by the city to which he had at last returned.

In the *Madonna and Child with Saint Anne*, as the painting is called today, Leonardo had again broken new ground with both his composition and the theological interpretation of a traditional religious theme.[37] Rather than presenting Mary and her mother, Saint Anne, in a static configuration—seated next to each other with Jesus in Mary's arms between them, or with Saint Anne seated higher in a majestic, hierarchical composition—Leonardo upset tradition by adding a lamb as a fourth figure. Jesus, having slipped to the ground, reaches for the

Figure 4-3: Madonna and Child with Saint Anne,
c. 1508 onward, Musée du Louvre, Paris

lamb as Mary tries to restrain him, and Saint Anne seems to hold her back.

The theological message embodied in Leonardo's highly original composition can be seen as a continuation of his long meditation on the destiny of Christ, which he had begun with the *Virgin of the Rocks*. Mary, in an anxious gesture, attempts to pull her son away from the lamb, the symbol of the Passion, while Saint Anne, representing the Mother Church, knows that Mary's gesture is futile—the Passion is Christ's destiny and cannot be avoided.

The completion of the painting took Leonardo more than a decade, during which he made numerous drawings with variations on compositional and theological themes. After the original cartoon, which is now lost, he produced a larger one, now in the National Gallery in London, in which Mary and Saint Anne are seated side by side and the lamb is replaced by Saint John the Baptist. But eventually he returned to his original idea. The final painting (Fig. 4-3), now in the Louvre, is a complex and masterful synthesis of his previous variations. The figures almost blend into each other in their rhythmic balance, with Leonardo's dreamy mountains, foreshadowing the landscape of the *Mona Lisa*, in the background.

TRAVELS IN CENTRAL ITALY

When Leonardo arrived in Florence, he found a city that was quite different from the one he had left eighteen years earlier. In 1494 the French king, Charles VIII, at that time still in alliance with Ludovico Sforza, had expelled the Medici and returned Florence to a republic. In the ensuing confusion, the city fell under the spell of the fanatical teachings of the Dominican monk Girolamo Savonarola, who managed to transform the republic into a fundamentalist theocracy.[38] For the next four years, Savonarola ruled as a virtual dictator until he was excommunicated by the pope, tried for heresy, and burned at the stake.

In the meantime, Pope Alexander VI had enlisted his son, the young military commander Cesare Borgia, to help him build a papal empire in central Italy. Intelligent, cruel, and ruthlessly opportunistic,

Cesare subdued one city after another for the papacy, from Piombino on the west coast to Rimini on the Adriatic. He was well aware, however, that unless his new conquests were systematically fortified, they were vulnerable to attack from hostile neighbors. To protect them, Cesare turned to the military engineer with the greatest reputation, Leonardo da Vinci.

In 1502, Leonardo was hired by Cesare to travel throughout central Italy, inspect the ramparts, canals, and other fortifications of the newly conquered cities, and make suggestions for their improvements. To confirm his appointment, Cesare provided him with a passport that gave him complete freedom of movement, encouraged him to take any initiative he deemed appropriate, and allowed him to travel in comfort with his entourage. For Leonardo, this appointment must have sounded like a tremendous opportunity, and he took full advantage of it, even though he must have known that the conflict between Borgia's cruel and violent nature and his own compassion and pacifism would eventually become unbearable.

During the next six to eight months, Leonardo traveled extensively in Tuscany and the adjacent Romagna—Piombino, Siena, Arezzo, Cesena, Pesaro, Rimini—making exquisite maps of various regions, working at schemes to build canals and drain marshes, studying the movements of waves and tides, and filling his Notebooks with drawings of ingenious new fortifications designed to withstand the impact of cannonballs that were now being fired at increased velocities.[39] During those months he kept a fairly detailed account of his movements and projects in a pocket-sized notebook, now known as Manuscript L.

In October, Leonardo joined Cesare Borgia in Imola, where the troops had taken up winter quarters. He spent the rest of the year designing new fortifications for the citadel and drawing a highly original and very beautiful circular map of the town. In Imola he also met the famous politician and writer Niccolò Machiavelli, one of the most influential figures of the Renaissance. Born in Florence, Machiavelli had entered the political service of the republic as a diplomat and rapidly risen in importance. He was sent on many prominent missions in Italy and France, during which he shrewdly observed the fine details of power politics, which he later described and analyzed in his best-known work, *The Prince*. His "ideal" Renaissance prince was an amoral and cunning tyrant, apparently modeled on Cesare Borgia.

A brilliant intellectual, Machiavelli was also a renowned poet and playwright; Leonardo was likely fascinated by him, and they remained on friendly terms for many years. When they met in Imola, Machiavelli had been sent to Romagna as an envoy of the Florentine republic, probably to keep an eye on the devious Borgia, in whose company he remained for the whole winter. There is no record of the many conversations this extraordinary trio—Cesare Borgia, Niccolò Machiavelli, and Leonardo da Vinci—must have had during their long winter evenings at Imola. However, it seems that they brought Leonardo face-to-face with the numerous crimes that had accompanied Borgia's rise to power.

Until then, Leonardo had always traveled independently of the army, working mostly on defensive systems without ever witnessing a battle. But in the extended company of both Borgia and Machiavelli, he must have heard firsthand accounts of Cesare's many massacres and murders. Perhaps he was so repelled by them that he felt he had to leave Borgia's employ. In his Notebooks, Leonardo mentions neither when he left Cesare, nor why, but by February 1503 he was back in Florence, and he withdrew money from his account, possibly because he had left Borgia abruptly, without being paid.

Leonardo did not have to wait long for a new appointment. Florence was at war with Pisa and had laid siege to the town, which was of great strategic importance because of its port. After several months of siege the Pisans still refused to surrender. The Florentine Signoria (the city's government) asked Leonardo to come up with a military solution. In June he visited the region and, as in Friuli three years earlier, drew a detailed map of its topography before devising a strategic plan.[40]

When he returned to Florence, he proposed to divert the Arno away from Pisa, which would deprive the town of its water supply and also provide Florence with a pathway to the sea. He argued that this strategy would end the siege quickly and without bloodshed. Leonardo's plan had the enthusiastic support of Machiavelli. It was accepted by the city fathers, and work on the project began in August. However, during the subsequent months it encountered many difficulties, from a shortage of manpower and military protection to unexpected floods. After half a year, the scheme was abandoned.

FLIGHTS OF FANCY

Leonardo used his study of the Arno valley to revive his old dream of creating a navigable waterway between Florence and Pisa. He drew numerous beautifully colored maps, showing how the proposed canal would avoid the steep hills west of Florence and instead run in a large arc past Prato and Pistoia, and cut through the heights of Serravalle before rejoining the Arno east of Pisa. He imagined that this waterway would provide irrigation for parched land as well as energy for numerous mills that could produce silk and paper, drive potters' wheels, saw wood, and sharpen metal.[41] It was his hope that the multiple benefits of such an "industrial" canal would bring peace and prosperity to the warring cities. Leonardo's dream of peace through technology was never realized, but he would probably have been pleased to know that five hundred years later the *autostrada* linking Florence with Lucca and Pisa would follow exactly the route he proposed for his waterway.

While he drew his maps of the Arno watershed, Leonardo studied the smooth and turbulent flows of water in rivers, the erosion of rocks, and the deposits of gravel and sand. On a larger scale, he speculated about the formation of the earth out of the waters of the sea and the movement of the "watery humors" through the macrocosm. He studied strata of rock formations and their fossil contents, which he recognized as telltale signs of life in the distant geological past. He saw mountain lakes as cutoff portions of the primeval sea, and pictured in his maps and paintings how they gradually found their way back to the oceans through narrow gorges.

In October 1503, while the war with Pisa dragged on, Leonardo received the tremendously prestigious commission for *The Battle of Anghiari*, the large fresco to be painted for the Signoria in its new council chamber at the Palazzo Vecchio. The artist accepted immediately. He registered his name once more with the painters' guild of San Luca and was given sumptuous premises for himself and his household in the convent of Santa Maria Novella, including the spacious Sala del Papa (Hall of the Pope), which he used as his studio.

The following summer, Leonardo recorded the death of his father in a brief and rather formal statement: "On the 9th day of July 1504, on a Wednesday at seven o'clock, died Ser Piero da Vinci, notary to the Palazzo del Podestà, my father. . . . He was 80 years old and left ten sons and two daughters."[42] From all we know, Leonardo was never close to his father, an ambitious man who was mostly interested in his own career. Nevertheless, it is surprising that he did not add any personal reflections to this entry in his private notebook. The distant tone of the note is reinforced by the unusual fact that it is not written in Leonardo's customary mirror writing, but rather is written from left to right, as if it were a draft for a public statement.

Leonardo worked on the large cartoon for the fresco and on painting its central portion, *The Struggle for the Standard*, for about three years. But with the horrors of Cesare Borgia's massacres still fresh in his mind, his *Battle of Anghiari* would not be a celebration of the military glory of Florence, as the city fathers expected. Instead, it would stand for all the world to see as his definitive condemnation of that *pazzia bestialissima*, the madness of war.[43]

During these years, Leonardo continued to reflect on the basic characteristics of the flow of water. In so doing, he realized that Euclidean geometry was insufficient to describe the shapes of waves and eddies. Around 1505 he began a new Notebook, now known as Codex Forster I, with the words "A book entitled 'On Transformation,' that is, of one body into another without diminution or increase of matter."[44] In forty folios of this Notebook he discussed and drew a great variety of transformations of geometrical shapes into one another—half circles into crescents, cubes into pyramids, spheres into cubes, and others. These pages were the beginning of his long fascination with a new type of geometry, a geometry of forms and transformations known today as topology.[45]

During the same years, Leonardo pursued with great intensity two engineering projects that excited his imagination. One was his long-contemplated plan for a waterway between Florence and Pisa; the other

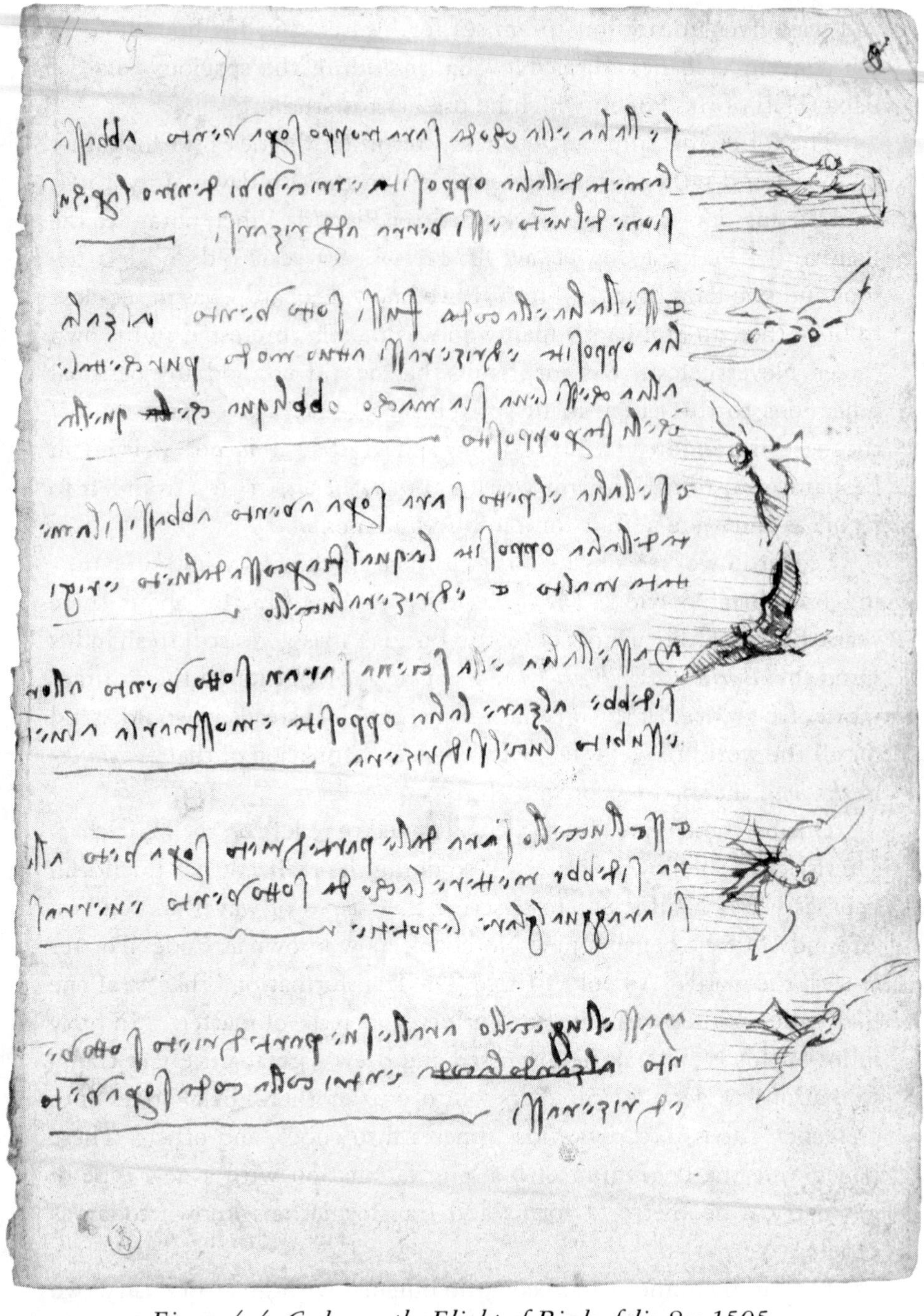

Figure 4-4: Codex on the Flight of Birds, folio 8r; 1505,
Biblioteca Reale, Turin

was his work on flying machines, which he took up with renewed vigor while he was also exploring the geometry of transformations and painting his battle scene in the Palazzo Vecchio.

When he had built flying machines in Milan and tested them in his workshop in the Corte Vecchia, Leonardo's main concern had been to find out how a human pilot could flap mechanical wings with enough force and velocity to compress the air underneath and be lifted up. For these tests he had designed various types of wings modeled after those of birds, bats, and flying fish. Now, ten years later, he embarked on careful and methodical observations of the flight of birds. He spent hours in the hills surrounding Florence, near Fiesole, observing the behavior of birds in flight, and he filled several Notebooks with drawings and comments that analyzed the birds' turning maneuvers, their ability to maintain their equilibrium in the wind, and the detailed mechanisms of active flight. His aim was to design a flying machine that would be able, like a bird, to maneuver with agility, keep its balance in the wind, and move its wings with enough force to allow it to fly.[46]

Leonardo summarized his observations and analyses in a small Notebook called *Codice sul volo degli uccelli* (Codex on the Flight of Birds), which is full of gorgeous drawings of birds in flight as well as of complex mechanisms designed to mimic their precise movements (see Fig. 4-4). His observations and analyses led him to the conclusion that human flight with mechanical wings might not be possible because of the limitations of our anatomy. Birds, he observed, have powerful pectoral muscles to move their wings with a force humans cannot summon. However, he speculated that "soaring flight," or gliding, might be possible. He would return to his research on human flight once more during the last phase of his life, combining the study of natural flight with theoretical studies of wind and air in an attempt to outline a comprehensive "science of the winds."[47]

Leonardo continued to work on *The Battle of Anghiari* throughout 1505. However, because of defective materials, the painting suffered (the colors could not be fixed and began to run), and he was unable to repair the damage.[48] At the same time, the French king, Louis XII, who was a great admirer of the artist, requested Leonardo's presence at his court in Milan from the Signoria. The Florentines resisted, arguing that they had spent large sums of money for the fresco in their council chamber and needed it to be finished. A diplomatic tussle ensued that lasted several months, but eventually the Signoria was forced to relent. In May 1506, abandoning his fresco, Leonardo left once more for an extended sojourn in Milan.

A STAGE OF MATURITY

King Louis XII was represented at his court in Milan by his lieutenant, Charles d'Amboise, whom Louis had appointed as its governor. Charles was a powerful ruler, but convivial and keenly interested in promoting the arts. And, like his king, he was a great admirer of Leonardo. He received the artist warmly at the French court and treated him royally. Leonardo was given a generous allowance that was not tied to specific commissions, was consulted on all kinds of artistic and technical projects, and his company and service were eagerly sought by every important person at court. Leonardo was delighted to be back in Milan, the city where he had achieved great fame fifteen years earlier, and he easily fell back into the lifestyle of the court artist and engineer that he knew so well from his days at the Sforza court.

Once more there were plenty of masques and pageants for which he was asked to design splendid sets and costumes. As he had done before, Leonardo also worked on improving the locks and dams of some of the Lombard canals, and to show his gratitude to Charles d'Amboise, he designed a villa with luxurious gardens for the governor. According to the surviving notes, his garden designs were quite extraordinary. They included scented groves of oranges and lemons, a large aviary covered by a copper net to keep exotic birds inside while letting them fly around freely, a fan of revolving sails to create a pleasant breeze in the hot summers, a table with running water to cool wine, automatic musical instruments powered by water, and so on.[49]

At age fifty-five, Leonardo's appearance must have approached that of the archetypal sage in his famous Turin self-portrait.[50] Although his eyesight had weakened (he had worn glasses for a few years), his energies, artistic creativity, and intellectual drive continued undiminished. The sympathetic understanding and generosity of Charles d'Amboise gave him the freedom to dedicate as much time as he desired to his studies and to pursue them in any direction he wished. This unprecedented freedom, combined with his mature age, brought forth a period of broad systemic reflection, of revision and synthesis, allowing him to map out comprehensive treatises on many of his favorite subjects: the flow of water, the geometry of transformations, the movement of the human body, the growth of plants, and the science of painting.

The six years Leonardo spent at the French court in Milan marked a stage of maturity both in his science and his art. During those years the artist slowly developed and refined three of his mature master paintings: the *Madonna and Child with Saint Anne*, the *Leda*, and his most famous painting, the *Mona Lisa*. In these masterworks, Leonardo perfected the characteristics that established his uniqueness as a painter—the serpentine forms that brought movement and grace into his figures, the delicate smiles and gestures that mirrored the "movements of the soul," and the subtle melting of shades, or sfumato, that became a unifying principle of his compositions. In all three of these works, Leonardo used his extensive knowledge of geology, botany, and human anatomy to explore the mystery of the procreative power of life, in the macrocosm as well as in the female body. As he continued to work on them year after year, he turned each painting into a meditation on the origin of life.[51]

In 1507, Leonardo met a young man, Francesco Melzi, who became his pupil, personal assistant, and inseparable companion. Melzi was the son of a Lombard aristocrat who owned a large estate at Vaprio, near Milan. When they met, Francesco was around fifteen and, according to Vasari, a *bellissimo fanciullo* ("a very beautiful boy"), who showed considerable talent as a painter. The adolescent boy and the elderly artist were immediately attracted to each other, and soon after their first meeting, Francesco announced to his parents that he wished to join Leonardo's household. For an aristocratic family, such a move was highly unusual, but surprisingly they did not object. Persuaded perhaps by Leonardo's fame or his personal charisma, they not only allowed their son to join him, but invited the master and his entourage to stay at their spacious villa for almost two years after he left Milan. From that point on, Melzi never left Leonardo's side. He took care of the master's affairs, wrote entries in the Notebooks from his dictation, nursed him when he was ill, and eventually was entrusted with Leonardo's legacy.

Toward the end of 1507, Leonardo's beloved uncle Francesco died in Vinci and left his entire estate to his favorite nephew. But the family, led by Ser Piero's youngest son, challenged the will, and Leonardo had to go to Florence to plead his case. He was obliged to stay there for several months, until judgment was finally reached in his favor.[52] During these months, Leonardo was the guest of the wealthy Florentine patron Piero di Braccio Martelli, an accomplished mathematician, who was also extending his hospitality to the sculptor Giovan Francesco Rustici.

According to Vasari, Leonardo was very fond of Rustici, who had been his fellow apprentice in Verrocchio's workshop. Rustici, Vasari tells us, was not only an excellent sculptor but also a delightful eccentric who loved to host fanciful feasts and play elaborate pranks. He kept a large menagerie in his studio that included an eagle, a raven, numerous snakes, and a porcupine trained like a dog, which would occasionally rub its pricks against people's legs under the table. Leonardo, who loved animals and was himself used to playing practical jokes, felt very much at home in the relaxed and playful ambience of the Casa Martelli and gladly participated in Rustici's spirited entertainments. According to Vasari, he also helped the sculptor model a group of bronze statues for the Baptistery of St. John in Florence during that time.[53]

Leonardo's main activity in Martelli's house, however, was of a far more serious nature. He used his ample free time to bring some order into his vast collection of notes, dating from the previous twenty years. He threw himself into this enormous task with great energy, systematically reviewing the contents of all his Notebooks. But he soon realized that rearranging the entire collection was too ambitious a job. He decided, therefore, to limit himself to a more manageable task, assembling a few selections on his favorite subjects—water, anatomy, painting, and botany—about which he would write comprehensive treatises. "Begun in Florence, in the house of Piero di Braccio Martelli, on the 22nd of March 1508," he wrote on the opening page of a new codex, now known as Codex Arundel. "This will be a collection without any order, made up of numerous sheets that I have copied here in the hope of later putting them in order in their proper places, according to the subjects they treat."⁵⁴ Over the following years, Leonardo mapped out the structure of his treatises in some detail and began to compose them. He may have finished some, although no full treatises are extant among the existing Notebooks today.

While reviewing his notes in Martelli's house in Florence, Leonardo decided that human anatomy was an area he needed to revisit thoroughly. During the next four years he performed more dissections than ever before, and his anatomical drawings reached their highest degree of accuracy. He planned to publish a formal treatise on anatomy, and outlined it in great detail. During his first phase of anatomical studies, twenty years earlier, he had been concerned with the physiology of vision, the pathways of the nerves, and the "seat of the soul." Now he concentrated on the grand theme of the human body in motion.

In his outline, Leonardo described in meticulous detail how he would demonstrate "in 120 books" the combined actions of nerves, muscles, tendons, and bones. "My configuration of the human body will be demonstrated to you just as if you had the natural man before you," he announced, and he explained why this would require numerous dissections.

> You must understand that such knowledge will not leave you satisfied on account of the very great confusion that results from the mix-up of membranes with veins, arteries, nerves, tendons, muscles, bones, and blood. . . .
>
> Therefore it is necessary to perform more dissections, of which you need 3 to have full knowledge of the veins and arteries, destroying with the utmost diligence all the rest; and another 3 to have knowledge of the membranes; and 3 for the tendons, muscles, and ligaments; 3 for the bones and cartilages; and 3 for the anatomy of the bones which have to be sawn through to demonstrate which is hollow and which is not. . . .
>
> Through my plan . . . there will be placed before you 3 or 4 demonstrations of each part from different aspects in such a way that you will retain a true and full knowledge of what you want to know about the human body.⁵⁵

We do not know how many of the 120 chapters (or "books") of his treatise Leonardo composed. However, the superb drawings that survived,
which are now in the Windsor Collection, make it evident that his
promises were not exaggerated.

In his Anatomical Studies, Leonardo gives a vivid description of
the dreadful conditions under which he had to work. As there were no
chemicals to preserve the cadavers, they would begin to decompose before he had time to examine and draw them properly. To avoid accusa-
tions of heresy, he worked at night, lighting his dissection room by
candles, which must have made the experience even more macabre.
"You will perhaps be impeded by your stomach," he writes, addressing
an imaginary apprentice, "and if this does not impede you, you will
perhaps be impeded by the fear of living through the night hours in
the company of these corpses, quartered and flayed and frightening to
behold."

It is evident that Leonardo needed a steely will to overcome his
own aversion, but he persevered and carried out his dissections with
the most delicate care and attention to detail, "taking away in its minutest particles all the flesh" to expose blood vessels, muscles, or bones
until the corpse's state of decay was too advanced to continue. "One
single body was not sufficient for enough time," he explains, "so it was
necessary to proceed little by little with as many bodies as would render the complete knowledge. This I repeated twice in order to observe
the differences."[56]

While he was still in Florence going through his notes and plan-
ning his treatises, Leonardo was able to perform a postmortem on an
old man he met by chance at the hospital of Santa Maria Nuova, where
he had done his earlier anatomical studies, and who died in his presence. This dissection became a milestone in his anatomical work and
led him to some of his most important medical discoveries. The story
itself is highly significant and very moving. It shows how Leonardo was
capable of performing his most precise dissections and scientific analyses without losing sight of human dignity:

> And this old man, a few hours before his death, told me that he
> was over a hundred years old and that he felt nothing wrong with
> his body other than weakness. And thus, while sitting on a bed in

the hospital of Santa Maria Nuova in Florence, without any movement or other sign of any mishap, he passed out of this life.—And
I made an anatomy of him in order to see the cause of so sweet a
death.[57]

Based on this anatomy, he brilliantly diagnosed that the old man had
died from a thickening and narrowing of his blood vessels, the condition that became known as arteriosclerosis more than three hundred
years after Leonardo discovered it.[58]

LAST YEARS IN MILAN

Upon his return to Milan, Leonardo continued his anatomical studies.
He also began to assemble his numerous notes and instructions on
painting into a sizable collection, known as *Libro A* (it has since been
lost). From this collection, Francesco Melzi compiled the famous *Trattato della pittura (Treatise on Painting)* after Leonardo's death.[59] Among
the many subjects in the *Trattato* are extensive observations on the forms
and visual appearance of plants and trees. Most of these observations,
which became known as Leonardo's "botany for painters," originated in
Milan during the years 1508–12, when he devoted considerable time to
botanical thought and drawings. Carlo Pedretti concluded that Melzi
must have copied the botanical chapters of the *Trattato* from an entire
lost manuscript on botany written by Leonardo.[60]

At the same time that he was working on his notes on anatomy,
botany, and painting, and continuing work on the *Leda* and the *Mona
Lisa*, Leonardo was asked by one of the king's principal generals,
Marshal Trivulzio, to design for him a tomb with a life-size equestrian
statue.[61] And so for the second time, almost fifteen years after abandoning the casting of *il cavallo*, Leonardo embarked on making extensive
studies and designs for an equestrian statue in bronze. It was a project
he would develop for three years, during which work on building the
chapel for the Trivulzio monument had begun. But once again, external circumstances intervened. Political turmoil would soon engulf the
city, and the bronze statue would never be cast.

In 1510, Leonardo had the good fortune to meet a brilliant young anatomist, Marcantonio della Torre, who had recently been appointed professor of medicine at the University of Pavia. Leonardo engaged Marcantonio in extensive discussions on anatomy, much as he had done with Luca Pacioli on geometry fifteen years earlier. Just as Pacioli had introduced him to the Latin editions of Euclid, the Greek authority on geometry, so della Torre likely introduced him to the Latin editions of Galen, the Greek authority on anatomy and medicine.[62]

Unfortunately, their discussions were short-lived. In the following year, della Torre died of the plague in Riva, where he had gone to treat victims of an epidemic. Nevertheless, this short association had a significant influence on Leonardo's understanding of anatomy. His dissections took on a new level of sophistication, and he expanded his research far beyond the areas involved in the movement of the human body. He dissected various animals to compare their anatomies to human anatomy. And he began to delve further into the body to study the functions of the internal organs, respiration, and the flow of blood.

During this time the political landscape of Italy shifted again, and war broke out. In 1509, Louis XII, in alliance with the Vatican, had achieved a brilliant victory over the Venetians. But in 1510, Pope Julius II made peace with Venice and persuaded several European rulers to form a Holy League in order to drive the French "barbarians" from Italy. The French troops resisted for a while, but in December 1511 the League, using Swiss mercenaries to do the fighting, stormed Milan, expelled the French, and nominally installed Maximiliano Sforza, the young son of Ludovico, on the ducal throne his father had occupied.

Leonardo, finding himself once again unwelcome in the city that had treated him so well, retired to the Melzi estate in Vaprio on the river Adda, some twenty miles distant. Thanks to the generosity of the Melzi family, he and his entourage resided there comfortably for almost two years. While the political constellations in Italy continued to change, Leonardo calmly went about his research, dissecting animals, studying the turbulent waters of the Adda, and making a series of exquisite small-scale drawings of the surrounding regions. He also carried out extensive botanical studies in the spacious gardens of the estate and the surrounding areas. In exchange for the family's hospitality,

Leonardo produced splendid designs for the enlargement of the Villa Melzi, and for landscaping the gardens, some of which were realized in later years.[63]

FRUSTRATION IN ROME

Although Leonardo was comfortable in Vaprio, it was clear that he could not stay there indefinitely. Sooner or later he would have to find another patron who could provide him with the financial means to support himself, his household, and his continuing scientific research. Fortunately, such an opportunity soon presented itself. In February of 1513, Pope Julius II died in Rome, and Giovanni de' Medici, the younger son of Lorenzo il Magnifico, was elected to the papacy under the name of Leo X. His brother Giuliano became commander in chief of the papal troops. With their support, the Medici, after an absence of almost twenty years, were able to reestablish themselves as the rulers of Florence.

Soon after his brother ascended to the papacy, Giuliano de' Medici invited Leonardo to the papal court in Rome. The two had likely met at the court in Milan, and Giuliano was well aware of Leonardo's reputation as a military engineer. Giuliano de' Medici was also an eager student of natural philosophy. Leonardo could not have hoped for a more powerful and sympathetic patron, and when invited was only too glad to join the papal court.

In September 1513 he embarked on the journey to Rome with several of his pupils, including Francesco Melzi, and with numerous chests and trunks containing his personal belongings—his painting materials, probably some tools and scientific instruments, his voluminous Notebooks, and several paintings in various stages of completion, including the *Leda*, the *Mona Lisa*, and the *Saint Anne*. After traveling many weeks, the caravan reached Rome sometime in November or December.

Giuliano de' Medici had prepared spacious quarters in the Belvedere, a luxurious villa near the papal palace inside the Vatican. Leonardo's suite included several bedrooms, a kitchen, and a large studio and workshop where he could paint and conduct experiments. He was treated with deference and respect, and given everything he needed, including a regular allowance, without specific obligations. And yet, for Leonardo, this was not a happy time.

At sixty-one, he was now an old man. His long beard was white, his eyesight was failing. And though he was well respected—even venerated—as a great sage, he was no longer in fashion as an artist. His reputation as a painter had been eclipsed by younger rivals like Michelangelo and Raphael, who were both at the height of their fame. Both had painted magnificent frescoes in the Vatican—Michelangelo in the Sistine Chapel and Raphael in the so-called Stanze (Rooms), the private apartments of Pope Julius II. The new pope, Leo X, attracted scores of young artists to Rome and handed out lavish commissions, but none of them went to the old master from Florence. Although Leonardo once again was living in great comfort at court, he was no longer the center of the court's attention. He felt lonely and depressed. It was during this time of uncertainty and discontent that he drew his celebrated self-portrait.[64]

Nonetheless, Leonardo continued his scientific studies with undiminished energy. Having been occupied with multiple projects for the past thirty years, working in this way had become second nature to him. His age may have slowed him down, but it certainly did not restrict or diminish his mental processes. After settling into his new home, he began extensive botanical studies in the sumptuous gardens of the Belvedere. He continued to explore the geometry of transformations, and designed a large parabolic mirror for capturing solar energy to boil water, which he thought could be useful to the dyers of textiles. And, he invented a machine for making rope, and a rolling mill for producing metal strips from which coins could be minted.[65]

He also continued his dissections, probably at the hospital of Santo Spirito, which was in the immediate vicinity of the Vatican. These dissections marked the last phase of his anatomical research, in which he concentrated on the processes of reproduction and the development of the embryo. Leonardo's studies included highly original speculations about the origin of the embryo's cognitive processes or, in his terminology, of the embryo's soul.[66] Unfortunately, these speculations contradicted the official Church doctrine about the divine nature of the human soul and were thus considered heretical by Pope Leo X. As a result, Leonardo was banned from conducting further autopsies or human dissections.[67]

Thus, in addition to being eclipsed as an artist, Leonardo now found himself prevented from continuing his research in embryology, his most advanced anatomical work. He may also have suffered from an illness in 1514.[68] At any rate, he was given to morbid thoughts, filling his Notebooks with apocalyptic tales of floods and other terrifying catastrophes. However, simply writing about storms and floods was not enough for Leonardo. He also had to draw them and analyze them scientifically. The result was a series of a dozen extraordinary drawings in somber black chalk known as the "deluge drawings," which are now a part of the Royal Collection at Windsor Castle and are accompanied by Leonardo's powerful narrative of his apocalyptic visions. The narrative is strongly reminiscent of Leonardo's description of how to paint a battle, composed twenty years earlier.[69] Several pages long, it is full of horror, drama, and violence; there are highly emotional passages interspersed with detached, analytical ones, with precise descriptions of cascades and water and air currents, and detailed instructions on how to paint optical effects generated by storm clouds and falling rain. The overwhelming impression evoked by Leonardo's narrative is that of despair, of the futility and frailty of human beings confronting the cataclysmic forces of the deluge. He writes in one passage:

> One will see the dark gloomy air beaten by the rush of different and convoluting winds, which are mingled with the weight of the continuous rain, and which are carrying helter-skelter an infinite number of branches torn from the trees, entangled with countless autumn leaves. The ancient trees will be seen uprooted and torn to pieces by the fury of the winds. . . . Oh how many will you see closing their ears with their hands to shut out the tremendous noises made in the darkened air by the raging of the winds. . . . Others, with gestures of hopelessness, took their own lives, despairing of being able to endure such suffering; and of these, some flung themselves from high rocks, others strangled themselves with their own hands. . . . [70]

The drawings that illustrate his apocalyptic narrative are dark, violent, menacing, and disturbing. Nonetheless, they are astonishingly accurate in their renderings of water and air turbulence. Throughout his life, Leonardo had carefully studied the forms of waves, eddies, waterfalls, vortices, and air currents. Here, in old age, he summed up his knowledge of turbulence. Beyond their expressive emotional power, the deluge drawings can be seen as sophisticated mathematical diagrams, presenting a visual catalog of turbulent flows that would not look out of place in a modern textbook on fluid dynamics (see Fig. 4-5).

In Rome, Leonardo finished the three masterpieces he had brought

Figure 4-5: Deluge Study, c. 1515,
Windsor Collection, Landscapes, Plants,
and Water Studies, folio 59r

with him from Milan—the *Saint Anne*, the *Mona Lisa*, and the *Leda*.[71] And he painted *Saint John the Baptist*, his last and perhaps most intriguing work. Like all of Leonardo's great paintings, *Saint John the Baptist* is unique in several ways. Bereft of all religious symbolism, the saint is neither the traditional child nor the ascetic of the desert, but is shown as a graceful young man whose charming face and naked torso display a seductive, sensuous beauty. Not surprisingly, the painting has often been seen as incongruous, sometimes even blasphemous.

From an artistic point of view, the picture exemplifies several of the painter's original contributions to Renaissance art—a dramatic use of chiaroscuro to make the figure stand out against a strikingly dark background, a subtle and intriguing spiral movement of the body, and the full use of sfumato to create a pervading sense of mystery. But Leonardo's "manifesto on the art of painting," as David Arasse calls it,[72] goes beyond mere technical achievements. About ten years earlier Leonardo had written a famous passage in his *Treatise on Painting* about the artist's power to inflame the viewer to love:

> The painter . . . seduces the spirits of men to fall in love with and to love a painting that does not represent a living woman. It has happened to me that I have painted a picture with a religious theme, bought by a lover who wanted to remove the attributes of divinity from it so that he could kiss it without guilt; but in the end, his conscience overcame his sighs and desires, and he had to remove the picture from his house.[73]

In *Saint John the Baptist*, Leonardo demonstrates this power to inflame the viewer once again. And this time the subject is not a woman, but an angelic, mysterious, and sensuous young man. The saint's alluring smile and enigmatic gesture—the index finger pointing heavenward—draw viewers in emotionally with a magnetism that many have found disturbing, probably because of its androgynous nature. However, it is also quite captivating and moving. Having kept his sexual feelings private throughout his life, Leonardo, it seems to me, finally declares himself to the world in his last painting. *Saint John the Baptist* is his personal genius and embodies his desire, which is fully revealed in its androgynous haunting beauty, grace, and transcendence.

LAST JOURNEYS

During his years in Rome, Leonardo was consulted by his patron Giuliano de' Medici and by other members of the Medici family about various architectural and engineering projects, which involved making trips to Civitavecchia, the port of Rome, as well as longer journeys to Parma, Piacenza, Florence, and Milan. That he could manage to travel that much at his advanced age, when such journeys were arduous and long, in addition to continuing his extensive scientific studies and his painting, is nothing short of miraculous.

While Leonardo patiently brushed fine layers of oil on his panels to perfect the magical luminosities of his last paintings, political events once again intervened in his life, changing it decisively for the last time. In January 1515 the French king Louis XII died. He was succeeded by his cousin François I. The young king—not yet twenty when he ascended the throne—aspired to be a noble warrior in the mold of the French chivalric knights. He enthusiastically went into battle in the front lines of his troops. Yet he also loved poetry, classical literature, and philosophy as well as music, dancing, and other courtly pleasures.

Soon after he was crowned king, François crossed the Alps with his troops to reconquer Lombardy. The French army swept aside the Italian troops and Swiss mercenaries, and in July, François I captured Maximiliano Sforza and entered Milan in triumph. But in a magnanimous gesture, he did not throw Maximiliano into prison but welcomed him at his court as a cousin.[74] The pope had initially allied himself with the Milanese to fight the French troops. But when François emerged victorious, he realized the power of the new king and proposed peace talks, which were held in October in Bologna.

Leonardo may well have accompanied Pope Leo X to Bologna, although there is no clear documentation of his presence in the papal suite. If he did make the journey, however, he would have met the young king; and soon François would become his last and most generous patron. What we know from the historical record is that Giuliano de' Medici asked Leonardo to create an unusual entertainment for the event. Although Leonardo had very little time for the project, he produced a unique piece of art and technology—a mechanical lion. As Vasari described it, "After making a few steps, [the lion] opened its breast to reveal a cluster of lilies."

Powered by springs and a system of wheels, the lion was a masterpiece of Leonardo's stagecraft, and its symbolism was ideal for the peace talks being conducted between the French king and the pope. The lion alluded to the name of the pope, Leo; the stylized lily (or *fleur de lis*) was the symbol of French royalty, and also of Florence. By revealing the lilies in its heart, Leonardo's lion offered, with a grand flourish, a powerful symbol of the union between France and Florence, and between the French king and the Medici pope. The automaton, which has since disappeared, greatly impressed the assembled statesmen. It was mentioned repeatedly and with great enthusiasm by commentators even a hundred years later.[75]

François I clearly was enchanted and flattered by Leonardo's mechanical lion. If the artist was indeed present, the king may have personally offered him the position of *peintre du Roy* (royal painter) at his court in France. In any event, offer it he did. But Leonardo did not accept the king's offer immediately. However, when Giuliano de' Medici died a few months later, he no longer hesitated. He knew that he could not find a more generous and understanding patron than the young French ruler.

Sometime toward the end of 1516, Leonardo put his affairs in order and prepared to make the move across the Alps. He packed his trunks with everything he owned, including all of his Notebooks and his now-completed master paintings, knowing that he was not likely to return to his native lands. He set off on the long journey on horse-back with the faithful Melzi and a couple of servants, his chests and trunks carried by several mules. From Rome the caravan took the familiar route north to Florence and Milan, the cities in which Leonardo had spent most of his life. From Milan, the travelers proceeded to Turin, crossed the Alps to Grenoble, and reached the Rhône valley at Lyon. There they probably continued westward until they reached the river Cher and followed it to the Loire, ending up at Amboise, near Tours, after a journey of about three months.[76]

THE PHILOSOPHER AND THE KING

During the fifteenth and sixteenth centuries, the mild climate and natural beauty of the Loire valley attracted successive generations of French royalty and nobility, who built splendid castles and elegant mansions along the river. The Château d'Amboise was the home of French kings and queens for over 150 years. François I had spent his childhood and youth there, and used it as his principal residence.

The king received Leonardo at Amboise with boundless generosity. He installed the artist and his entourage in the spacious manor of Cloux, known today as Clos-Lucé, adjacent to the château. The manor house had comfortable rooms with high-vaulted ceilings, including a studio, a library, a sitting room, and several bedrooms. The property included elegant gardens, a vineyard, meadows and trees, and a stream for fishing.[77] The manor's gardener was Italian, as were several members of the court, allowing Leonardo to speak in his native tongue.

François also granted his famous guest a generous income. In return, he asked nothing but the pleasure of his company, which he enjoyed almost every day. There was a secret underground tunnel between Cloux and the royal castle, which allowed the king to visit Leonardo easily for long conversations whenever he wished to do so. Just as Alexander the Great, another young warrior-king, had been tutored by Aristotle, the great philosopher of antiquity, so François I was now tutored by Leonardo da Vinci, the great sage and genius of the

Renaissance. He never tired of hearing Leonardo explain to him the subtleties of his science of living forms—the complexities of turbulent water and air, the formation of rocks and the origin of fossils, the intricacies of human movement and the flight of birds, the nature of light and perspective, the canons of beauty and proportion, the pathways of the senses and the vital spirits that sustain our life, and the origin of human will and power in the seat of the soul.

The king treasured his conversations with Leonardo, as we know from the firsthand account of the Florentine goldsmith Benvenuto Cellini, who worked at the court of François I twenty years after Leonardo's death. Cellini wrote,

> I cannot resist repeating the words which I heard the King say about him, in the presence of the Cardinal of Ferrara and the Cardinal of Lorraine and the King of Navarre; he said that he did not believe that a man had ever been born who knew as much as Leonardo, not only in the spheres of painting, sculpture and architecture, but that he was also a very great philosopher.[78]

Leonardo, who had always been famous as an artist and engineer, was deeply appreciated and acclaimed by the king of France for his intellectual achievements as a philosopher, or, as we would say today, a scientist.

One of the few documents about Leonardo's final years at Amboise is the travel diary of Antonio de Beatis, secretary to the Cardinal of Aragon, who visited the artist with the cardinal in October 1517. Beatis wrote that Leonardo appeared to be "over 70 years old" (in reality he was 65) and that he could no longer work in color, "for he is paralyzed in the right arm," but that he could still draw, and was assisted by a pupil (no doubt Francesco Melzi) who "worked to excellent effect" under the master's supervision.[79] Art historians surmise that Leonardo's paralysis, probably as a result of a stroke, did not prevent him from writing and drawing, which he did with his left hand. But it would have affected the nuanced painting he was famous for, which would have required the freedom to move both arms. For Leonardo, this handicap, combined with his failing eyesight, must have been deeply depressing.

Beatis reported that Leonardo showed the cardinal three master paintings—"the portrait of a certain Florentine lady" (the *Mona Lisa*), *Saint John the Baptist*, and the *Madonna and Child with Saint Anne*. The cardinal and his secretary were amazed by Leonardo's anatomical drawings as well as his writings on other subjects.[80] Then he added: "All these books, written in Italian, will be a source of pleasure and profit when they appear."[81] This leaves one with the impression that Leonardo discussed with the cardinal his plans to publish the Notebooks.

Indeed, Leonardo spent most of his working time at Cloux systematically reorganizing his Notebooks, most likely in view of future publication. In spite of his diminished health, he did so with characteristic enthusiasm and intellectual vigor, making plans for at least half a dozen new treatises or discourses.[82] From the titles he listed, it is clear that he was reviewing his entire life's work—his science of the "qualities of forms"[83]—trying to summarize it in a few representative treatises.

Leonardo began his list with the planned *Treatise on Painting* as well as a *Treatise on Light and Shade*. He decided to lay out, at least in principle, the mathematical foundations of his science, and to do so, planned to write two mathematical treatises. The first, a *Book on Perspective*, would deal with the laws of perspective and geometrical optics that needed to be mastered in order to understand vision, the representation of solid objects, and the rendering of light and shade. The second, a *Treatise on Continuous Quantity* with a companion volume titled *De ludo geometrico (On the Game of Geometry)*, would discuss the geometry of transformations, which Leonardo considered to be the appropriate mathematics for describing the qualities of living forms.[84] He had explored this new type of geometry for over ten years and continued to do so at Cloux. With regard to anatomy, Leonardo proposed to write a *Discourse on the nerves, muscles, tendons, membranes, and ligaments* as well as a *Special book on the muscles and movements of the limbs*. Together, these two books were to represent the author's definitive treatment of the human body in motion.

Since historians do not know how many treatises were contained in Leonardo's lost Notebooks, it is difficult to judge to what extent the plan he outlined at Cloux would have allowed him to publish the results of his lifelong scientific research as an integrated body of knowledge. However, it is evident that the treatises he proposed, together with those that were well advanced and have been preserved, would have gone a long way toward accomplishing such a goal. In Leonardo's mind, his science of living forms was certainly an integrated whole. At the end of his life, his problems were no longer conceptual; they were simply the limitations of time and energy. As he wrote several years before his death, "I have been impeded neither by avarice nor by negligence, but only by time."[85] And yet, Leonardo never gave up. In June 1518 he wrote what may have been the last entry in his Notebooks: "I shall go on."[86]

During his time at Amboise, Leonardo also advised the king on various architectural and engineering projects, in which he revived his conception of buildings and cities as "open systems" (to use our modern term), in which people, material goods, food, water, and waste need to move and flow easily for the system to remain healthy.[87] He produced designs for rebuilding the royal château, including water closets connected by flushing channels within the walls and ventilating shafts that reached all the way up to the roof.[88] In December 1517 he accompanied the king to Romorantin, some fifty miles from Amboise, where François I wanted to build a new capital and royal residence. Leonardo stayed in Romorantin for several weeks, working on plans for a splendid palace and for an ideal "healthy" city, based on the revolutionary designs he had developed in Milan more than thirty years earlier.[89]

Like most Renaissance courts, that of François I indulged in lavish pageants and dazzling spectacles, perhaps even more so than other courts because of the energetic and convivial nature of its young king. Leonardo contributed to these festivities, creating spectacular performances, designing costumes and royal emblems, and showing off his stage magic. To do so, he had recourse to the large repertoire of designs and inventions he had produced during his years at the Sforza court. This included his most famous creation, the "Masque of the Planets," which was performed at Amboise in a new production in May 1518.

But in the midst of the gaiety and pomp, Leonardo's physical strength continued to decline. His conversations with the king, however, went on. Nor was he perturbed by contemplating his approaching death. "Just as a well-spent day brings a happy sleep," he had written thirty years earlier, "so a well-employed life brings a happy death."[90] In

April 1519, shortly after his sixty-seventh birthday, Leonardo went to see a notary and carefully recorded his last will and testament. He set out in great detail the customary arrangements for his burial, left the savings remaining in his account at Santa Maria Nuova to his half brothers, and made various bequests to his servants.[91] To Francesco Melzi, whom he named as executor of his estate, he left all his personal belongings as well as his entire artistic and intellectual legacy, including his paintings and the complete collection of his Notebooks.

A few days after completing his will, on May 2, 1519, Leonardo da Vinci died in the manor of Cloux—according to legend, in the arms of the king of France.

THE FATE OF THE NOTEBOOKS

After Leonardo's death, Francesco Melzi stayed at Amboise for several months to take care of Leonardo's affairs. He first notified Leonardo's family, conveying his grief to them in a moving letter:

> He was like the best of fathers to me, and the grief that I felt at his death seems to me impossible to express. As long as there is breath in my body, I shall feel the eternal sadness it caused and with true reason, for he gave me every day proof of a passionate and ardent affection. Each of us must mourn the loss of a man that nature is powerless to recreate.[92]

Before returning to Milan, Melzi entrusted to the king the paintings his master had brought to France; and there they remained, eventually ending up at the Louvre. The Notebooks, by contrast, were scattered all over Europe. Some of them were disassembled, cut into pieces arbitrarily, and reassembled into various collections. In the process, over the centuries more than half of the manuscripts disappeared. The dispersion of Leonardo's Notebooks is convoluted and distressing, and like his biography, it has been documented by scholars only fairly recently, with a great deal of detective work.[93]

When Melzi returned to Lombardy, he set aside a special room in his villa at Vaprio to exhibit his master's Notebooks. Over the years he proudly showed them to visitors, including the artists and writers Vasari and Giovanni Lomazzo. Francesco hired two scribes to help him classify Leonardo's notes and compile the anthology known today as *Trattato della pittura (Treatise on Painting)*. The work, even though incomplete, was acquired by the duke of Urbino and then by the Vatican, where it was cataloged as Codex Urbinas and eventually published in 1651.

After Melzi's death in 1570, his son Orazio, who did not share his father's reverence for the great Leonardo, carelessly stuffed the Notebooks into several chests in the villa's attic. When it became known that batches of Leonardo's exquisite drawings could easily be obtained from Orazio, souvenir hunters turned up at Vaprio; they were allowed to take whatever they wanted. Pompeo Leoni of Arezzo, sculptor at the court of Madrid, obtained close to fifty bound volumes in addition to about two thousand single sheets, which he took to Spain in 1590. Thus, at the turn of the sixteenth to the seventeenth century, Spain had the largest concentration of Leonardo's writings and drawings.

Leoni sorted and rearranged the manuscripts according to his own tastes, cutting them up, throwing away what he deemed uninteresting, and pasting what he liked on large folios, which he bound into two volumes. The first, known as Codex Atlanticus because of its large, atlas-size folios, changed hands a couple of times after Leoni's death before ending up at the Ambrosiana Library in Milan. The second volume was bought from Leoni's heirs by the British art collector Lord Arundel, who donated it to the Royal Collection at Windsor Castle, where the pages were detached and mounted individually. Lord Arundel also bought another large collection of manuscripts in Spain, which now bears his name, Codex Arundel, and is housed in the British Library.

Leoni also sold several complete Notebooks. Twelve of those were eventually given to the Ambrosiana Library; others disappeared. Pages were torn from some and ended up in various European libraries and museums. One collection, acquired in 1750 by Prince Trivulzio and known as Codex Trivulzianus, is now in the Trivulziana Library in Milan, which bears the name of the prince's family.

By the eighteenth century, Leonardo's manuscripts were in great demand, especially among English art collectors. Lord Lytton purchased three bound Notebooks and later sold them to a certain John Forster, who in turn bequeathed them to the Victoria and Albert Museum. They are now known as Codices Forster I, II, and III. Another complete Notebook, which had been obtained directly from Orazio Melzi, passed through the hands of a succession of Italian artists before it was bought by the Earl of Leicester, and thus acquired the name Codex Leicester.

When Napoleon Bonaparte entered Milan in 1796 at the height of his Italian campaign, he ordered, with an imperial gesture, the transfer of all the Notebooks from the Ambrosiana Library to Paris. The Codex Atlanticus was later returned to the Ambrosiana, but the twelve complete Notebooks remained at the Bibliothèque Nationale in Paris, where they have been designated by the initials A–M (excluding J).

In the mid-nineteenth century, Guglielmo Libri, professor of mathematics and historian of science, stole several folios from Manuscripts A and B at the Bibliothèque Nationale. He also removed the small *Codice sul volo degli uccelli* (Codex on the Flight of Birds), which had been attached to Manuscript B. After the theft, Libri fled to England where he assembled the single folios into two collections and sold them to Lord Ashburnham. Eventually they were returned to Paris and reattached to Manuscripts A and B. Nonetheless, they are still known today as Ashburnham I and II. The Codex *sul volo* was disassembled by Libri. Its pieces passed through several hands, including those of the Russian prince Theodore Sabachnikoff, who donated the pieces to the Royal Library in Turin, where the entire codex was finally reassembled.

In 1980 the Codex Leicester was sold at auction by the heirs of the earl. It was bought by the American petroleum magnate and collector Armand Hammer, who renamed it Codex Hammer. After Hammer's death, the codex was auctioned again and was bought by the software billionaire Bill Gates. Gates restored the original name, Codex Leicester, but then proceeded to cut up the Notebook into individual pieces in the fashion of Leoni and other wealthy art collectors.

The Codex Leicester is the only Notebook remaining in private possession today. The other manuscripts—Notebooks in their original bound forms of various sizes, the large artificial collections, torn pages, and isolated folios—are all housed in libraries and museums. More than half of the original manuscripts have been lost, although some may still exist, gathering dust unseen in private European libraries. Indeed, two complete Notebooks were discovered in the labyrinth of the stacks in the National Library in Madrid as recently as 1965. Designated Codices Madrid I and II, they brought to light many previously unknown aspects of Leonardo's works, including studies in mathematics, mechanical and hydraulic engineering, optics, and perspective, as well as inventories of Leonardo's personal library.[94]

While Leonardo's paintings have been admired by countless art lovers during his lifetime and throughout the centuries, his Notebooks came fully to light only in the late nineteenth century, when they were finally transcribed and published. Today the writings of this brilliant pioneer of modern science are available to scholars in excellent facsimile editions and clear transcriptions. His scientific and technical drawings are frequently exhibited today, sometimes supplemented by wooden models of the machines he designed. Nevertheless, more than five hundred years after his birth, the science of Leonardo is still not widely known, and is often misunderstood.

PART TWO

LEONARDO, THE SCIENTIST

FIVE

Science in the Renaissance

To appreciate Leonardo's science, it is important to understand the cultural and intellectual context in which he created it. Scientific ideas do not occur in a vacuum. They are always shaped by cultural perceptions and values, and by the technologies available at the time. The entire constellation of concepts, values, perceptions, and practices—the "scientific paradigm" in the terminology of science historian Thomas Kuhn—provides the context that is necessary for scientists to pose the great questions, organize their subjects, and define legitimate problems and solutions.[1] All science is built upon such an intellectual and cultural foundation.

Hence, when we recognize ancient or medieval ideas

reflected in Leonardo's scientific writings, this does not mean that he was less of a scientist, as has sometimes been asserted. On the contrary: Like every good scientist, Leonardo consulted the traditional texts and used their conceptual framework as his starting point. He then tested the traditional ideas against his own scientific observations. And, in accordance with scientific method, he did not hesitate to modify the old theories when his experiments contradicted them.

THE REDISCOVERY OF THE CLASSICS

Before we examine how Leonardo developed his scientific method, we need to understand the principal ideas of ancient and medieval natural philosophy, which formed the intellectual context within which he operated.[2] Only then will we be able to truly appreciate the transformative nature of his accomplishments.

The ideas of Greek philosophy and science, on which the Renaissance worldview was based, were ancient knowledge. Yet for Leonardo and his contemporaries, they were fresh and inspiring, because most of them had been lost for centuries. They had been rediscovered only recently in the original Greek texts and in Arabic translations. As the Italian humanists studied a wide variety of classical texts and their Arabic elaborations and critiques, the Renaissance rediscovered the classics, as well as the concept of critical thinking.

During the Early Middle Ages (sixth through tenth centuries A.D.), also known as the Dark Ages, Greek and Roman literature, philosophy, and science were largely forgotten in Western Europe. But the ancient texts had been preserved in the Byzantine Empire, along with the knowledge of classical Greek.[3] And so the Italian humanists repeatedly journeyed to the East, where they acquired hundreds of classical manuscripts and brought them to Florence. They also established a chair of Greek at the Studium Generale, as the University of Florence was called, and attracted eminent Greek scholars to help them read and interpret the ancient texts.

In antiquity, the Romans were in awe of Greek art, philosophy, and science, and their noble families often employed Greek intellectuals as tutors for their children. But the Romans themselves hardly produced any original science. However, Roman architects and engineers wrote many important treatises, and Roman scholars condensed the scientific legacy of Greece into large encyclopedias that were popular during the Middle Ages and the Renaissance. These Latin texts were eagerly consulted by the humanist artists and intellectuals, and some were translated into the Italian vernacular.

In the seventh century, powerful Muslim armies, inspired by the new religion of Islam, burst forth from the Arabian peninsula and in successive invasions conquered peoples in the Middle East, across North Africa, and in southern Europe. As they built their vast empire, they not only spread Islam and the Arabic language, but also came in contact with the ancient texts of Greek philosophy and science in the Byzantine libraries. The Arabs deeply appreciated Greek learning, translated all the important philosophical and scientific works into Arabic, and assimilated much of the science of antiquity into their culture.

In contrast to the Romans, the Arab scholars not only assimilated Greek knowledge but examined it critically and added their own commentaries and innovations. Numerous editions of these texts were housed in huge libraries throughout the Islamic empire. In Moorish Spain, the great library of Córdoba alone contained some six hundred thousand manuscripts.

When the Christian armies confronted Islam in their military crusades, their spoils often included the works of Arab scholars. Among the treasures left behind by the Moors in Toledo when they retreated was one of the finest Islamic libraries, filled with precious Arabic translations of Greek scientific and philosophical texts. The occupying forces included Christian monks, who quickly began to translate the ancient works into Latin. A hundred years later, by the end of the twelfth century, much of the Greek and Arabic philosophical and scientific heritage was available to the Latin West.

Islamic religious leaders emphasized compassion, social justice, and a fair distribution of wealth. Theological speculations were seen as being far less important and therefore discouraged.[4] As a result, Arab scholars were free to develop philosophical and scientific theories without fear of being censored by their religious authorities.

Christian medieval philosophers did not enjoy such freedom.

Unlike their Arab counterparts, they did not use the ancient texts as the basis for their own independent research, but instead evaluated them from the perspective of Christian theology. Indeed, most of them were theologians, and their practice of combining philosophy—including natural philosophy, or science—with theology became known as Scholasticism. While early Scholastics, led by Saint Augustine, attempted to integrate the philosophy of Plato into Christian teachings, the height of the Scholastic tradition was reached in the twelfth century, when the complete writings of Aristotle became available in Latin, usually translated from Arabic texts. In addition, the commentaries on Aristotle by the great Arab scholars Avicenna (Ibn Sina) and Averroës (Ibn Rushd) were translated into Latin.

The leading figure in the movement to weave the philosophy of Aristotle into Christian teachings was Saint Thomas Aquinas, one of the towering intellects of the Middle Ages. Aquinas taught that there could be no conflict between faith and reason, because the two books on which they were based—the Bible and the "book of nature"—were both authored by God. Aquinas produced a vast body of precise, detailed, and systematic philosophical writings in which he integrated Aristotle's encyclopedic works and medieval Christian theology into a magnificent whole.

The dark side of this seamless fusion of science and theology was that any contradiction by future scientists would necessarily have to be seen as heresy. In this way, Thomas Aquinas enshrined in his writings the potential for conflicts between science and religion—which indeed arose three centuries later in Leonardo's anatomical research,[5] reached a dramatic climax with the trial of Galileo, and have continued to the present day.

THE INVENTION OF PRINTING

The sweeping intellectual changes that took place in the Renaissance and prepared the way for the Scientific Revolution could not have happened without a technological breakthrough that changed the face of the world—the invention of printing. This momentous advance, which took place around the time of Leonardo's birth, actually involved a double invention, that of typography (the art of printing from movable type) and that of engraving (of printable pictures). Together, these inventions marked the decisive threshold between the Middle Ages and the Renaissance.

Printing introduced two fundamental changes to the distribution of texts: rapid diffusion and standardization. Both were of tremendous importance for the spread of scientific and technological ideas. Once a page had been composed by the typesetters, it was easy to produce and distribute hundreds or thousands of copies. Indeed, after Johannes Gutenberg printed his famous forty-two-line Bible in Mainz around 1450, the art of printing spread across Europe like wildfire. By 1480 there were over a dozen printers in Rome, and by the end of the century Venice boasted around one hundred printers, who turned this city of great wealth into the foremost printing center of Europe. It has been estimated that the Venetian printers alone produced about 2 million volumes during the fifteenth century.[6]

For the rise of science, the production of standard texts was as important as their wide dissemination. With the use of the printing press, texts could not only be copied exactly, but were also laid out identically in each copy, so that scholars in different geographical locations could refer to a particular passage on a specific page without ambiguity. This had never been easy, nor dependable, in hand-copied medieval manuscripts.

The production of standard copies of images that served as illustrations of texts was perhaps even more important, and this is where the invention of engraving became an indispensable complement to typography. Whereas the pictures in ancient manuscripts often lost detail with each new manual copy, the use of woodcuts and copper plates now made it possible to reproduce illustrations of plants, anatomical details, mechanical devices, scientific apparatus, and mathematical diagrams with complete accuracy. Those images were valuable standards to which scholars could easily refer.

Leonardo was well aware of these tremendous advantages of printing and keenly interested in the technical details of the printing process throughout his life.[7] Among his earliest drawings of mechanical devices in the Codex Atlanticus, from the years 1480–82, is one of a typographic press with an automatic page feeder, an innovation that

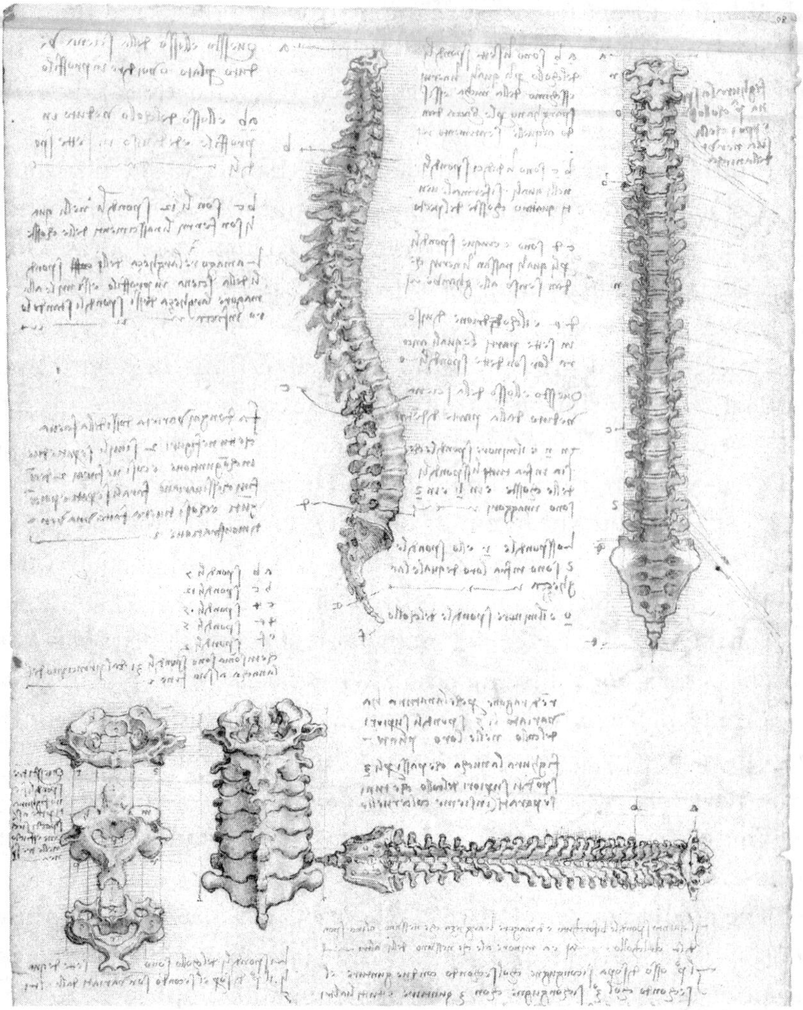

Figure 5-1: The vertebral column, c. 1510,
Anatomical Studies, folio 139v

was to reappear a couple of decades later. As he expanded his scientific research, Leonardo became increasingly aware of the need to disseminate printed versions of his treatises. Around 1505, while he painted *The Battle of Anghiari* in Florence and wrote his Codex on the Flight of Birds, he even invented a novel printing method for the simultaneous reproduction of texts and drawings. This was an extraordinary forerunner of the method introduced in the late eighteenth century by the

Romantic poet and artist William Blake, who was also a professional engraver.[8]

A few years later, at the height of his anatomical work in Milan, Leonardo added a technical note about the reproduction of his drawings to his famous assertion of the superiority of drawing over writing.[9] He insisted that his anatomical drawings should be printed from copper plates, which would be more expensive than woodcuts but much more effective in rendering the fine details of his work. "I beg you who come after me," he wrote on the sheet that contains his magnificent drawings of the vertebral column (Fig. 5-1), "not to let avarice constrain you to make the prints in [wood]."[10]

THE WORLD OF EXPLORATION

While explorations of the rediscovered classical texts greatly extended the intellectual frontiers of the Italian humanists, their physical frontiers were also being extended by the geographical discoveries of the famous Portuguese explorers and those who followed them. The Renaissance was the golden age of geographical exploration. By 1600 the surface of the known world had doubled since medieval times. Entirely new regions, new climates, and new aspects of nature were being discovered. These explorations generated a strong interest in biology, or "natural history" as it was called at the time, and the great ocean voyages led to numerous improvements in shipbuilding, cartography, astronomy, and other sciences and technologies associated with navigation.

In addition to the explorers' seafaring voyages, new regions of the Earth were being discovered, even in the very heart of Europe when the first mountaineers ventured into the higher altitudes of the Alps. During the Middle Ages it had been commonly believed that the high mountains were dangerous, not only because of the severity of their climates but also because they were the abodes of gnomes and devils. Now, with the new humanist curiosity and confidence in human capabilities, the first Alpine expeditions were being undertaken, and by the end of the sixteenth century, close to fifty summits had been reached.[11]

Leonardo fully embraced the humanist passion for exploration, in both the physical and mental realms. He was one of the first European mountaineers[12] and traveled frequently within Italy, exploring the vegetation, waterways, and geological formations of the regions he visited. In addition, he delighted in composing fictitious tales of journeys to mountains and deserts in faraway countries.[13]

These few examples from Leonardo's many interests and activities show us that he was well aware of the intellectual, technological, and cultural achievements of his time. From his early days as an apprentice in Verrocchio's workshop through the years he spent at various European courts, he was in regular contact with leading artists, engineers, philosophers, historians, and explorers, and thus thoroughly familiar with the wide range of ideas and practices that we now associate with the Renaissance.

THE ANCIENT VIEW OF THE UNIVERSE

The foundation of the Renaissance worldview was the conception of the universe that had been developed in classical Greek science: that the world was a *kosmos*, an ordered and harmonious structure. From its beginnings in the sixth century B.C., Greek philosophy and science understood the order of the cosmos to be that of a living organism rather than a mechanical system. This meant that all its parts had an innate purpose to contribute to the harmonious functioning of the whole, and that objects moved naturally toward their proper places in the universe. Such an explanation of natural phenomena in terms of their goals, or purposes, is known as teleology, from the Greek *telos* (purpose). It permeated virtually all of Greek philosophy and science.

The view of the cosmos as an organism also implied for the Greeks that its general properties are reflected in each of its parts. This analogy between macrocosm and microcosm, and in particular between the Earth and the human body, was articulated most eloquently by Plato in his *Timaeus* in the fourth century B.C., but it can also be found in the teachings of the Pythagoreans and other earlier schools. Over time, this idea acquired the authority of common knowledge, which continued throughout the Middle Ages and into the Renaissance.

In early Greek philosophy, the ultimate moving force and source of all life was identified with the soul, and its principal metaphor was that of the breath of life. Indeed, the root meaning of both the Greek *psyche* and the Latin *anima* is "breath." Closely associated with that moving force—the breath of life that leaves the body at death—was the idea of knowing. For the early Greek philosophers, the soul was both the source of movement and life, and that which perceives and knows. Because of the fundamental analogy between micro- and macrocosm, the individual soul was thought to be part of the force that moves the entire universe, and accordingly the knowing of an individual was seen as part of a universal process of knowing. Plato called it the *anima mundi*, the "world soul."

As far as the composition of matter was concerned, Empedocles in the fifth century B.C. claimed that the material world was composed of varying combinations of four elements—earth, water, air, and fire. When left to themselves, the elements would settle into concentric spheres with the earth at the center, surrounded successively by the spheres of water, air, and fire. Farther outside were the spheres of the planets and beyond them was the sphere of the stars.

According to the four-element theory, the great variety of qualities we observe in material objects is the result of combinations of four pairs of qualities associated with the elements: cold and dry (earth), hot and dry (fire), cold and wet (water), and hot and wet (air). Half a century after Empedocles, an alternative theory of matter was proposed by Democritus, who taught that all material objects are composed of atoms of numerous shapes and sizes, and that all observable qualities are derived from the particular combinations of atoms inside the objects. His theory was so antithetical to the traditional teleological views of matter that it was pushed into the background, where it remained throughout the Middle Ages and the Renaissance. It would surface again only in the seventeenth century, with the rise of Newtonian physics.[14]

Even if the properties of material objects could be seen as arising from various combinations of the basic qualities inherent in the four elements, the Greek philosophers still faced the problem of how these combinations of elements acquired the specific forms we see in nature. The first philosopher to address the problem of form was Pythagoras in the sixth century B.C., who founded a cultlike school of mathematics, known as Pythagoreans. He and his disciples believed that numerical patterns and ratios were at the origin of all forms. With this association between the concrete world of natural forms and the abstract realm of numerical relationships began the link between science and mathematics that would become the foundation of classical physics in the seventeenth century.

The Pythagoreans divided the universe into two realms: the heavens, in which the stars revolve in celestial spheres according to perfect, unchanging mathematical laws; and the Earth, in which phenomena are complex, ever changing, and imperfect. Plato added his own refinement to this picture. Since the circle is the most perfect geometrical figure, he argued, the planets, like the stars, must move in circles.

ARISTOTLE'S SYNTHESIS OF SCIENCE

For science at the time of the Renaissance, the most important Greek philosopher was Aristotle. A student of Plato, Aristotle was by far the most brilliant in Plato's Academy. But he was quite different not only from his teacher, but also from all his predecessors. Aristotle was the first philosopher to write systematic, professorial treatises about the main branches of learning of his time. He synthesized and organized the entire scientific knowledge of antiquity in a scheme that would remain the foundation of Western science for two thousand years. And when this body of knowledge was fused with Christian theology in the Middle Ages, it acquired the status of religious dogma.

To integrate the main disciplines of his time—biology, physics, metaphysics, ethics, and politics—into a coherent theoretical framework, Aristotle created a formal system of logic and a set of unifying principles. He stated explicitly that the goal of his logic was to learn the art of scientific investigation and reasoning. It was to serve as the rational instrument for all scientific work.

As a scientist, Aristotle was first and foremost a biologist, whose observations of marine life were unsurpassed until the nineteenth century. Like Pythagoras, he distinguished between matter and form, but as a biologist he knew that living form is more than shape, more than a static configuration of component parts.[15] His highly original approach to the problem of form was to posit that matter and form are linked through a process of development. In contrast with Plato, who believed in an independent realm of ideal forms, Aristotle held that form has no separate existence but is immanent in matter. Nor can matter exist separately from form. By means of form, the essence of matter becomes real, or actual. Aristotle called this process of the self-realization of matter *entelechy* (self-completion). Matter and form, in his view, are the two sides of this process of development, separable only through abstraction.

Aristotle associated his *entelechy* with the traditional Greek concept of the soul as the source of life.[16] The soul, for him, is the source not only of bodily motion but also of the body's formation: It is the form that realizes itself in the changes and movements of the organic body. Leonardo, as I shall show, adopted the Aristotelian concept of the soul, expanded it, and transformed it into a scientific theory based on empirical evidence.[17]

Aristotle conceived of the soul as being built up in successive levels, corresponding to levels of organic life. The first level is the "vegetative soul," which controls, as we would say today, the mechanical and chemical changes of the body's metabolism. The soul of plants is restricted to this metabolic level of a vital force. The next higher form is the "animal soul," characterized by autonomous motion in space and by sensation, that is, feelings of pleasure and pain. The "human soul," finally, includes the vegetable and animal souls, but its main characteristic is reason.

In terms of physics and astronomy, Aristotle adopted the Pythagorean antithesis between the terrestrial and the heavenly worlds. From the Earth to the sphere of the Moon, he taught, all things constantly change, generating new forms and then decaying again; above the Moon, the crystalline spheres of the planets and stars revolve in eternal, unchanging motions. He subscribed to the Platonic idea that the perfection of the celestial realm implies that the planets and stars move in perfect circles. Aristotle also accepted Plato's view that divine souls reside in the heavenly bodies, and that they influence life on Earth. This idea lies at the root of medieval astrology, which was still very popular during the Renaissance. Leonardo, however, emphatically rejected it.[18]

Following Empedocles, Aristotle maintained that all forms in the world arise from various combinations of the four elements—earth, water, air, and fire—and he saw the ever-changing mixtures of elements as the source of the imperfection and accidental nature of material forms. The four elements did not always remain in their assigned realms, he stated, but were constantly disturbed and being pushed into neighboring spheres, whereupon they would naturally try to return to their proper places. With this argument, Aristotle tried to explain why rain falls downward through the air, while air drifts upward in water, and the flames of fire rise up into the air. He strongly opposed the attempt by Democritus to reduce the qualities of matter to quantitative relations between atoms. It was because of Aristotle's great authority that the atomism of Democritus was eclipsed by teleological explanations of physical phenomena throughout antiquity and the Middle Ages.

For Aristotle, all activities that occurred spontaneously were natural, guided by the goals inherent in physical phenomena, and hence observation was the proper means of investigating them. Experiments that altered natural conditions in order to bring to light some hidden properties of matter were unnatural. As such, they could not be expected to reveal the essence of the phenomena. Experiments, Aristotle taught, were therefore not proper means of investigation, and indeed the experimental method was not essential to Greek science.

Aristotle's treatises were the foundation of philosophical and scientific thought in the Renaissance. But the humanist scholars also read Plato and various texts from the earlier traditions of Greek natural philosophy as well as the more recent treatises by Arab scientists. Thus, different schools of thought soon arose that followed one or another of the ancient philosophers. In particular, there was a lively debate between the Platonists, for whom only ideas were real and the world of the senses was illusory, and the Aristotelians, for whom the senses provided reality and ideas were mere abstractions.

Florence under the Medici was the center of Platonism. Milan, under the influence of the universities of Padua and Bologna, was predominantly Aristotelian. Leonardo, who spent many years in both cities, was well aware of the philosophical debates between the two schools. Indeed, the tension between the Platonic fascination with mathematical precision and the Aristotelian attention to qualitative forms and their transformations surfaces again and again in his writings.[19]

Renaissance science as a whole was characterized by a literary rather than an empirical approach. Instead of observing nature, the Italian humanists preferred to read the classical texts. In the words of historian of science George Sarton, "To study geometry was to study Euclid; a geographical atlas was an edition of Ptolemy; the physician did not study medicine, he studied Hippocrates and Galen."[20]

The classical treatises rediscovered in the Renaissance covered a wide range of subjects, from art and literature to philosophy, science, architecture, and engineering. As far as science, or "natural philosophy," was concerned, the Renaissance scholars studied Greek and Arabic texts within three broad areas: mathematics and astronomy, natural history, and medicine and anatomy.

MATHEMATICS AND ASTRONOMY
AT THE TIME OF LEONARDO

Greek theoretical mathematics began during the lifetime of Plato, in the fifth and fourth centuries B.C. The Greeks tended to geometrize all mathematical problems and seek answers in terms of geometrical figures. For example, they represented quantities by lengths of lines and products of two quantities by the area of rectangles. These methods even enabled them to deal with irrational numbers,[21] representing the number $\sqrt{2}$, for example, by the diagonal of a square with sides of length 1.

Several centuries earlier the Babylonians had developed a different approach to solving mathematical problems, now known as algebra, which began with simple arithmetic operations and then evolved into more abstract formulations with numbers represented by letters. The Greeks learned these numerical and algebraic methods together with Babylonian astronomy, but they transformed them into their geometrical language and continued to see mathematical problems in terms of geometry. Plato's Academy, the principal Greek school of natural philosophy for nine centuries, is said to have had a sign above its entrance, "Let no one enter here who does not know geometry."

The culmination of the early phase of Greek mathematics was reached around 300 B.C. with Euclid, who presented all of the geometry and other mathematics known in his day in a systematic, orderly sequence in his celebrated *Elements*. The thirteen volumes of this classical textbook were not only widely read during the Renaissance, but remained the foundation for the teaching of geometry until the end of the nineteenth century. About one hundred years after Euclid, Greek mathematics reached its final climax with Archimedes, a brilliant mathematician who wrote many important treatises in what we would now call mathematical physics. But he was never as popular as Euclid. His mathematical work was so advanced that it was not understood until many centuries later, and his great fame as an inventor eclipsed his reputation as a mathematician.

With the rise of Islam during the seventh and subsequent centuries, the Arab world became the center of mathematical studies. Arab mathematicians translated and synthesized the Greek texts and also commented on important influences from Mesopotamia and India. Of particular importance was the work of Muhammad al-Khwarzimi in the ninth century, whose *Kitab al jabr* was the most influential work on algebra from this period. The Arabic *al jabr* (binding together) in its title is the root of our modern word "algebra."[22]

Two centuries later, Persia produced an outstanding algebraist in the poet Omar Khayyam, the world-renowned author of the *Rubaiyat*, who was famous in his time for classifying cubic equations and solving many of them. Another Islamic scholar of that period who was very influential in the Renaissance was the Arab mathematician Alhazen (Ibn al-Haitham), who wrote a brilliant treatise on the "science of perspective," which included detailed discussions of geometrical optics and of the geometrical principles of vision and the eye's anatomy.

In the Renaissance, thus, mathematicians had access to two different approaches for solving mathematical problems, geometry and algebra. However, until the seventeenth century, geometry was considered to be more fundamental. All algebraic reasoning was justified in terms of geometrical figures in the tradition of Greek mathematics. In the seventeenth century, this dependence of algebra on geometry was reversed by René Descartes, the founder of modern philosophy and a brilliant mathematician, who invented a method for associating algebraic equations with curves and surfaces.[23] This method, now known as analytic geometry, involves using Cartesian coordinates, the system invented by Descartes and named after him. Long before Descartes, however, the fields of geometry and algebra were related because both of them were necessary for the development of an accurate science of astronomy.

For astronomy was surely the principal physical science throughout antiquity. The Babylonians successfully applied their numerical methods to compile astronomical tables. The Greeks used their geometrical approach to construct elaborate cosmological models, involving the use of trigonometry—which the Greek astronomers had learned from Hindu mathematicians—to determine the distances between celestial bodies from their observed angular positions.

When the conquests of Alexander the Great made the observations and mathematical methods of the Babylonian astronomers available to the Greeks, they found it impossible to reconcile this improved data with their Platonic idea of circular planetary orbits. Several Greek astronomers therefore abandoned the Platonic-Aristotelian view and began to devise complex geocentric systems of cycles and epicycles to account for the movements of the sun, moon, and planets. The culmination of this development was reached in the second century A.D. with the Ptolemaic system, which predicted the motion of the planets with considerable accuracy.

Ptolemy's thirteen-volume treatise, *He mathematike syntaxis (The Mathematical Collection)* summarized much of this ancient astronomical knowledge. It remained the authoritative text on astronomy for fourteen centuries. (It is indicative of the prestige of Islamic science that the text was known throughout the Middle Ages and the Renaissance under its Arabic title, *Almagest*.) Ptolemy also published the *Geography*, which contained detailed discussions of cartographic techniques and an elaborate map of the known world. The book was printed in the fifteenth century under the title *Cosmography* and became the most popular geographical book printed from movable type during the Renaissance.

NATURAL HISTORY

Throughout antiquity and in the centuries that followed, the study of the living world was known as natural history, and those who pursued it were known as naturalists. This was often an amateur activity rather than a professional occupation. It was only in the nineteenth century that the term "biology" began to be widely used, and even then, biologists often continued to be called "naturalists."

In the fifteenth century, books about natural history still tended to display some fascination with the fabulous, often imaginary beasts that had populated medieval bestiaries. At the time of Leonardo, the rediscovery of classical natural history texts, together with the explorations of new floras and faunas in the Americas, began to stimulate more serious interest in the study of living things. The ideas of the ancient natural philosophers about plants and animals were represented in great detail in the encyclopedic works of Aristotle, Theophrastus, Pliny the Elder, and Dioscorides.[24]

Aristotle was the classical author most widely available to Renaissance scholars. His numerous works included several treatises on animals, including the *Historia animalium (History of Animals)* and *De anima (Of the Soul)*. While Aristotle's observations of plants were less accurate than his observations of animals, his disciple and successor Theophrastus was a keen botanical observer. His treatise *De historia plantarum (Of the History of Plants)* was a pioneering work that made Theophrastus famous as the "father of botany."

In the first century A.D., the Roman naturalist Pliny the Elder (Gaius Plinius) wrote a monumental encyclopedia titled *Natural History*, comprising 37 books in which almost 500 Greek and Roman authors are cited. It became the favorite scientific encyclopedia in the Middle Ages, not only because of its rich content but also because it was written in an informal style. While it lacked scientific rigor, it was much easier and more pleasant to read than the learned volumes of Aristotle and the other Greek philosophers. For most Renaissance humanists, Pliny's name meant natural history itself. And his encyclopedia was the most convenient entry point to further research.

Botany, from ancient times up to the end of the sixteenth century, was often considered a subdiscipline of medicine, since plants were mainly studied for their use in the healing arts. For centuries the authoritative text in this field was the *Materia Medica* by the Greek physician Dioscorides, who was a contemporary of Pliny.

MEDICINE AND ANATOMY

In prehistoric cultures around the world, the origin of illness and the process of healing were associated with forces belonging to the spirit world, and a great variety of healing rituals and practices were developed to deal with illness accordingly.[25] In Western medicine, a revolutionary change occurred in Greece in the fifth century B.C., with the emergence of the scientific medical tradition associated with Hippocrates. There is no doubt that a famous physician by that name practiced and taught medicine around 400 B.C. on the island of Cos, but the voluminous writings attributed to him, known as the Hippocratic Corpus, were probably written by several authors at different times.

At the core of Hippocratic medicine was the conviction that illnesses are not caused by supernatural forces, but are natural phenomena that can be studied scientifically and influenced by therapeutic procedures and wise management of one's life.[26] Thus medicine should be practiced as a scientific discipline and should include the prevention of illness, as well as its diagnosis and treatment. This attitude has formed the basis of scientific medicine to the present day.

Health, according to the Hippocratic writings, requires a state of balance among environmental influences, the way in which we live, and the various components of human nature. One of the most important volumes in the Hippocratic Corpus, the book on *Airs, Waters and Places*, represents what we might now call a treatise on human ecology. It shows in great detail how the well-being of individuals is influenced by environmental factors—the quality of air, water, and food, the topography of the land, and general living habits. During the last two decades of the fifteenth century, this and several other volumes from the Hippocratic Corpus were available to scholars in Latin, most of them derived from Arabic translations.[27]

The culmination of anatomical knowledge in antiquity was reached in the second century A.D. with Galen (Claudius Galenus), a Greek physician who resided chiefly in Rome, where he had a large practice. His work in anatomy and physiology, based partly on dissections of animals, greatly increased the ancient knowledge of the arteries, brain, nerves, and spinal cord. Galen wrote over one hundred treatises in which he summarized and systematized the medical knowledge of his time in accordance with his own theories. By the end of the ninth century, all his works had been translated into Arabic, and Latin translations followed in due course. The authority of the Galenic teachings was unchallenged until Leonardo's time, although they were not founded on detailed knowledge of human organs. His dogmatic doctrines actually impeded medical progress. Nor was Galen successful in correlating his medical theories with corresponding therapies.

The medical bible throughout the Middle Ages and the Renaissance was the *Canon of Medicine*, written by the physician and philosopher Avicenna (Ibn Sina) in the eleventh century. A vast encyclopedia that codified the complete Greek and Arabic medical knowledge, Avicenna's *Canon* was more elaborate than Galen's works and had the advantage of being a single monumental opus rather than a collection dispersed in many separate treatises.

Medical teaching at the great universities was based on the classical texts of Hippocrates, Galen, and Avicenna, and concentrated on interpreting the classics, without questioning them or comparing them with clinical experience. Practicing physicians, on the other hand, many of them without medical degrees, used their own eclectic combinations of therapies.[28] The best of them simply relied on the Hippocratic notions of clean living and the ability of the body to heal itself.

As medical theory and practice increasingly diverged, human anatomy gradually became an independent field of study. Leonardo da Vinci, who became the greatest Renaissance anatomist, never practiced medicine. In fact, Leonardo had a very low opinion of doctors. "Strive to preserve your health," he wrote on a sheet of anatomical drawings, "in which you will be the more successful the more you are wary of physicians."[29]

One of the earliest texts on anatomy was the *Anatomia* by Mondino de' Luzzi, a professor at Bologna in the fourteenth century. He was one of the few medieval teachers who actually performed anatomical dissections himself.[30] His text, much influenced by the Arab interpreters of Galen, gave rudimentary instructions for dissections without, however, specifying the exact position and nature of individual organs. Yet, because of its succinctness and utility, Mondino's *Anatomia* was a standard textbook in medical schools in the fourteenth and fifteenth centuries.

LEONARDO AND THE CLASSICS

During the years of his extensive self-education in Milan,[31] Leonardo familiarized himself with the principal classical texts. He not only accumulated a considerable personal library, but also consulted classical manuscripts in the private libraries of wealthy aristocrats and monasteries whenever he had an opportunity, or borrowed them from other scholars. His Notebooks are full of reminders to himself to borrow or consult certain books. Since he had only the most rudimentary knowledge of Latin, he studied Italian translations whenever he could obtain them, or sought out scholars who could help him with the Latin texts.

We know from Leonardo's own accounts that he knew Plato's *Timaeus* well. He also owned several of Aristotle's works, in particular the *Physics*. His knowledge of the mathematical writings of Plato, Pythagoras, Archimedes, and Euclid was derived mostly from Luca Pacioli's famous Renaissance textbook, which was written in Italian. When Leonardo and Pacioli became friends, Pacioli helped Leonardo deepen his understanding of mathematics, particularly geometry, by guiding him through the complete Latin edition of Euclid's *Elements*.[32]

Leonardo's interest in astronomy was largely confined to studying optical effects in the visual perception of the heavenly bodies. But he was well aware of the Ptolemaic model of planetary motions. He owned several books on astronomy and cartography, including Ptolemy's celebrated *Cosmography* and a work by the Arabian astronomer Albumazar (Abu-Mashar).[33] With regard to natural history, Leonardo, like most Renaissance humanists, was well acquainted with the works of Aristotle, Pliny the Elder, and Dioscorides. He studied an Italian edition of Pliny's encyclopedic *Natural History*, printed in Venice in 1476, and read Dioscorides' popular *Materia Medica*. His own work in botany, however, went far beyond those classical texts.[34]

Many of Leonardo's greatest scientific achievements were in the field of anatomy, and it was this subject that he studied most carefully in the classical texts. He owned an Italian edition of Mondino's *Anatomy* and used it as an initial guide for dissections of the nervous system and other parts of the body. Through Mondino, he became acquainted with the theories of Galen and Avicenna, and subsequently studied an Italian edition of Avicenna's classic *Canon of Medicine*. Eventually Leonardo probably read some of Galen's work in Latin, with the help of the young anatomist Marcantonio della Torre, whom he met during his second period in Milan.[35] Having thoroughly studied the three principal medical authorities of his time—Galen, Avicenna, and Mondino—Leonardo had a solid foundation in classical and medieval anatomy, on which he built his own extraordinary accomplishments.

Leonardo da Vinci shared with his fellow humanists their great confidence in the capabilities of the human individual, their passion for voyages of exploration, and their excitement about the rediscovery of the classical texts of antiquity. But he differed dramatically from most of them by refusing to blindly accept the teachings of the classical authorities. He studied them carefully, but then he tested them by subjecting them to rigorous comparisons with his own experiments and his direct observations of nature. In doing so, I would argue, Leonardo single-handedly developed a new approach to knowledge, known today as the scientific method.

Science Born of Experience

Today's modern word "science" is derived from the Latin *scientia*, which means "knowledge," a meaning that was retained throughout the Middle Ages and the Renaissance. The modern understanding of science as an organized body of knowledge, acquired through a particular method, evolved gradually during the eighteenth and nineteenth centuries. The characteristics of the scientific method were fully recognized only during the twentieth century and are still frequently misunderstood, especially by the general public.

THE SCIENTIFIC METHOD

The scientific method represents a particular way of gaining knowledge about natural phenomena. First, it involves the systematic observation of the phenomena being studied and the recording of these observations as evidence, or scientific data. In some sciences, such as physics, chemistry, and biology, systematic observation includes conducting controlled experiments; in others, such as astronomy or paleontology, this is not possible.

Next, scientists attempt to interconnect the data in a coherent way, free of internal contradictions. The resulting representation is known as a scientific model. Whenever possible, we try to formulate our models in mathematical language, because of the precision and internal consistency inherent in mathematics. However, in many cases, especially in the social sciences, such attempts have been problematic, as they tend to confine the scientific models to such a narrow range that they lose much of their usefulness. Thus we have come to realize over the last few decades that neither mathematical formulations nor quantitative results are essential components of the scientific method.

Last, the theoretical model is tested by further observations and, if possible, additional experiments. If the model is found to be consistent with all the results of these tests, and especially if it is capable of predicting the results of new experiments, it eventually becomes accepted as a scientific theory. The process of subjecting scientific ideas and models to repeated tests is a collective enterprise of the community of scientists, and the acceptance of the model as a theory is done by tacit or explicit consensus in that community.

In practice, these steps, or stages, are not neatly separated and do not always occur in the same order. For example, a scientist may formulate a preliminary generalization, or hypothesis, based on intuition or initial empirical data. When subsequent observations contradict the hypothesis, the researcher may try to modify the hypothesis without giving it up completely. But if the empirical evidence continues to contradict the hypothesis or the scientific model, the scientist is forced to discard it in favor of a new hypothesis or model, which is then subjected to further tests. Even an accepted theory may eventually be overthrown when contradictory evidence comes to light. This method of basing all models and theories firmly on empirical evidence is the very essence of the scientific approach.

All scientific models and theories are limited and approximate. This realization has become crucial to the contemporary understanding of science.[1] Twentieth-century science has shown repeatedly that all natural phenomena are ultimately interconnected, and that their essential properties, in fact, derive from their relationships to other things. Hence, in order to explain any one of them completely, we would have to understand all the others, which is obviously impossible. This insight has forced us to abandon the Cartesian belief in the certainty of scientific knowledge and to realize that science can never provide complete and definitive explanations. In science, to put it bluntly, we never deal with truth, in the sense of a precise correspondence between our descriptions and the described phenomena. We always deal with limited and approximate knowledge.

This may sound frustrating, but for many scientists the fact that we *can* formulate approximate models and theories to describe an endless web of interconnected phenomena, and that we are able to systematically improve our models or approximations over time, is a source of confidence and strength. As the great biochemist Louis Pasteur put it, "Science advances through tentative answers to a series of more and more subtle questions which reach deeper and deeper into the essence of natural phenomena."[2]

LEONARDO'S EMPIRICAL APPROACH

Five hundred years before the scientific method was recognized and formally described by philosophers and scientists, Leonardo da Vinci single-handedly developed and practiced its essential characteristics—study of the available literature, systematic observations, experimentation, careful and repeated measurements, the formulation of theoretical models, and frequent attempts at mathematical generalizations.

The full extent of Leonardo's method has come to light only recently with the accurate dating of his notes, which now makes it possible to follow the evolution of his ideas and techniques. For centuries, published selections from his Notebooks were arranged according to subject matter and often presented contradictory statements from different periods of Leonardo's life. But during the last three decades the Notebooks have finally been dated properly.

The critical examination and dating of old manuscripts, known as paleography, has grown into a sophisticated science.[3] In the case of the Notebooks, the dating involves not only evaluating actual dates, references to external events, and various cross-references in the text, but also a meticulous analysis of the evolution of Leonardo's style of writing and drawing over his lifetime; his use of different types of paper (often with distinctive watermarks) and of different kinds of pens, ink, and other writing materials at different times; as well as comparing and piecing together a host of stains, tears, special folds, and all kinds of marks added by various collectors over the centuries.

As a result of this painstaking work, performed for several decades under the leadership of Carlo Pedretti, all of Leonardo's manuscripts are now published in facsimile editions together with carefully transcribed and annotated versions of the original texts. Passages from different periods of Leonardo's life—sometimes even on the same folio of a manuscript—have been dated accurately. These scholarly publications have made it possible to recognize the developments of Leonardo's theoretical models, and the gradual perfection of his methods of observation and representation on the page, and thus to appreciate aspects of his scientific approach that could not be recognized before.[4]

One revolutionary change Leonardo brought to natural philosophy in the fifteenth century was his relentless reliance on direct observation of nature. While the Greek philosophers and scientists had shunned experimentation, and most of the Renaissance humanists uncritically repeated the pronouncements of the classical texts, Leonardo never tired of emphasizing the importance of *sperienza*, the direct experience of natural phenomena. From his earliest entries, when he began his scientific investigations, to his final days, he sprinkled his Notebooks with declarations about the critical importance of methical observation and experimentation.

"All our knowledge has its origin in the senses," he noted in his first Notebook, the Codex Trivulzianus.[5] "Wisdom is the daughter of experience," we read in the Codex Forster,[6] and in his *Treatise on Painting*, Leonardo asserted: "To me it seems that those sciences are vain and full of errors that are not born of experience, mother of all certainty. . . . that is to say, which do not at their beginning, middle, or end pass through any of the five senses."[7] Such an approach to the study of nature was unheard-of in Leonardo's day, and would fully emerge again only in the seventeenth century, the era of the Scientific Revolution.

Leonardo despised the established philosophers who merely quoted the classical texts in Latin and Greek. "They strut about puffed up and pompous," he wrote scornfully, "decked out and adorned not with their own labors but with those of others."[8] He recognized that learning from skilled masters was important in the arts, but he also observed that such masters were rare. "The surer way," he suggested, "is to go to the objects of nature, rather than those that are imitated with great deterioration, and so acquire sad habits; for he who can go to the well does not go to the water jar."[9]

When he was over sixty and living in Rome, Leonardo, one day, was working on problems of mechanics, filling the pages of a small notebook with a series of elaborate diagrams of scales and pulleys. "I shall now define the nature of composite scales . . . ," he wrote at one point. And then—as if suddenly mindful of future readers who needed to be taught about science—he interrupted himself to add his now famous manifesto on his scientific method:

> But first I shall do some experiments before I proceed farther, because my intention is to cite experience first and then with reasoning show why such experience is bound to operate in such a way. And this is the true rule by which those who speculate about the effects of nature must proceed.[10]

In the intellectual history of Europe, Galileo Galilei, who was born 112 years after Leonardo, is usually credited with being the first to develop this kind of rigorous empirical approach and is often hailed as the "father of modern science." There can be no doubt that this honor would have been bestowed on Leonardo da Vinci had he published his scientific writings during his lifetime, or had his Notebooks been widely studied soon after his death.

The empirical approach came naturally to Leonardo. He was gifted with exceptional powers of observation and a keen visual memory, complemented by his great drawing skills.[11] Art historian Kenneth Clark suggests that Leonardo had an "inhumanly sharp eye with which . . . he followed the movements of birds or of a wave, understood the structure of a seed-pod or skull, noted down the most trivial gesture or most evasive glance."[12]

What turned Leonardo from a painter with exceptional gifts of observation into a scientist was his recognition that his observations, in order to be scientific, needed to be carried out in an organized, methodical fashion. Scientific experiments are performed repeatedly and in varying circumstances so as to eliminate accidental factors and technical flaws as much as possible. The parameters of the experimental setting are varied in order to bring to light the essential unchanging features of the phenomena being investigated. This is exactly what Leonardo did. He never tired of carrying out his experiments and observations again and again, with fierce attention to the minutest details, and he would often vary his parameters systematically to test the consistency of his results. "We can only marvel at the master's voracious appetite for details," wrote art historian Erich Gombrich. "His range of activities and his insatiable thirst for knowledge seem never to have come in conflict with that awe-inspiring power of concentration that made him study one plant, one muscle, one sleeve or indeed one geometrical problem as if nothing else would ever concern him."[13]

In the Notebooks, Leonardo repeatedly commented on how a good experiment should be conducted, and in particular he stressed the need for careful repetitions and variations. Thus we read in Manuscript A: "Before you make a general rule of this case, test it two or three times and observe whether the tests produce the same effects." In Manuscript M he notes: "This experiment should be made several times, so that no accident may occur to hinder or falsify the test."[14]

Being a brilliant inventor and mechanical engineer, Leonardo was able to design ingenious experiments with the simplest means. For example, grains of millet or sprigs of straw, thrown into flowing water, helped him visualize and draw the shapes of the flow lines; specially designed floats, suspended at different depths of a flowing river, allowed him to measure the water's speed at different levels and at different distances from the banks.[15] He built glass chambers with their bases lined with sand and rear walls painted black for observing fine details of water movements in a controlled laboratory setting.[16]

Leonardo had to invent and design most of his measuring instruments. These included a device for measuring wind speed, a hygrometer to measure the humidity of the air, and various types of odometers to record distances traveled. In the course of surveying land, Leonardo would sometimes attach a pendulum to his thigh, which moved the teeth in a cogwheel to count the number of his steps. At other times he would use a cart with a cogwheel, and the cogwheel was designed to advance one cog with every ten *braccia* (about twenty feet) traveled, until a pebble audibly dropped into a metal basin at a distance of one mile.[17] In addition, he made many attempts to improve clock mechanisms for time measurement, which was still in its infancy in his day.[18]

In his scientific observations and experiments, Leonardo showed the same patience and subtle attention to detail that he practiced as a painter. This is especially noticeable in his anatomical research. For example, in one dissection he poured wax into the cavities of the brain known as cerebral ventricles to determine their shape. "Make two vent holes in the horns of the greater ventricles and insert melted wax with the syringe," he noted in his Anatomical Studies. "Then, when the wax has set, dissect off the brain and you will see the shape of the three ventricles exactly."[19] He invented an equally ingenious technique for dissecting the eye. As physician Sherwin Nuland describes it:

> In dissecting the eye, a notoriously difficult organ to cut, Leonardo hit upon the idea of first immersing it in egg white and then boiling the whole, so as to create a coagulum [thickened mass] before cutting into the tissue. Similar embedding techniques are routinely used today to enable accurate slicing of fragile structures.[20]

The systematic approach and careful attention to detail that Leonardo applied to his observations and experiments are characteristic of his entire method of scientific investigation. He would usually start from commonly accepted concepts and explanations, often summarizing what he had gathered from the classical texts before proceeding to verify it with his own observations. Sometimes he jotted down these summaries in the form of quick sketches, or even as elaborate drawings.

Before the accurate dating of the Notebooks, these drawings were often seen as indications of Leonardo's own lack of scientific knowledge rather than as the "citations" of received opinion that they are.

For example, the well-known "coitus figure" in the Windsor Collection of anatomical drawings, which shows the male reproductive organs with anatomies that are mostly erroneous, was long viewed as reflecting Leonardo's poor understanding of anatomy. More recently, however, the drawing was recognized by the historian of medicine and Leonardo scholar Kenneth Keele as Leonardo's illustration of what he had read in Plato's *Timaeus*. He had used it as the starting point for his own anatomical explorations of human reproductive processes.[21]

After testing the traditional ideas repeatedly with careful observations and experiments, Leonardo would either adhere to tradition if he found no contradictory evidence or would formulate his own alternative explanations. Sometimes he would dispense with comments altogether, relying entirely on the persuasive power of his drawings.

Leonardo generally worked on several problems simultaneously and paid special attention to similarities of forms and processes in different areas of investigation—for example, between the forces transmitted by pulleys and levers and those transmitted by muscles, tendons, and bones; between patterns of turbulence in water and in air; between the flow of sap in a plant or tree and the flow of blood in the human body.

When he made progress in his understanding of natural phenomena in one area, he was always aware of the analogies and interconnecting patterns to phenomena in other areas and would revise his theoretical ideas accordingly. This method led him to tackle many problems not just once but several times during different periods of his life, modifying his theories in successive steps as his scientific thought evolved over his lifetime.

Leonardo's method of repeatedly reassessing his theoretical ideas in various areas meant that he never saw any of his explanations as "final." Even though he believed in the certainty of scientific knowledge, as did most philosophers and scientists for the next three hundred years, his successive theoretical formulations in many fields are quite similar to the theoretical models that are characteristic of modern science. For example, he proposed several different models for the functioning of the heart and its role in maintaining the flow of blood, including one that pictured the heart as a stove housing a central fire, before he concluded that the heart is a muscle pumping blood through the arteries.[22] Leonardo also used simplified models—or approximations, as we would say today—to analyze the essential features of complex natural phenomena. For instance, he represented the flow of water through a channel of varying cross sections by using a model of rows of men marching through a street of varying width.[23]

Like modern scientists, Leonardo was always ready to revise his models when he felt that new observations or insights required him to do so. In his art as in his science, he always seemed to be more interested in the process of exploration than in the completed work or final results. Thus many of his paintings and all of his science remained unfinished work in progress.

This is a general characteristic of the modern scientific method. Although scientists publish their work in various stages of completion in papers, monographs, and textbooks, science as a whole is always work in progress. Old models and theories continue to be replaced by new ones, which are judged superior but are nevertheless limited and approximate, destined to be replaced in their turn as knowledge progresses.

Since the Scientific Revolution in the seventeenth century, this progress in science has been a collective enterprise. Scientists continually exchanged letters, papers, and books, and discussed their theories at various gatherings. This continual exchange of ideas is well documented and thus makes it fairly easy for historians to follow the progress of science through the centuries. With Leonardo, the situation is quite different. He worked alone and in secrecy, did not publish any of his findings, and only rarely dated his notes. In addition, he frequently copied excerpts from scholarly works into his Notebooks without proper attribution, even without identifying them as quotations, so that historians long took some of those copied passages for Leonardo's own original ideas.

Having pioneered the scientific method in solitude, Leonardo did not see science as a collective, collaborative enterprise. During his lifetime, therefore, any progress in his science was evident to him alone. Scholars today have had to engage in meticulous detective work to reconstruct the evolution of his scientific thought.

THE NOTEBOOKS

Leonardo recorded the results of his observations and experiments, his theoretical models, and his philosophical speculations in thousands of pages of notes, some in the form of well-organized treatises in various stages of completion, but most of them as disjointed notes and drawings without any apparent order, sometimes scribbled on the same folio at different times. Even though scholarly editions with clear transcriptions of all the Notebooks are now available, and most of the pages have been carefully dated, Leonardo's notes and drawings are so extensive, and their topics so diverse, that much work remains to be done to fully analyze their scientific contents and evaluate their significance.

The original text is difficult to read not only because it is written in mirror writing and is often disjointed, but also because Leonardo's spelling and syntax are highly idiosyncratic. He always seems to be in a hurry to jot down his thoughts, makes plenty of banal slips and errors, and often strings words together without any spaces between them. Punctuation is practically absent in his handwriting. The period (the only punctuation he uses) may occur very frequently in some manuscripts and be totally absent in others. In addition, like anyone used to taking regular and extensive personal notes, he employs his own code of abbreviations and shorthand notations.

In the fifteenth century, standard Italian spelling had not yet been established,[24] and scribes allowed themselves considerable variations. Accordingly, Leonardo varies his spellings quite indiscriminately, recording the sound of the spoken word in his own idiosyncratic ways rather than following any written tradition.

Taken together, these idiosyncrasies present considerable obstacles to the reader of Leonardo's original text. Fortunately, however, scholars have provided us with two kinds of transcriptions which, reproduced side by side, solve all these problems while following Leonardo's words

Figure 6-1: Spiraling foliage of Star of Bethlehem, c. 1508, Windsor Collection, Landscapes, Plants, and Water Studies, folio 16r

as closely as possible.[25] The so-called "diplomatic" transcription gives a printed version of the text exactly the way Leonardo wrote it, with all the abbreviations, idiosyncratic spellings, errors, crossed-out words, and other anomalies. The "critical" transcription next to it is a cleaned-up version of the text in which the abbreviations and errors have been eliminated, and Leonardo's archaic and erratic spellings have been replaced by their modern Italian counterparts, including modern punctuation, whenever this could be done without affecting the original Florentine pronunciation.

From these critical transcriptions emerges a flowing text, liberated from the obstacles mentioned, which anybody who is reasonably fluent in Italian can read without too many difficulties. Such reading makes it evident that Leonardo's language is highly eloquent, often witty, and at times movingly beautiful and poetic. It is worth reading his writings aloud to appreciate their beauty, because Leonardo's medium was the spoken word rather than the carefully composed written text. To make his arguments, he used the persuasive power of his drawings as well as the elegant cadences of his native Tuscan.

Let me now turn to the key characteristics of the science Leonardo discussed and developed in his Notebooks.

A SCIENCE OF LIVING FORMS

From the very beginning of Western philosophy and science, there has been a tension between mechanism and holism, between the study of matter (or substance, structure, quantity) and the study of form (or pattern, order, quality).[26] The study of matter was championed by Democritus, Galileo, Descartes, and Newton; the study of form by Pythagoras, Aristotle, Kant, and Goethe. Leonardo followed the tradition of Pythagoras and Aristotle, and he combined it with his rigorous empirical method to formulate a science of living forms, their patterns of organization, and their processes of growth and transformation. He was deeply aware of the fundamental interconnectedness of all phenomena and of the interdependence and mutual generation of all parts of an organic whole, which Immanuel Kant in the eighteenth century would define as "self-organization."[27] In the Codex Atlanticus, Leonardo eloquently summarized his profound understanding of life's basic processes by paraphrasing a statement by the Ionian philosopher Anaxagoras: "Everything comes from everything, and everything is made of everything, and everything turns into everything, because that which exists in the elements is made up of these elements."[28]

The Scientific Revolution replaced the Aristotelian worldview with the concept of the world as a machine. From then on the mechanistic approach—the study of matter, quantities, and constituents—dominated Western science. Only in the twentieth century did the limits of Newtonian science become fully apparent, and the mechanistic Cartesian worldview begin to give way to a holistic and ecological view not unlike that developed by Leonardo da Vinci.[29] With the rise of systemic thinking and its emphasis on networks, complexity, and patterns of organization, we can now more fully appreciate the power of Leonardo's science and its relevance for our modern era.

Leonardo's science is a science of qualities, of shapes and proportions, rather than absolute quantities. He preferred to *depict* the forms of nature in his drawings rather than *describe* their shapes, and he analyzed them in terms of their proportions rather than measured quantities. Proportion was seen by Renaissance artists as the essence of harmony and beauty. Leonardo filled many pages of his Notebooks with elaborate diagrams of proportions between the various parts of the human figure, and he drew corresponding diagrams to analyze the body of the horse.[30] He was far less interested in absolute measurements, which, in any case, were not as accurate, nor as important, in his time as they are in the modern world. For example, the standard units of length and weight—the *braccio* (arm) and the pound—both varied in different Italian cities from Florence to Milan to Rome, and they had different values in neighboring European countries.[31]

Leonardo was always impressed by the great diversity and variety of living forms. "Nature is so delightful and abundant in its variations," he wrote in a passage about how to paint trees, "that among trees of the same kind there would not be found one plant that resembles another nearby, and this is so not only of the plant as a whole, but among the branches, the leaves, and the fruit, not one will be found that looks precisely like another."[32]

Leonardo recognized this infinite variety as a key characteristic of living forms, but he also tried to classify the shapes he studied into different types.

Figure 6-2: Flow of water and flow of human hair, c. 1513,
Windsor Collection, Landscapes, Plants, and
Water Studies, folio 48r

He made lists of different body parts, such as lips and noses, and identified different types of human figures, varieties of plant species, and even classes of water vortices.[33] Whenever he observed natural forms, he recorded their essential features in drawings and diagrams, classified them into types if possible, and tried to understand the processes and forces underlying their formation.

In addition to the variations within a particular species, Leonardo paid attention to similarities of organic forms in different species and to similarities of patterns in different natural phenomena. The Notebooks contain countless drawings of such patterns—anatomical similarities between the leg of a man and that of a horse, spiraling whirlpools and spiraling foliages of certain plants (Fig. 6-1), the flow of water and the flow of human hair (Fig. 6-2), and so on. On a folio of anatomical drawings, he notes that the veins in the human body behave like oranges, "in which, as the skin thickens, so the pulp diminishes the older they become."[34] Among his studies for *The Battle of Anghiari*, we find a comparison of expressions of fury in the faces of a man, a horse, and a lion (Fig. 6-3).

These frequent comparisons of forms and patterns are usually described as analogies by art historians, who point out that explanations in terms of analogies were common among artists and philosophers in the Middle Ages and the Renaissance.[35] This is certainly true. But Leonardo's comparisons of organic forms and processes in different species are much more than simple analogies. When he investigates similarities between the skeletons of different vertebrates, he studies what biologists today call homologies—structural correspondences between different species, due to their evolutionary descent from a common ancestor.

The similarities of expressions of fury in the faces of animals and humans are homologies as well, derived from commonalities in the evolution of face muscles. Leonardo's analogy between the skin of human veins and the skin of oranges during the process of aging is based on the fact that in both cases he was observing the behavior of living tissues. In all these cases, he realized intuitively that living forms in different species exhibit similarities of patterns. Today we explain these patterns in terms of microscopic cellular structures and of metabolic and evolutionary processes. Leonardo, of course, did not have access to those levels of explanation, but he correctly perceived that throughout the creation (or evolution, as we would say today) of the great diversity of forms, nature used again and again the same basic patterns of organization.

Leonardo's science is utterly dynamic. He portrays nature's forms—in mountains, rivers, plants, and the human body—in ceaseless movement and transformation.

Form, for him, is never static. He realizes that living forms are continually being shaped and transformed by underlying processes. He studies the multiple ways in which rocks and mountains are shaped by turbulent flows of water, and how the organic forms of plants, animals, and the human body are shaped by their metabolism. The world Leonardo portrays, both in his art and in his science, is a world in de-

Figure 6-3: Fury in the faces of a man, a horse, and a lion, c. 1503–4,
Windsor Collection, Horses and Other Animals, folio 117r

velopment and flux, in which all configurations and forms are merely stages in a continual process of transformation. "This feeling of movement inherent in the world," writes art historian Daniel Arasse, "is absolutely central to Leonardo's work, because it reveals an essential aspect of his genius, thereby defining his uniqueness among his contemporaries."[36] At the same time, Leonardo's dynamic understanding of organic forms reveals many fascinating parallels to the new systemic understanding of life that has emerged at the forefront of science over the past twenty-five years.

In Leonardo's science of living forms, life's patterns of organization and its fundamental processes of metabolism and growth were the unifying conceptual threads that interlinked his knowledge of macro- and microcosm. In the macrocosm, the main themes of his science were the movements of water and air, the geological forms and transformations of the Earth, and the botanical diversity and growth patterns of plants. In the microcosm, his main focus was on the human body—its beauty and proportions, the mechanics of its movements, and how it compared to other animal bodies in motion, in particular birds in flight.

THE MOVEMENTS OF WATER

Leonardo was fascinated by water in all its manifestations. He recognized its fundamental role as life's medium and vital fluid, as the matrix of all organic forms. "It is the expansion and humor of all living bodies," he wrote. "Without it nothing retains its original form."[37] Throughout his life, he strove to understand the mysterious processes underlying the creation of nature's forms by studying the movements of water through earth and air.

As an engineer, Leonardo worked extensively on schemes of canalization, irrigation, the drainage of marshes, and the uses of waterpower for pumping, milling, and sawing. Like other noted engineers in the Renaissance, he was very familiar with the beneficial as well as the destructive effects of the power of water. But he was the only one to go beyond empirical rules of hydraulic engineering and embark on sustained theoretical studies of the flow of water. His examinations and exquisite drawings of the flows of rivers, eddies, spiraling vortices, and other patterns of turbulence establish Leonardo as a pioneer in a field that did not even exist in his time—the discipline known today as fluid dynamics.

Throughout his life, Leonardo observed the flows of rivers and tides, drew beautiful and accurate maps of entire watersheds, and investigated currents in lakes and seas, flows over weirs and waterfalls, and the movement of waves as well as flows through pipes, nozzles, and orifices. His observations, drawings, and theoretical ideas would fill hundreds of pages in his Notebooks.

Through this lifelong study, Leonardo gained a full understanding of the main characteristics of fluid flow. He recognized the two principal forces operating in flowing water—the force of gravity and the fluid's internal friction, or viscosity—and he correctly described many phenomena generated by their interplay. He also realized that water is incompressible and that, even though it assumes an infinite number of shapes, its mass is always conserved.

In a branch of science that did not even exist before him, Leonardo's deep insights into the nature of fluid flow must be ranked as a momentous achievement. That he also drew many turbulent structures erroneously and imagined some flow phenomena that do not occur in reality does not diminish his great accomplishments, especially in view of the fact that even today scientists and mathematicians encounter considerable difficulties in their attempts to predict and model the complex details of turbulent flows.

At the center of Leonardo's investigations of turbulence lies the water vortex, or whirlpool. Throughout the Notebooks, there are countless drawings of eddies and whirlpools of all sizes and types—in the currents of rivers and lakes, behind piers and jetties, in the basins of waterfalls, and behind objects of various shapes immersed in flowing water. These often very beautiful drawings are testimony to Leonardo's endless fascination with the ever-changing and yet stable nature of this fundamental type of turbulence. I believe that this fascination came from a deep intuition that the dynamics of vortices, combining stability and change, embody an essential characteristic of living forms.[38]

Leonardo was the first to understand the detailed motions of water vortices, often drawing them accurately even in complex situations. He correctly distinguished between flat circular eddies in which the water essentially rotates as a solid body, and spiral vortices (such as the whirlpool in a bathtub) that form a hollow space, or funnel, at their center. "The spiral or rotary movement of every liquid," he noted, "is so much swifter as it is nearer to the center of its revolution. What we

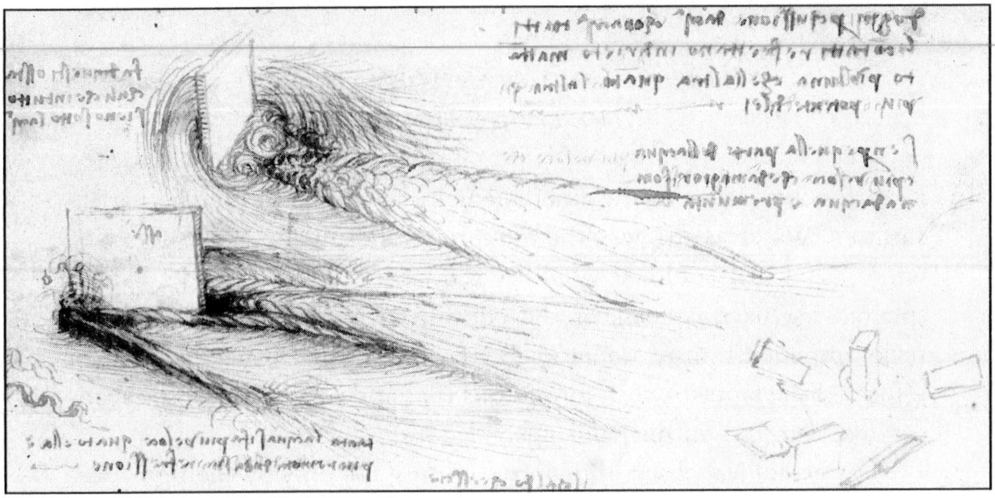

Figure 6-4: Turbulent wakes behind a rectangular plank, c. 1509–11, Windsor Collection, Landscapes, Plants, and Water Studies, folio 42r

are here proposing is a fact worthy of admiration, since the circular movement of the wheel is so much slower as it is nearer to the center of the rotating object."[39] Such detailed studies of vortices in turbulent water were not taken up again for another 350 years, until the physicist Hermann von Helmholtz developed a mathematical analysis of vortex motion in the mid-nineteenth century.

Leonardo produced several elaborate drawings of highly complex patterns of turbulence, generated by placing various obstacles into flowing water. Figure 6-4, from the Windsor Collection, shows the turbulent flows around a rectangular plank inserted at two different angles. (Additional variations are suggested in the small sketches to the right of the main drawing.) The upper drawing clearly shows a pair of counter-rotating vortices at the head of a stream of random wake. The essential details of this complex pattern of turbulence are completely accurate—an amazing testimony to Leonardo's powers of observation and conceptual clarity.

THE FORMS AND TRANSFORMATIONS OF
THE LIVING EARTH

Leonardo saw water as the chief agent in the formation of the Earth's surface. "Water wears away the mountains and fills up the valleys," he wrote, "and if it could, it would like to reduce the Earth to a perfect sphere."[40] This awareness of the continual interaction of water and rocks impelled him to undertake extensive studies in geology, which informed the fantastic rock formations that appear so often in the shadowy backgrounds of his paintings.

His geological observations are stunning not only by their great accuracy, but also because they led him to formulate general principles that were rediscovered only centuries later and are still used by geologists today.[41] Leonardo recognized temporal sequences in the strata of soil and rock, and corresponding sequences in the fossils deposited in those strata, and he recorded many fine details concerning erosion and deposits by rivers.

He was the first to postulate that the forms of the Earth are the result of processes taking place over long epochs of what we now call geological time. With this view he came close to an evolutionary perspective more than three hundred years before Charles Darwin, who also found inspiration for evolutionary thought in geology. For Leonardo, geological time began with the formation of the living Earth, a process to which he alluded in his paintings with a sense of awe and mystery.

"Describe a landscape with wind and water," Leonardo exhorted his fellow painters, "and at the setting and rising of the sun."[42] He was a true master in rendering these atmospheric effects. Like his predecessors and contemporaries, he frequently introduced flowers and herbs into his paintings for their symbolic meanings, but unlike most of his fellow painters, he was always careful to present plants in their proper ecological habitats with seasonal appropriateness and great botanical accuracy.[43]

The Notebooks contain numerous drawings of trees and flowering plants indigenous to Italy, many of them masterpieces of detailed botanical imagery. Most of these drawings were made as studies for paintings, but some also include detailed notes explaining the plants' characteristics. Unlike the formal decorative plant motifs that were common in Renaissance paintings, Leonardo's flowers, herbs, and trees display a vitality and grace that could only be achieved by a painter who had profound botanical and ecological knowledge.

Indeed, Leonardo's mind was not satisfied with merely depicting plants in paintings, but turned to a genuine inquiry into their intrinsic nature—the patterns of metabolism and growth that underlie their organic forms. He made detailed observations of the effects of sunlight, water, and gravity on plant growth; he examined the sap of trees and discovered that a tree's age could be determined from the number of rings in the cross-section of its trunk; he investigated patterns of leaves and branches around their stems, known to botanists today as the study of phyllotaxis; and he related patterns of branching to the activity of a tree's "humor"—an extraordinary insight into effects of hormonal activity that became known only in the twentieth century. As in so many other fields, Leonardo carried his scientific thinking far beyond that of his peers, establishing himself as the first great theorist in botany.[44]

MACRO- AND MICROCOSM

Whenever Leonardo explored the forms of nature in the macrocosm, he also looked for similarities of patterns and processes in the human body. In so doing, he went beyond the general analogies between macro- and microcosm that were common knowledge in his time, drawing parallels between very sophisticated observations in both realms. He applied his knowledge of turbulent flows of water to the movement of blood in the heart and aorta.[45] He saw the "vital sap" of plants as their essential life fluid and observed that it nourishes the plant tissues, as the blood nourishes the tissues of the human body. He noticed the structural similarity between the stalk (known to botanists as the funiculus) that attaches the seed of a plant to the tissues of the fruit, and the umbilical cord that attaches the human fetus to the placenta.[46] He took these observations as compelling testimonies to the unity of life at all scales of nature.

Leonardo's wide-ranging and meticulous observations of the human body must be ranked among his greatest scientific achievements. In order to study the organic forms of the human body, he dissected numerous corpses of humans and animals, and examined their bones, joints, muscles, and nerves, drawing them with an accuracy and clarity never seen before. At the same time, his anatomical drawings are superb works of art, due to his unique ability to represent forms and movements in stunning visual perspective with subtle gradations of light and shade, which gives his drawings a vivid quality rarely achieved in modern anatomical illustrations.

Looking through Leonardo's drawings and notes in over a thousand pages of anatomical manuscripts, we can discern several broad themes. The first is that of beauty and proportion, which held great fascination for Renaissance artists. They saw proportion in painting, sculpture, and architecture as the essence of harmony and beauty, and there were many attempts to establish a canon of proportions for the human figure. Leonardo threw himself into this project with his usual vigor and attention to detail, taking a wealth of measurements to establish a comprehensive system of correspondences between all parts of the body. At the same time, he explored the relationship between proportion and beauty in his paintings. "The beautiful proportions of an angelic face in painting," he wrote, "produce a harmonious concord, which reaches the eye simultaneously, just as [a chord in] music affects the ear."[47]

The second grand theme of Leonardo's anatomical research was the human body in motion. As noted earlier, Leonardo's science of living forms is a science of movement and transformation, whether he studied mountains, rivers, plants, or the human body. Hence, to understand the human form meant for him to understand the body in motion. He demonstrated in countless elaborate and stunning drawings how nerves, muscles, tendons, and bones work together to move the body.

NATURE'S MECHANICAL INSTRUMENTS

Leonardo never thought of the human body as a machine.[48] However, he clearly recognized that the anatomies of animals and humans involve mechanical functions. In his anatomical drawings, he sometimes replaced muscles by threads or wires to better demonstrate the directions of their forces (see Fig. I-1 on p. 10, and Fig. 9-4 on p. 251). He showed how joints operate like hinges and applied the principle of levers to explain the movements of the limbs. "Nature cannot give movement to animals without mechanical instruments," he declared.[49] Hence, he felt that, in order to understand the movements of the animal body, he needed to explore the laws of mechanics. Indeed, for Leonardo, this was the principal role of this branch of science: "The instrumental or mechanical science is very noble and most useful above all others, because by means of it all animated bodies that have movement perform all their operations."[50]

To investigate the mechanics of muscles, tendons, and bones, Leonardo immersed himself in a long study of the "science of weights," known today as statics, which is concerned with the analysis of loads and forces on physical systems in static equilibrium, such as balances, levers, and pulleys. In the Renaissance this knowledge was very important for architects and engineers, as it is today, and the medieval science of weights comprised a large collection of works compiled in the late thirteenth and the fourteenth centuries.

In his usual fashion, Leonardo absorbed the key ideas from the best and most original texts, commented on many of their postulates in his Notebooks, verified them experimentally, and refuted some incorrect proofs.[51] The classical law of the lever, in particular, appears repeatedly in the Notebooks. In the Codex Atlanticus, for example, Leonardo states, "The ratio of the weights that hold the arms of the balance parallel to the horizon is the same as that of the arms, but it is inverse."[52]

Leonardo applied this law to calculate the forces and weights necessary to establish equilibria in numerous simple and compound systems involving balances, levers, pulleys, and beams hanging from cords.[53] In addition, he carefully analyzed the tensions in various segments of the cords, probably for the purpose of estimating similar tensions in the muscles and tendons of human limbs.

Leonardo applied the lever law not only to situations where the forces act in a direction perpendicular to the lever arms, but also to forces acting at various angles. The Codex Arundel and Manuscript E in particular contain numerous diagrams of varying complexities, with weights exerting forces at different angles via cords and pulleys. He recognized that in such cases, the relevant length in the lever law is not the actual length of the lever arm, but the perpendicular distance from the line of the force to the axis of rotation. He called that distance the "potential lever arm" (*braccio potenziale*) and marked it clearly in many diagrams. In modern statics, the potential lever arm is known as the "moment arm," and the product of moment arm and force is called the "moment," or "torque." Leonardo's discovery of the principle that the sum of the moments about any point must be zero for a system to be in static equilibrium was his most original contribution to statics. It went well beyond the medieval science of weights of his time.

LEONARDO'S MACHINES

Leonardo applied his knowledge of mechanics not only to his investigations of the movements of the human body, but also to his studies of machines. Indeed, the uniqueness of his genius lay in his synthesis of art, science, and design.[54] In his lifetime, he was famous as an artist, and also as a brilliant mechanical engineer who invented and designed countless machines and mechanical devices, often involving innovations that were centuries ahead of his time.[55] Today, Leonardo's technical drawings are frequently exhibited around the world, often supplemented by wooden models that show in impressive detail how the machines work as Leonardo had intended.[56]

As noted earlier, Leonardo was the first to separate individual mechanisms from the machines in which they were embedded.[57] In these studies, he always insisted that any improvement of existing devices must be based on sound knowledge of the principles of mechanics. He paid special attention to the transmission of power and motion from one plane into another, which was a major challenge of Renaissance engineering. In his design of a water-powered milling machine (Fig. 8-3 on p. 218), for example, the motion is transmitted three times between horizontal and vertical axes with the help of a combination of toothed wheels and worm gears. The corresponding transfer of power is clearly indicated by Leonardo in a small diagram below the main drawing.[58]

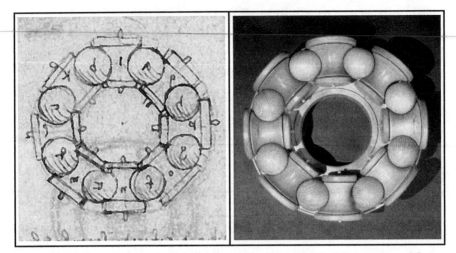

Figure 6-5: Rotary ball bearing, Codex Madrid I, folio 20v; model
by Muséo Techni, Montreal, 1987

Among Leonardo's many mechanical innovations, there are several involving the conversion of the rotary motion of a crank into a straight back-and-forth movement, which could be used, for example, in automatic manufacturing processes.[59] And then there is Leonardo's well-known, highly ingenious design of a two-wheeled hoist (Fig. 2-3 on p. 41), which performs the opposite conversion: The motion of a vertical operating lever rocking back and forth is converted into the smooth hoisting of a heavy load by means of two toothed wheels and a caged lantern gear. This is one of Leonardo's most famous technical drawings. It displays the mechanism both in its assembled form and in an exploded view that exposes the complex combination of gears and plates.[60]

In the Renaissance, hoists, cranes, and other large machines were made of wood, and friction between their movable parts was a major problem. Leonardo invented numerous sophisticated devices for reducing friction and wear, including automatic lubrication systems, adjustable bearings, and mobile rollers of various shapes—spheres, cylinders, truncated cones, and the like. Figure 6-5 shows an elegant example of a rotary bearing composed of eight concave-sided spindles rotating on their own axes, interspersed by balls that can rotate freely but are prevented from lateral movements by the spindles. When a platform is put on this ball bearing, friction is reduced to such an extent that the platform can be turned easily even when carrying a heavy load.

All the great Renaissance engineers were aware of the effects of friction, but Leonardo was the only one who undertook systematic empirical studies of frictional forces. He found by experiment that, when an object slides against a surface, the amount of friction is determined by three factors: the roughness of the surfaces, the weight of the object, and the slope of an inclined plane:

> In order to know accurately the quantity of the weight required to move a hundred pounds over a sloping road, one must know the nature of the contact which this weight has with the surface on which it rubs in its movement, because different bodies have different frictions. . . .

> Different slopes make different degrees of resistance at their contact; because, if the weight that must be moved is upon level ground and has to be dragged, it undoubtedly will be in the first strength of resistance, because everything rests on the earth and nothing on the cord that must move it. . . . But you know that, if one were to draw it straight up, slightly grazing and touching a perpendicular wall, the weight is almost entirely on the cord that draws it, and only very little rests upon the wall where it rubs.[61]

Leonardo's conclusions are fully borne out by modern mechanics. Today the force of friction is defined as the product of the frictional coefficient (measuring the roughness of the surfaces) and the force perpendicular to the contact surface (which depends both on the object's weight and the slope of the surface).

Leonardo's studies of power transmission led him to investigate the medieval belief that power could be harnessed through perpetual motion machines. At first he accepted this idea. He designed a host of complex mechanisms to keep water in perpetual motion by means of various feedback systems. But eventually he realized that any mechanical system will gradually lose its power because of friction. In the end,

Leonardo scoffed at attempts to build perpetual motion machines. "I have found among the excessive and impossible delusions of men," he wrote in the Codex Madrid, "the search for continuous motion, which is called by some the perpetual wheel."[62]

Leonardo extended his keen interest in friction to his extensive studies of fluid flows. The Codex Madrid contains meticulous records of his investigations and analyses of the resistance of water and air to moving solid bodies, as well as of water and fire moving in air.[63] Well aware of the internal friction of fluids, known as viscosity, Leonardo dedicated numerous pages in the Notebooks to analyzing its effects on fluid flow. "Water has always a cohesion in itself," he wrote in the Codex Leicester, "and this is the more potent as the water is more viscous."[64]

Air resistance was of special interest to Leonardo, because it played an important role in one of his great passions—the flight of birds and the design of flying machines. "In order to give the true science of the movement of birds in the air," he declared, "it is necessary first to give the science of the winds."[65]

THE DREAM OF FLYING

The dream of flying like a bird is as old as humanity itself. But nobody pursued it with more intensity, perseverance, and commitment to meticulous research than Leonardo da Vinci. His "science of flight" involved numerous disciplines—from fluid dynamics to human anatomy, mechanics, the anatomy of birds, and mechanical engineering. He diligently pursued these studies throughout most of his life, from the early years of his apprenticeship in Florence to his old age in Rome.[66]

The first intense period of research on flying machines began in the early 1490s, about a decade after Leonardo's arrival in Milan.[67] His experiments during this period combined mechanics and the anatomy of the human body. He carefully investigated and measured the body's ability to generate various amounts of force in order to find out how a human pilot might be able to lift a flying machine off the ground by flapping its mechanical wings.

Leonardo realized that the air under a bird's wing is compressed by

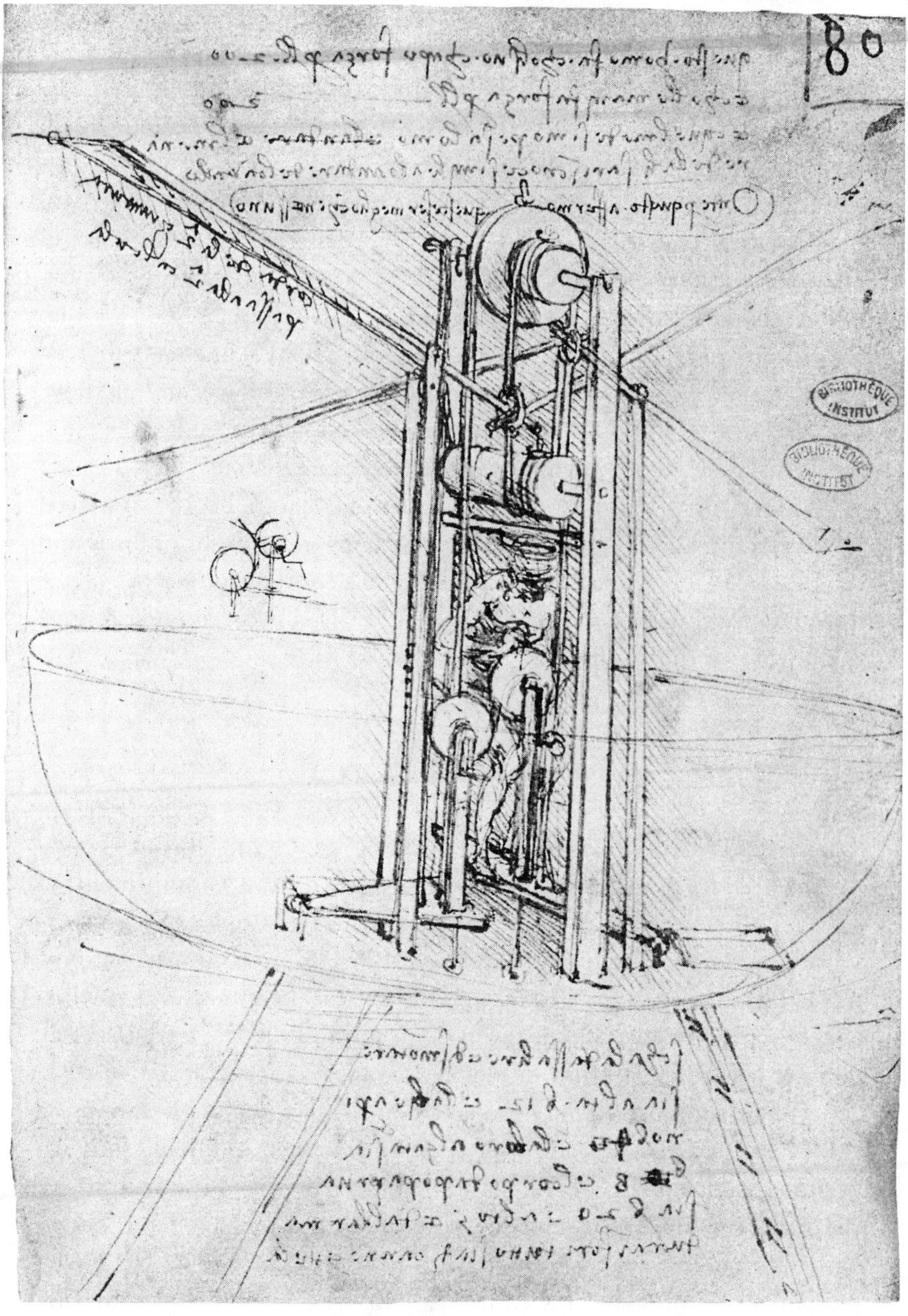

Figure 6-6: Leonardo's "flying ship," Ms. B, folio 80r

the downstroke. "See how the wings, striking against the air, sustain the heavy eagle in the thin air on high," he noted in the Codex Atlanticus, and then he added a remarkable observation: "As much force is exerted by the object against the air as by the air against the object."[68] Leonardo's observation was restated by Isaac Newton two hundred years later and has since been known as Newton's third law of motion.[69]

The result of these investigations was Leonardo's so-called flying ship, his first design of a flying machine (see Fig. 6-6). From the human point of view, the design is rather strange. Crouched down in the center of the craft, the pilot generates the necessary force by pushing two pedals with his feet while simultaneously turning two handles with his hands. As historian Domenico Laurenza points out, "There is no note, no mention to be found . . . of how the pilot will steer the machine in flight; he becomes almost an automatic pilot: he simply has to generate the force to lift off the ground."[70]

During these years, Leonardo designed a series of much more realistic flying machines in which the pilot is placed horizontally (see Fig. 6-7). These designs involve more varied and subtle movements. Human arms and legs are used to make the wings flap. Other movements turn the wings, angling them in the upstroke and opening them to the air in the downstroke, as birds do when flapping in flight. Yet other movements are used to maintain balance and change direction.

These drawings (in Manuscript B and the Codex Atlanticus) represent Leonardo's most sophisticated designs of flying machines. They became the basis of several models built by modern engineers.[71] Figure 6-8 shows one of these models, built from materials that were available in the Renaissance. Unfortunately, the limitations of these materials—wooden struts, leather joints and thongs, and skin of strong cloth—make it evident why Leonardo could not create a viable model of his flying machines, even though they were based on sound aerodynamic principles. The combined weight of the machine and its pilot was simply far too heavy to be lifted by human muscle power.

Eventually, Leonardo became aware that he could not achieve the required power-to-weight ratio for successful flight. Ten years after his experiments with flying machines in Milan, he entered into another in-

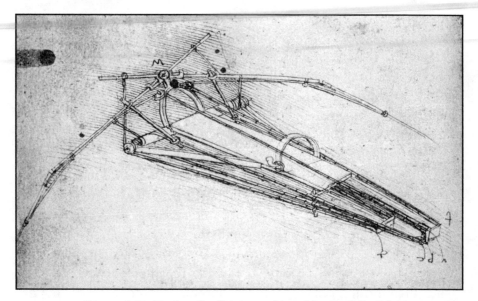

Figure 6-7: Design for flying machine, Ms. B, folio 74v

tense period of research in Florence, which involved his making careful and methodical observations of birds in flight, down to the finest anatomical and aerodynamic details.[72]

In the resulting Notebook, Codex on the Flight of Birds, Leonardo concludes that human flight with mechanical wings might not be possible because of the limitations of our anatomy. Birds have powerful pectoral muscles, he notes, that allow them to flee rapidly from predators, or to carry heavy prey, but they need only a fraction of that force to sustain themselves in the air during normal flight.[73]

His observations led Leonardo to speculate that, even though human beings would not be able to fly by flapping mechanical wings, "soaring flight," or gliding, might be possible, since this required much less force. During his last years in Florence he began to experiment with designs of flying machines that had fixed wings, not unlike a modern hang glider.

Based on these designs, British engineers recently built a glider and tested it successfully in a flight from the chalk cliffs in southeast England known as the Sussex Downs. This maiden flight of "Leonardo's glider," reportedly, exceeded the first attempts by the Wright brothers in 1900.[74]

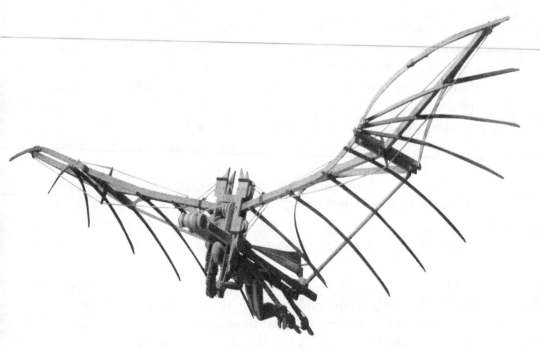

*Figure 6-8: Working model of the flying machine,
Museum of the History of Science, Florence*

Although the machines with movable mechanical wings were not
destined to fly, the models built from Leonardo's designs are extraordinary testimonies to his genius as a scientist and engineer. In the words
of art historian Martin Kemp: "Using mechanical systems, the wings
flap with much of the sinuous and menacing grace of a gigantic bird of
prey. . . . [Leonardo's] designs retain their conceptual power as archetypal expressions of man's desire to emulate the birds, and remain capable of inspiring a sense of wonder even in a modern audience, for
whom the sight of tons of metal flying through the air has become a
matter of routine."[75]

THE MYSTERY OF HUMAN LIFE

The third grand theme in Leonardo's anatomical research (in addition
to the themes of harmony and proportion, and the body in motion) is

his persistent quest for understanding the nature of life. It is the leit-motiv of his anatomies of the body's internal organs, and in particular of his investigations of the heart—the bodily organ that has served as the foremost symbol of human existence and emotional life throughout the ages.

Leonardo's careful and patient studies of the movements of the heart and the flow of blood, undertaken in old age, are the culmination of his anatomical work. He not only understood and pictured the heart like no one before him, but also observed subtleties in its actions and in the flow of blood that would elude medical researchers for centuries.

Because he did not see the body as a machine, Leonardo's main concern was not the mechanical transportation of blood, but the twin problems, as he saw them, of how the actions of the heart maintained the blood at body temperature and how they produced the "vital spirits" that keep us alive. He accepted the ancient notion that these vital spirits arise from a mixture of blood and air—which is essentially correct, if we identify them with oxygenated blood—and he developed an ingenious theory to solve both problems.

In the absence of any knowledge of chemistry, Leonardo used his extensive understanding of turbulent flows of water and air, and of the role of friction, in his attempt to explain the origin of both the blood-air mixture and the body temperature. This included a meticulous description of many subtle features of blood flow—including the coordinated actions of the heart's four chambers (when all his contemporaries knew only of two), and the corresponding synchronized actions of the coronary valves—which he pictured in a series of superb drawings. According to the eminent physician and Leonardo scholar Kenneth Keele:

> Leonardo's success in cardiac anatomy [is] so great that there are aspects of the work which are not yet equaled by modern anatomical illustration. . . . His consistent practice of illustration of the heart and its valves, both in systole and in diastole, with a comparison of the position of the parts, has rarely if ever been performed in any anatomical textbook.[76]

Leonardo missed some crucial details about the mechanics of blood circulation, which were discovered by William Harvey a hundred years later, and without chemistry he could not explain the oxygen exchange between the blood and the tissues of the lungs and body. But amazingly, he recognized many subtle features of cellular metabolism without even knowing about cells—for example, that heat energy supports the metabolic processes, that oxygen (the "vital spirits") sustains them, that there is a constant flow of oxygen from the heart to the body's periphery, and that the blood returns with waste products from the tissue metabolism. In other words, Leonardo developed a theory of the functioning of the heart and the flow of blood that allowed him to understand some of the essential features of biological life.

During the last decade of his life, while he was engaged in his most advanced studies of the human heart, Leonardo also became intensely interested in another aspect of the mystery of life—its origin in the processes of reproduction and embryonic development. That he had always considered embryology as an integral part of his studies of the human body is evident from the grandiose outline of a planned (but never assembled) treatise on the movements of the body, written about twenty years earlier. This long and detailed outline begins with the following sweeping declaration:

> This work should begin with the conception of man, and should describe the nature of the womb, and how the child lives in it, and to what stage it resides in it, and in what way it acquires life and food, and its growth, and what interval there is between one degree of growth and another, and what it is that pushes it out of the body of the mother.[77]

Leonardo's embryological studies, based largely on dissections of cows and sheep, included most of the topics he had listed and led him to remarkable observations and conclusions. While most authorities in his day believed that all inherited characteristics derived from the father, he asserted unequivocally: "The seed of the mother has equal power in the embryo to the seed of the father."[78]

He described the life processes of the fetus in the womb, including its nourishment through the umbilical cord, in astonishing detail, and he also made a series of measurements on animal fetuses to determine their rates of growth. Leonardo's embryological drawings are graceful and touching revelations of the mysteries surrounding the origins of human life (see Fig. E-1 on p. 261). In the words of physician Sherwin Nuland,

> [His] depiction of a five-month fetus in the womb is a thing of beauty. . . . It stands as a masterwork of art, and, considering the very little that was at the time understood of embryology, a masterwork of scientific perception as well.[79]

Leonardo knew very well that, ultimately, the nature and origin of life would remain a mystery, no matter how brilliant his scientific mind was. "Nature is full of infinite causes that have never occurred in experience,"[80] he declared in his late forties, and as he got older his sense of mystery deepened. Nearly all the figures in his last paintings have that smile that expresses the ineffable, often combined with a pointing finger. "Mystery to Leonardo," wrote Kenneth Clark, "was a shadow, a smile and a finger pointing into darkness."[81]

SEVEN

Geometry Done with Motion

Leonardo was well aware of the critical role of mathematics in the formulation of scientific ideas and in the recording and evaluation of experiments. "There is no certainty," he wrote in his Notebooks, "where one can not apply any of the mathematical sciences, nor those which are connected with the mathematical sciences."[1] In his Anatomical Studies, he proclaimed, in evident homage to Plato, "Let no man who is not a mathematician read my principles."[2]

Leonardo's approach to mathematics was that of a scientist, not a mathematician. He wanted to use mathematical language to provide consistency and rigor to the descriptions of his scientific observations. However, in his time there was no mathematical language appropriate to express the kind of science he was pursuing—explorations of the forms of nature in their movements and transformations. And so Leonardo used his powers of visualization and his great intuition to experiment with new techniques that foreshadowed branches of mathematics that would not be developed until centuries later. These include the theory of functions and the fields of integral calculus and topology, as I shall discuss below.

Leonardo's mathematical diagrams and notes are scattered throughout his Notebooks. Many of them have not yet been fully evaluated. While we have illuminating books by physicians on his anatomical studies and detailed analyses of his botanical drawings by botanists, a comprehensive volume on his mathematical works by a professional mathematician still needs to be written. Here, I can give only a brief summary of this fascinating side of Leonardo's genius.

GEOMETRY AND ALGEBRA

In the Renaissance, as we have seen, mathematics consisted of two main branches, geometry and algebra, the former inherited from the Greeks, while the latter had been developed mainly by Arab mathematicians.[3] Geometry was considered more fundamental, especially among Renaissance artists, for whom it represented the foundation of perspective, and thus the mathematical underpinning of painting.[4] Leonardo fully shared this view. And since his approach to science was largely visual, it is not surprising that his entire mathematical thinking was geometric. He never got very far with algebra, and indeed he frequently made careless errors in simple arithmetical calculations. The really important mathematics for him was geometry, which is evident from his praise of the eye as "the prince of mathematics."[5]

In this he was hardly alone. Even for Galileo, one hundred years after Leonardo, mathematical language essentially meant the language of geometry. "Philosophy is written in that great book which ever lies before our eyes," Galileo wrote in a much quoted passage. "But we cannot understand it if we do not first learn the language and characters in which it is written. This language is mathematics, and the characters are triangles, circles, and other geometrical figures."[6]

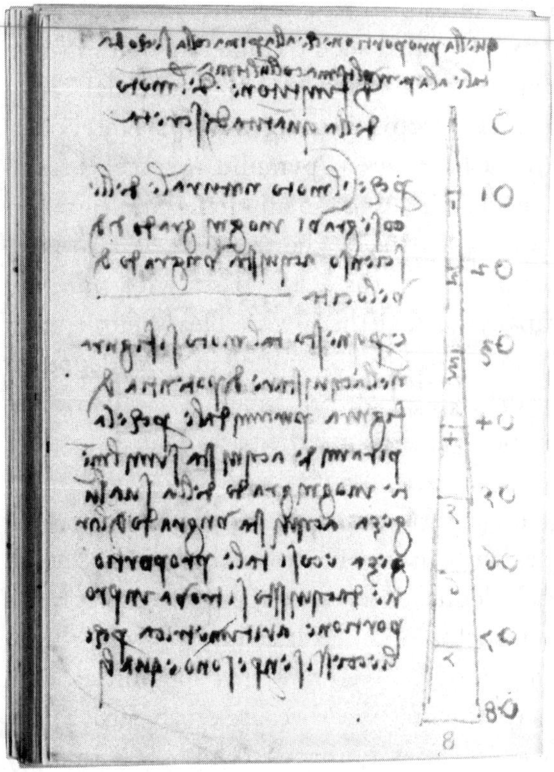

Figure 7-1: The "pyramidal law,"
Ms. M, folio 59v

Like most mathematicians of his time, Leonardo frequently used geometrical figures to represent algebraic relationships. A simple but very ingenious example is his pervasive use of triangles and pyramids to illustrate arithmetic progressions and, more generally, what we now call linear functions.[7] He was familiar with the use of pyramids to represent linear proportions from his studies of perspective, where he observed that "All the things transmit to the eye their image by means of a pyramid of lines. By 'pyramid of lines' I mean those lines which, starting from the edges of the surface of each object, converge from a distance and meet in a single point . . . placed in the eye."[8]

In his notes, Leonardo often represented such a pyramid, or cone, in a vertical section, that is, simply as a triangle, where the triangle's base represents the edge of the object and its apex a point in the eye. Leonardo then used this geometric figure—the isosceles triangle (i.e., a triangle with two equal sides)—to represent arithmetic progressions and linear algebraic relationships, thus establishing a visual link between the proportions of perspective and quantitative relationships in many fields of science, for example, the increase of the velocity of falling bodies with time, discussed below.

He knew from Euclidean geometry that in a sequence of isosceles triangles with bases at equal distances from the apex, the lengths of these bases, as well as the distances of their endpoints from the apex, form arithmetic progressions. He called such triangles "pyramids" and accordingly referred to an arithmetic progression as "pyramidal."

Leonardo repeatedly illustrates this technique in his Notebooks. For example, in Manuscript M he draws a "pyramid" (isosceles triangle) with a sequence of bases, labeled with small circles and numbers running from 1 to 8 (see Fig. 7-1). Inside the triangle, he also indicates the progressively increasing lengths of the bases with numbers from 1 to 8. In the accompanying text, he gives a clear definition of arithmetic progression: "The pyramid . . . acquires in each degree of its length a degree of breadth, and such proportional acquisition is found in the arithmetic proportion, because the parts that exceed are always equal."[9]

Leonardo uses this particular diagram to illustrate the increase of the velocity of falling bodies with time. "The natural motion of heavy things," he explains, "at each degree of its descent acquires a degree of velocity. And for this reason, such motion, as it acquires power, is represented by the figure of a pyramid."[10] We know that the phrase "each degree of its descent" refers to units of time, because on an earlier page of the same Notebook he writes: "Gravity that descends freely in every degree of time acquires . . . a degree of velocity."[11] In other words, Leonardo is establishing the mathematical law that for freely falling bodies there is a linear relationship between velocity and time.[12]

In today's mathematical language, we say that the velocity of a falling body is a linear function of time, and we write it symbolically as $v = gt$, where g denotes the constant gravitational acceleration. This language was not available to Leonardo. The concept of a function as a relation between variables was developed only in the late seventeenth century. Even Galileo described the functional relationship between velocity and time for a falling body in words and in the language of proportion, as did Leonardo 140 years before him.[13]

For most of his life, Leonardo believed that his "pyramidal" progression was a universal mathematical law describing all quantitative relationships between physical variables. He discovered only late in life that there are other kinds of functional relationships between physical variables, and that some of those, too, could be represented by pyramids. For example, he realized that a quantity could vary with the square of another variable, and that this relationship, too, was embodied in the geometry of pyramids. In a sequence of square pyramids with a common apex, the areas of the bases are proportional to the squares of their distances from the apex. As Kenneth Keele noted, there can be no doubt that with time Leonardo would have revised and extended many applications of his pyramidal law in the light of his new insights.[14] But as we shall see, Leonardo preferred to explore a different kind of mathematics during the last years of his life.

DRAWINGS AS DIAGRAMS

Leonardo realized very early on that the mathematics of his time was inappropriate for recording the most important results of his scientific research—the description of nature's living forms in their ceaseless movements and transmutations. Instead of mathematics, he frequently used his exceptional drawing facility to graphically document his observations in pictures that are often strikingly beautiful while, at the same time, they take the place of mathematical diagrams.

His celebrated drawing of "Water falling upon water" (Fig. 7-2), for example, is not a realistic snapshot of a jet of water falling into a pond, but an elaborate diagram of Leonardo's analysis of several types of turbulence caused by the impact of the jet.[15]

Similarly, Leonardo's anatomical drawings, which he called "demonstrations," are not always faithful pictures of what one would see in an actual dissection. Often, they are diagrammatic representations of the functional relationships between various parts of the body.[16]

For example, in a series of drawings of the deep structures of the shoulder (Fig. 7-3), Leonardo combines different graphical techniques—individual parts shown separated from the whole, muscles cut away to expose the bones, parts labeled with a series of letters, cord diagrams showing lines of forces, among others—to demonstrate the spatial extensions and mutual functional relationships of anatomical forms. These drawings clearly display characteristics of mathematical diagrams, used in the discipline of anatomy.

Leonardo's scientific drawings—whether they depict elements of machines, anatomical structures, geological formations, turbulent

Figure 7-2: "Water falling upon water," c. 1508–9, Windsor Collection, Landscapes, Plants, and Water Studies, folio 42r

flows of water, or botanical details of plants—were never realistic representations of a single observation. Rather, they are syntheses of repeated observations, crafted in the form of theoretical models. Daniel Arasse makes an interesting point: Whenever Leonardo rendered objects in their sharp outlines, these pictures represented conceptual models rather than realistic images. And whenever he produced realistic images of objects, he blurred the outlines with his famous sfumato technique, in order to represent them as they actually appear to the human eye.[17]

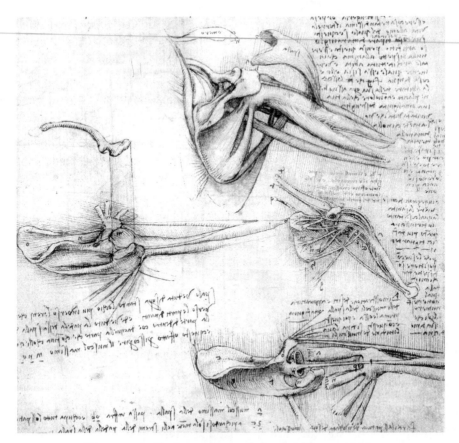

Figure 7-3: Deep structures of the shoulder, c. 1509,
Anatomical Studies, folio 136r

GEOMETRY IN MOTION

In addition to using his phenomenal drawing skills, Leonardo also pursued a more formal mathematical approach to represent nature's forms. He became seriously interested in mathematics when he was in his late thirties, after his visit to the library of Pavia. He furthered his studies of Euclidean geometry a few years later with the help of mathematician and friend Luca Pacioli.[18] For about eight years he diligently went through the volumes of Euclid's *Elements* and studied several works of Archimedes. But he went beyond Euclid in his own drawings and notes. As Kenneth Clark observed, "Euclidean order could not satisfy Leonardo for long, for it conflicted with his sense of life."[19]

What Leonardo found especially attractive in geometry was its ability to deal with continuous variables. "The mathematical sciences . . . are only two," he wrote in the Codex Madrid, "of which the first is arithmetic, the second is geometry. One encompasses the discontinuous quantities [i.e., variables], the other the continuous."[20] It was evident to Leonardo that a mathematics of continuous quantities would be needed to describe the incessant movements and transformations in nature. In the seventeenth century, mathematicians developed the theory of functions and the differential calculus for that very purpose.[21] Instead of these sophisticated mathematical tools, Leonardo had only geometry at his disposal, but he expanded it and experimented with new interpretations and new forms of geometry that foreshadowed subsequent developments.

In contrast to Euclid's geometry of rigid static figures, Leonardo's conception of geometric relationships is inherently dynamic. This is evident even from his definitions of the basic geometric elements. "The line is made with the movement of the point," he declares. "The surface is made by the transverse movement of the line; . . . the body is made by the movement of the extension of the surface."[22] In the twentieth century, the painter and art theorist Paul Klee used almost identical words to define line, plane, and body in a passage that is still used today to teach design students the primary elements of architectural design:

> The point moves . . . and the line comes into being—the first dimension. If the line shifts to form a plane, we obtain a two-dimensional element. In the movement from plane to spaces, the clash of planes gives rise to body.[23]

Leonardo also drew analogies between a segment of a line and a duration of time: "The line is similar to a length of time, and as the points are the beginning and end of the line, so the instants are the endpoints of any given extension of time."[24] Two centuries later this analogy became the foundation of the concept of time as a coordinate in Descartes' analytic geometry and in Newton's calculus.

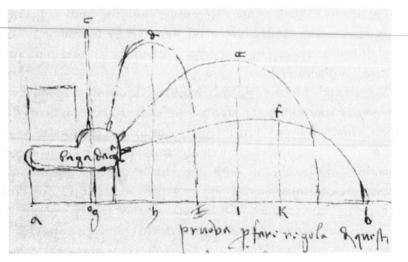

Figure 7-4: Family of water jets flowing out of a pressurized bag, Ms. C, folio 7r (sides have been reversed to make the similarity with modern diagrams of geometric curves more evident)

As mathematician Matilde Macagno points out,[25] on the one hand, Leonardo uses geometry to study trajectories and various kinds of complex motions in natural phenomena; on the other hand, he uses motion as a tool to demonstrate geometrical theorems. He called his approach "geometry which is demonstrated with motion" *(geometria che si prova col moto)*, or "done with motion" *(che si fa col moto)*.[26]

Leonardo's Notebooks contain a large number of drawings and discussions of trajectories of all kinds, including flight paths of projectiles, balls rebounding from walls, water jets descending through the air and falling into ponds, jets ricocheting across a water tank, and the propagation of sound and its reverberation as an echo. In all these cases, Leonardo pays careful attention to the geometries of the trajectories, their curves, angles of incidence and reflection, and so on. Of special significance are drawings of families of path-lines that depend on a single parameter; for example, a family of water jets flowing out of a pressurized bag, generated by different inclinations of a nozzle (see Fig. 7-4). These drawings can be seen as geometric precursors of the concept of a function of continuous variables, dependent on a parameter.

The concepts of functions, variables, and parameters were developed gradually in the seventeenth century from the study of geometric curves representing trajectories, and were clearly formulated only in the eighteenth century by the great mathematician and philosopher Gottfried Wilhelm Leibniz.[27]

The second, highly original branch of Leonardo's geometry is a geometry of continuous transformations of rectilinear and curvilinear shapes, which occupied him intensely during the last twelve years of his life. The central idea underlying this new type of geometry is Leonardo's conception of both movement and transformation as processes of continual transition, in which bodies leave one area in space and occupy another. "Of everything that moves," he explains, "the space which it acquires is as great as that which it leaves."[28]

Leonardo saw this conservation of volume as a general principle governing all changes and transformations of natural forms, whether solid bodies moving in space or pliable bodies changing their shapes. He applied it to the analysis of various movements of the human body, including in particular the contraction of muscles,[29] as well as to the flow of water and other liquids. Here is how he writes about the flow of a river: "If the water does not increase, nor diminish, in a river, which may be of varying tortuosities, breadths and depths, the water will pass in equal quantities in equal times through every degree of the length of that river."[30]

The realization that the same volume of water can take on an infinite number of shapes may well have inspired Leonardo to search for a new, dynamic geometry of transformations. It is striking that his first explorations of such a geometry in the Codex Forster coincide with increased studies of the shapes of waves and eddies in flowing water.[31] Leonardo evidently thought that, by developing a "geometry done with motion," based on the conservation of volume, he might be able to describe the continual movements and transformations of water and other natural forms with mathematical precision. He methodically set out to develop such a geometry, and in doing so anticipated some important developments in mathematical thought that would not occur until several centuries later.

"ON TRANSFORMATION"

Leonardo's ultimate aim was to apply his geometry of transformations to the movements and changes of the curvilinear forms of water and other pliable bodies. But in order to develop his techniques, he began with transformations of rectilinear figures where the conservation of areas and volumes can easily be proven with elementary Euclidean geometry. In so doing, he pioneered a method that would become standard practice in science during the subsequent centuries—to develop mathematical frameworks with the help of simplified unrealistic models before applying them to the actual phenomena under study.

Many of Leonardo's examples of rectilinear transformations are contained in the first forty folios of Codex Forster I under the heading "A book entitled 'On Transformation,' that is, of one body into another without diminution or increase of matter."[32] This sounds like conservation of mass, but in fact Leonardo's drawings in these folios all have to do with conservation of area or volume. For solid bodies and incompressible liquids, conservation of volume does imply conservation of mass, and the wording of his title shows us that Leonardo's geometrical explorations were clearly intended for the study of such material bodies.

He begins with transformations of triangles, rectangles (which he calls "table tops"), and parallelograms. He knows from Euclidean geometry that two triangles or parallelograms with the same base and height have the same area, even when their shapes are quite different. He then extends this reasoning to transformations in three dimensions, changing cubes into rectangular prisms and comparing the volumes of upright and inclined pyramids.

In his most sophisticated example, Leonardo transforms a dodecahedron—a regular solid with 12 pentagonal faces—into a cube of equal volume. He does so in four clearly illustrated steps (see Fig. 7-5): First, he cuts up the dodecahedron into 12 equal pyramids with pentagons as bases; then he cuts each of these pyramids into 5 smaller pyramids with triangular bases, so that the dodecahedron has now been cut into 60 equal pyramids; then he transforms the triangular base of each pyramid into a rectangle of equal area, thereby conserving the pyramid's volume; and in the last step, he ingeniously stacks the 60 rectangular pyramids into a cube, which evidently has the same volume as the original dodecahedron.

In a final flourish, Leonardo then reverses the steps of the whole procedure, beginning with a cube and ending up with a dodecahedron of equal volume. Needless to say, this set of transformations shows great imagination and considerable powers of visualization.

MAPPINGS OF CURVES AND CURVED SURFACES

As soon as Leonardo achieved sufficient confidence and facility with transformations of rectilinear figures, he turned to the main topic of his mathematical explorations—the transformations of curvilinear figures. In an interesting "transitional" example, he draws a square with an inscribed circle and then transforms the

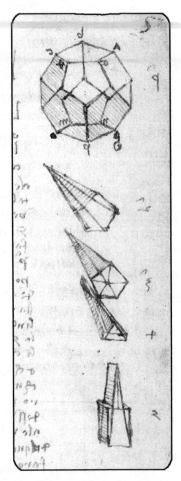

Figure 7-5: Transforming a dodecahedron into a cube, Codex Forster I, folio 7r

square into a parallelogram, thereby turning the circle into an ellipse. On the same folio, he transforms the square into a rectangle, which elongates the circle into a different ellipse. Leonardo explains that the relationship of the *figura ovale* (ellipse) with respect to the parallelogram is the same as that of the circle with respect to the square, and he asserts that the area of an ellipse can easily be obtained if the right equivalent circle is found.[33]

In the course of his explorations of circles and squares, Leonardo tried his hand at the problem of squaring the circle, which had fascinated mathematicians since antiquity. In its classical form, the challenge is to construct a square with an area equal to that of a given circle, and to do so by using only ruler and compass. We know today that this is not possible, but countless professional and amateur mathematicians have tried. Leonardo worked on the problem repeatedly over a period of more than a dozen years.

In one particular attempt, he worked by candlelight through the night, and by dawn he believed that he had finally found the solution. "On the night of St. Andrew," he excitedly recorded in his Notebook, "I found the end of squaring the circle; and at the end of the light of the candle, of the night, and of the paper on which I was writing, it was completed; at the end of the hour."[34] However, as the day progressed, he came to the realization that this attempt, too, was futile.

Even though Leonardo could not succeed in solving the classical problem of squaring the circle, he did come up with two ingenious and unorthodox solutions, both of which are revealing about his mathematical thinking. He divided the circle into a number of sectors, which in turn are subdivided into a triangle and a small circular segment. These sectors are then rearranged in such a way that they form an approximate rectangle in which the short side is equal to the circle's radius (r) and the long side is equal to half the circumference (C/2). As this procedure is carried out with larger and larger numbers of triangles, the figure will tend toward a true rectangle with an area equal to that of the circle. Today, we would write the formula for the area as $A = r \, (C/2) = r^2\pi$.

The last step in this process involves the subtle concept of approaching the limit of an infinite number of infinitely small triangles, which was understood only in the seventeenth century with the development of calculus. The Greek mathematicians all shied away from infinite numbers and processes, and thus were unable to formulate the mathematical concept of a limit. It is interesting, however, that Leonardo seems to have had at least an intuitive grasp of it. "I square the circle minus the smallest portion of it that the intellect can imagine," he wrote in the Windsor manuscripts, "that is, the smallest perceptible point."[35] In the Codex Atlanticus he stated: "[I have] completed here various ways of squaring the circles . . . and given the rules for proceeding to infinity."[36]

Leonardo's second method of squaring the circle is much more pragmatic. Again, he divides the circle into many small sectors, but then—perhaps encouraged by his intuitive grasp of the limiting process in the first method—he simply rolls half of the circumference on a line and constructs the rectangle accordingly, its short side being equal to the radius. Thus he arrives again at the correct formula, which he properly attributes to Archimedes.[37]

Leonardo's second method, which greatly appealed to his practical mind, involves what we now call the mapping of a curve onto a straight line. He compared it to measuring distances with a rolling wheel, and he also extended the process to two dimensions, mapping various curved surfaces onto planes.[38] On several folios of Manuscript G, he described procedures for rolling cylinders, cones, and spheres on plane surfaces to find their surface areas. He realized that cylinders and cones can be mapped onto a plane, line by line, without any distortion, while this is not possible for spheres. But he experimented with several methods of approximately mapping a sphere onto a plane, which corresponds to the cartographer's problem of finding accurate plane maps of the surface of the Earth.

One of Leonardo's methods involved drawing parallel circles on a portion of the sphere, thereby marking off a series of small strips, and then rolling the strips one by one, so that an approximate triangle is generated on the plane. The strips were probably freshly painted so that they left an imprint on the paper. As Macagno points out, this technique foreshadows the development of integral calculus, which began in the seventeenth century with various attempts to calculate the lengths of curves, areas of circles, and volumes of spheres.[39] Indeed, some of these efforts involved dividing curved surfaces into small segments by drawing a series of parallel lines, as Leonardo had done two centuries earlier.[40]

CURVILINEAR TRANSFORMATIONS

In today's mathematical language, the concept of mapping can be applied also to Leonardo's transformation of a circle into an ellipse, in which the points of one curve are mapped onto those of another together with the mapping of all other corresponding points from the square onto the parallelogram. Alternatively, the operation may be viewed as a continuous transformation—a gradual movement, or "flow," of one figure into the other—which was how Leonardo understood his "geometry done with motion." He used this approach in a variety of ways to turn rectilinear into curvilinear figures in such a manner that their areas or volumes are always conserved. These procedures are illustrated and discussed systematically in Codex Madrid II, but there are countless related drawings scattered throughout the Notebooks.[41]

Leonardo used these curvilinear transformations to experiment with an endless variety of shapes, turning rectilinear planar figures and solid bodies—cones, pyramids, cylinders, etc.—into "equal" curvilinear ones. On an interesting folio in Codex Madrid II, he illustrates his basic techniques by sketching several different transformations on a single page (see Fig. 7-6). In the last paragraph of the text on this folio, he explains that these are examples of "geometry which is demonstrated with motion" *(geometria che si prova col moto).*[42]

As Macagno and others have noted, some of these sketches are highly reminiscent of the swirling shapes of substances in rotating liquids (e.g., chocolate syrup in stirred milk), which Leonardo studied extensively. This strongly suggests once again that his ultimate aim was to use his geometry for the analysis of transformations of actual physical forms, in particular in eddies and other turbulent flows.

In these endeavors, Leonardo was greatly helped by his exceptional ability to visualize geometrical forms as physical objects, mold them like clay sculptures in his imagination, and sketch them quickly and accurately. "However abstract the geometrical problem," writes Martin Kemp, "his sense of its relationship to actual or potential forms in the physical universe was never far away. This accounts for his almost irresistible desire to shade geometric diagrams as if they portrayed existing objects."[43]

EARLY FORMS OF TOPOLOGY

When we look at Leonardo's geometry from the point of view of present-day mathematics, and in particular from the perspective of complexity theory, we can see that he developed the beginnings of the

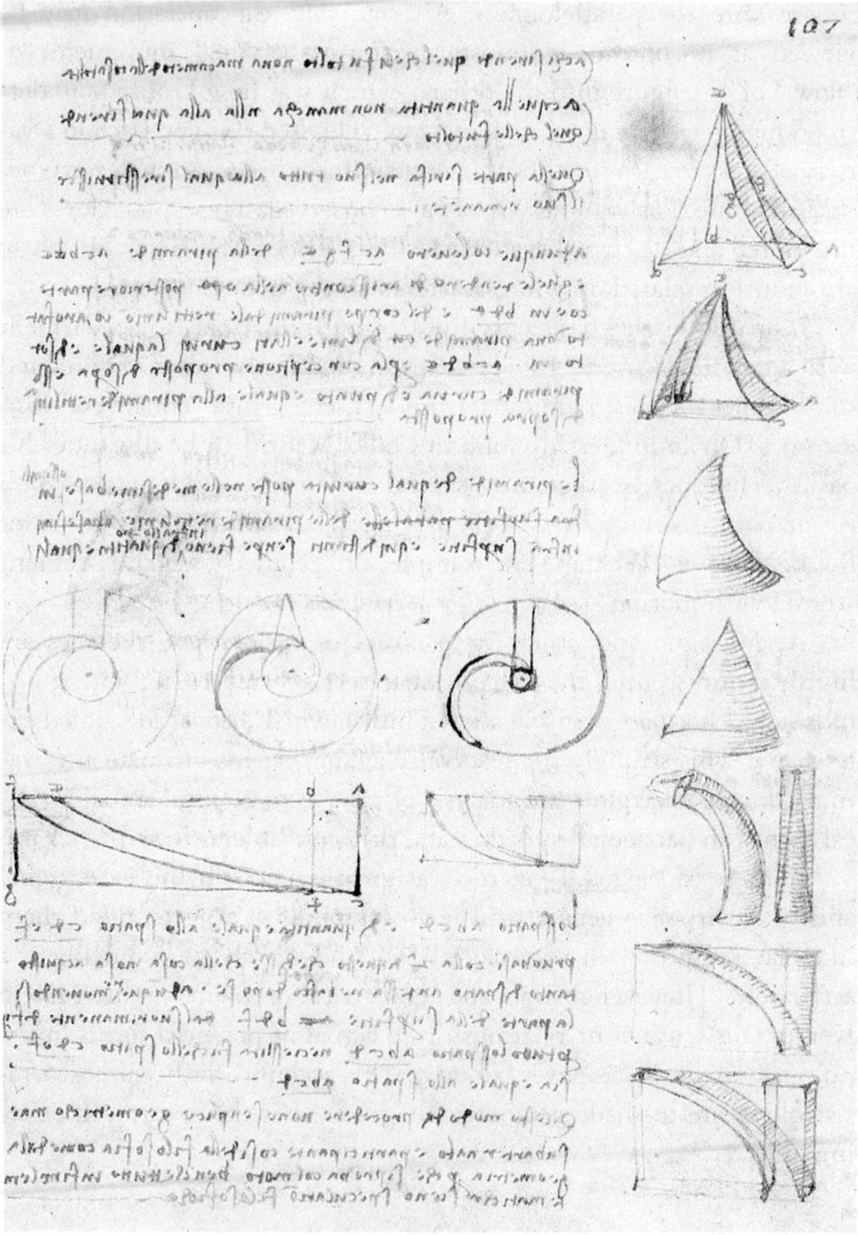

*Figure 7-6: Leonardo's catalog of transformations,
Codex Madrid II, folio 107r*

branch of mathematics now known as topology. Like Leonardo's geometry, topology is a geometry of continuous transformations, or mappings, in which certain properties of geometric figures are preserved. For example, a sphere can be transformed into a cube or a cylinder, all of which have similar continuous surfaces. A doughnut (torus), by contrast, is topologically different because of the hole in its center. The torus can be transformed, for example, into a coffee cup where the hole now appears in the handle. In the words of historian of mathematics Morris Kline:

> Topology is concerned with those properties of geometric figures that remain invariant when the figures are bent, stretched, shrunk, or deformed in any way that does not create new points or fuse existing points. The transformation presupposes, in other words, that there is a one-to-one correspondence between the points of the original figure and the points of the transformed figure, and that the transformation carries nearby points into nearby points. This latter property is called continuity.[44]

Leonardo's geometric transformations of planar figures and solid bodies are clearly examples of topological transformations. Modern topologists call the figures related by such transformations, in which very general geometric properties are preserved, topologically equivalent. These properties do not include area and volume, as topological transformations may arbitrarily stretch, expand, or shrink geometric figures. In contrast, Leonardo concentrated on operations that conserve area or volume, and he called the transformed figures "equal" to the original ones. Even though these represent only a small subset of topological transformations, they exhibit many of the characteristic features of topology in general.

Historians usually give credit for the first topological explorations to the philosopher and mathematician Leibniz who, in the late seventeenth century, tried to identify basic properties of geometric figures in a study he called *geometria situ* (geometry of place). But topological relationships were not treated systematically until the turn of the nineteenth to the twentieth century, when Henri Poincaré, the leading mathematician of the time, published a series of comprehensive papers on the subject.[45] Poincaré is therefore regarded as the founder of topology. The transformations of Leonardo's "geometry done with motion" are early forms of this important field of mathematics—three hundred years before Leibniz and five hundred years before Poincaré.

One subject that fascinated Leonardo from his early years in Milan was the design of tangled labyrinths of knots. Today this is a special branch of topology. To a mathematician, a knot is a tangled closed loop or path, similar to a knotted rope with its two free ends spliced together, precisely the structures Leonardo studied and drew. In designing such interlaced motifs, he followed a decorative tradition of his time.[46] But he far surpassed his contemporaries in this genre, treating his knot designs as objects of theoretical study and drawing a vast quantity of extremely complex interlaced structures.[47]

Topological thinking—thinking in terms of connectivity, spatial relationships, and continuous transformations—was almost second nature to Leonardo. Many of his architectural studies, especially his designs of radially symmetrical churches and temples, exhibit such characteristics.[48] So, too, do many of his numerous diagrams. Leonardo's topological techniques can also be found in his geographical maps. In the famous map of the Chiana valley (Fig. 7-7), now in the Windsor Collection, he uses a topological approach to distort the scale while providing an accurate picture of the connectivity of the terrain and its intricate waterways.

The central part is enlarged and shows accurate proportions, while the surrounding parts are severely distorted in order to fit the entire system of watercourses into the given format.[49]

DE LUDO GEOMETRICO

During the last twelve years of his life, Leonardo spent a great deal of time mapping and exploring the transformations of his "geometry done with motion." Several times he wrote of his intention to present the results of these studies in one or more treatises. During the years he spent in Rome, and while he was summing up his knowledge of complex turbulent flows in his famous deluge drawings,[50] Leonardo produced a magnificent compendium of topological transformations,

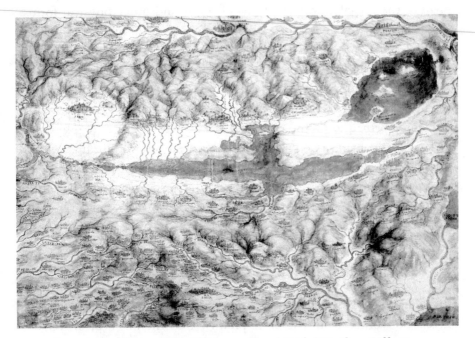

Figure 7-7: Map of the Chiana valley, 1504, Windsor Collection, Drawings and Miscellaneous Papers, Vol. IV, folio 439v

titled *De ludo geometrico* (*On the Game of Geometry*), on a large double folio in the Codex Atlanticus.[51] He drew 176 diagrams displaying a bewildering variety of geometric forms, built from intersecting circles, triangles, and squares—row after row of crescents, rosettes and other floral patterns, paired leaves, pinwheels, and curvilinear stars. Previously this endless interplay of geometric motifs was often interpreted as the playful doodling of an aging artist—"a mere intellectual pastime," in the words of Kenneth Clark.[52] Such assessments were made because art historians were generally not aware of the mathematical significance of Leonardo's geometry of transformations. Close examination of the double folio shows that its geometric forms, regardless of how complex and fanciful, are all based upon strict topological principles.[53]

When he created his double folio of topological equations, Leonardo was over sixty. He continued to explore the geometry of transformations during the last years of his life. But he must have realized that he was still very far from developing it to a point where it could be used to analyze the actual transformations of fluids and other physical forms. Today we know that for such a task, much more sophisticated mathematical tools are needed than those Leonardo had at his disposal. In modern fluid dynamics, for example, we use vector and tensor analysis, rather than geometry, to describe the movements of fluids under the influence of gravity and various shear stresses. However, Leonardo's fundamental principle of the conservation of mass, known to physicists today as the continuity equation, is an essential part of the equations describing the motions of water and air. As far as the ever-changing forms of fluids are concerned, it is clear that Leonardo's mathematical intuition was on the right track.

THE NECESSITY OF NATURE'S FORMS

Like Galileo, Newton, and subsequent generations of scientists, Leonardo worked from the basic premise that the physical universe is fundamentally ordered and that its causal relationships can be comprehended by the rational mind and expressed mathematically.[54] He used the term "necessity" to express the stringent nature of those ordered causal relationships. "Necessity is the theme and inventor of nature, the curb and the rule," he wrote around 1493, shortly after he began his first studies of mathematics.[55]

Since Leonardo's science was a science of qualities, of organic forms and their movements and transformations, the mathematical "necessity" he saw in nature was not one expressed in quantities and numerical relationships, but one of geometric shapes continually transforming themselves according to rigorous laws and principles. "Mathematical" for Leonardo referred above all to the logic, rigor, and coherence according to which nature has shaped, and is continually reshaping, her organic forms.

This meaning of "mathematical" is quite different from the one understood by scientists during the Scientific Revolution and the subsequent three hundred years. However, it is not unlike the understanding of some of the leading mathematicians today. The recent development of complexity theory has generated a new mathematical language in which the dynamics of complex systems—including the turbulent flows and growth patterns of plants studied by Leonardo—are no longer represented by algebraic relationships, but instead by geometric shapes, like the computer-generated strange attractors or fractals, which are analyzed in terms of topological concepts.[56]

This new mathematics, naturally, is far more abstract and sophisticated than anything Leonardo could have imagined in the fifteenth and sixteenth centuries. But it is used in the same spirit in which he developed his "geometry done with motion"—to show with mathematical rigor how complex natural phenomena are shaped and transformed by the "necessity" of physical forces. The mathematics of complexity has led to a new appreciation of geometry and to the broad realization that mathematics is much more than formulas and equations. Like Leonardo da Vinci five hundred years ago, modern mathematicians today are showing us that the understanding of patterns, relationships, and transformations is crucial to understand the living world around us, and that all questions of pattern, order, and coherence are ultimately mathematical.

EIGHT

Pyramids of Light

Leonardo's scientific method was based not only on the careful and systematic observation of nature—his much-exalted *sperienza*[1]—but also included a detailed and comprehensive analysis of the process of observation itself. As an artist and a scientist, his approach was predominantly visual, and he began his explorations of the "science of painting" by studying perspective: investigating how distance, light, and atmospheric conditions affect the appearance of objects. From perspective, he proceeded in two opposite directions—outward and inward, as it were. He explored the geometry of light rays, the interplay of light and shadow, and the very nature of light, and he also studied the anatomy of the eye, the physiology of vision, and the pathways of sensory impressions along the nerves to the "seat of the soul."

To a modern intellectual, used to the exasperating fragmentation of academic disciplines, it is amazing to see how Leonardo moved swiftly from perspective and the effects of light and shade to the nature of light, the pathways of the optic nerves, and the actions of the soul. Unencumbered by the mind-body split that Descartes would introduce 150 years later, Leonardo did not separate epistemology (the theory of knowledge) from ontology (the theory of what exists in the world), nor indeed philosophy from science and art. His wide-ranging examinations of the entire process of perception led him to formulate highly original ideas about the relationship between physical reality and cognitive processes—the "actions of the soul," in his language—which have reemerged only very recently with the development of a post-Cartesian science of cognition.[2]

THE SCIENCE OF PERSPECTIVE

Leonardo's earliest studies of perception stand at the beginning of his scientific work. "All our knowledge has its origin in the senses," he wrote in his very first Notebook, the Codex Trivulzianus,[3] begun in 1484. During the subsequent years he embarked on his first studies of the anatomy of the eye and the optic nerves. At the same time, he explored the geometries of linear perspective and of light and shadow, and demonstrated his profound understanding of these concepts in his first master paintings, the *Adoration of the Magi* and the *Virgin of the Rocks*.[4]

Leonardo's interest in the mathematics underlying perspective and optics intensified in the summer of 1490, when he met the mathematician Fazio Cardano at the University of Pavia.[5] He had long discussions with Cardano on the subjects of linear perspective and geometrical optics, which together were known as "the science of perspective." Soon after these discussions, Leonardo filled two Notebooks with a short treatise on perspective and with numerous diagrams of geometrical optics.[6] He returned to the study of optics and vision eighteen years later, around 1508, when he explored various subtleties of visual perception.

At that time, Leonardo revised his earlier notes and summarized his findings on vision in the small Manuscript D, which is similar in its brevity and elegant compact structure to the Codex on the Flight of Birds, composed around the same time.

Linear perspective was established in the early fifteenth century by the architects Brunelleschi and Alberti as a mathematical technique for representing three-dimensional images on a two-dimensional plane. In his classic work *De pictura (On Painting)*,[7] Alberti suggested that a painting should give the impression of being a window through which the artist looks at the visible world. All objects in the picture were to be systematically reduced as they receded into the distance, and all sight lines were to converge to a single "central point" (later called the "vanishing point"), which corresponded to the fixed viewpoint of the spectator.

As architectural historian James Ackerman points out, the geometry of perspective developed by the Florentine artists was the first scientific conception of three-dimensional space:

> As a method of constructing an abstract space in which any body can be related mathematically to any other body, the perspective of the artists was a preamble to modern physics and astronomy. Perhaps the influence was indirect and unconsciously transmitted, but the fact remains that artists were the first to conceive a generalized mathematical model of space and that it constituted an essential step in the evolution from medieval symbolism to the modern image of the universe.[8]

Leonardo used Alberti's definition of linear perspective as his starting point. "Perspective," he states, "is nothing else than seeing a place behind a pane of glass, quite transparent, on the surface of which the objects behind that glass are to be drawn."[9] A few pages later in the same Notebook, he introduces geometric reasoning with the help of the image of a "pyramid of lines," which was common in medieval optics.[10] The first statement about perspective, too, continues with a reference to visual pyramids. "These [objects]," Leonardo explains, "can be traced through pyramids to the point of the eye, and the pyramids are intersected on the glass pane."[11]

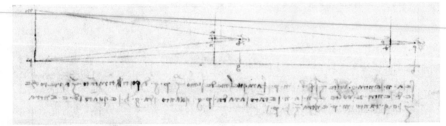

Figure 8-1: The geometry of linear perspective, Codex Atlanticus, folio 119r

To determine to what extent exactly the image of an object on the glass pane diminishes with the object's distance from the eye, Leonardo conducted a series of experiments, in which he methodically varied the three relevant variables in all possible combinations—the height of the object, the distance from the eye, and the distance between the eye and the vertical glass pane.[12] He sketched the experimental arrangements in several diagrams; for example, as shown in Figure 8-1, where the object is kept stationary and the observer's eye, together with the glass pane in front of it, is placed in two different locations. The corresponding "pyramids" (isosceles triangles) with the two different visual angles are clearly shown.

With these experiments, Leonardo established conclusively that the height of the image on the glass pane is inversely proportional to the object's distance from the eye, if the distance between the eye and the glass pane is kept constant. "I find by experience," he recorded in Manuscript A, "that, if the second object is as far from the first as the first is from the eye, although they are of the same size, the second will seem half the size of the first."[13] In another entry he records a series of distances with the corresponding reductions of the object's image, and then concludes: "As the space passed through doubles, the diminution doubles."[14]

These results, obtained during the late 1480s, mark Leonardo's first explorations of arithmetic, or "pyramidal," progressions. To establish them, he did not really have to perform all these experiments, because the inverse linear relationship between the distance of the object from the eye and the reduction of its image on the glass pane can easily be derived with elementary Euclidean geometry. But it would be

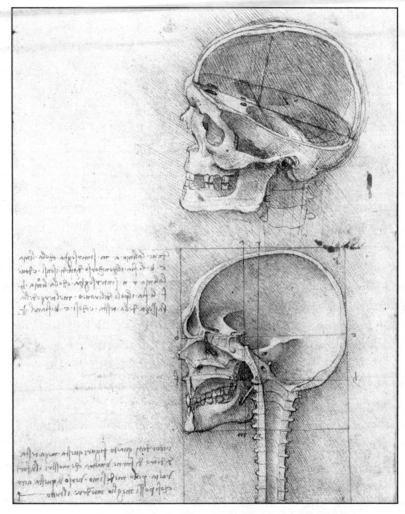

Figure 8-2: Section of the human skull,
Anatomical Studies, folio 43r

almost another ten years before Leonardo would acquire those mathematical skills.[15]

Leonardo demonstrated his thorough understanding of linear perspective not only in his art, but also in his scientific drawings. While he was conducting his experiments on the geometry of perspective, he also investigated the anatomical connections between the eye and the brain.

He documented his findings in a series of magnificent pictures of the human skull, in which the foreshortening of visual perspective is employed to great effect (see Fig. 8-2). Leonardo combined this technique with delicate renderings of light and shade to create a vivid sense of space within the skull, in which he exhibited anatomical structures that had never been seen before and located them with complete accuracy in three dimensions.[16] He used the same mastery of visual perspective and subtle renderings of light and shade in his technical drawings (see, for example, Fig. 8-3), depicting complex machines and mechanisms with an elegance and effectiveness never seen before.[17]

While he skillfully used Alberti's rules of perspective to produce radical innovations in the art of scientific illustration, Leonardo soon realized that for his paintings, these rules were too restrictive and fraught with contradictions.[18]

Alberti had suggested that the geometric horizon of a painting should be at the eye level of the painted figures so as to create the illusion of a continuity between the imaginary space and that of the spectators. However, frescoes and altarpieces were often placed quite high up, which made it impossible for the spectators to look at them from a viewpoint that would make the illusion work. Moreover, Alberti's system assumed a fixed viewpoint in front of the vanishing point, but most spectators were likely to move around and look at the painting from different angles, which would also destroy the illusion. In *The Last Supper*, Leonardo, well aware of the internal contradictions of linear perspective, played around with Alberti's rules to enhance the presence of the human figures and create elaborate illusions,[19] but after that he no longer painted any architectural motifs and went far beyond the linear perspective of the quattrocento.

To refine the theory of perspective, Leonardo questioned Alberti's simplistic assumption that the lines of all visual pyramids meet in a single mathematical point within the eye. Instead, he studied the actual physiology of visual perception. "Perspective," he noted, "is nothing else than a thorough knowledge of the function of the eye."[20] He took into account that natural vision is binocular—produced by two moving eyes rather than the single fixed eye of Alberti's geometry. He carefully investigated the actual pathways of the sensory impressions, and he also considered the effects of atmospheric conditions on visual perception.

From his studies of the anatomy of the eye and the physiology of

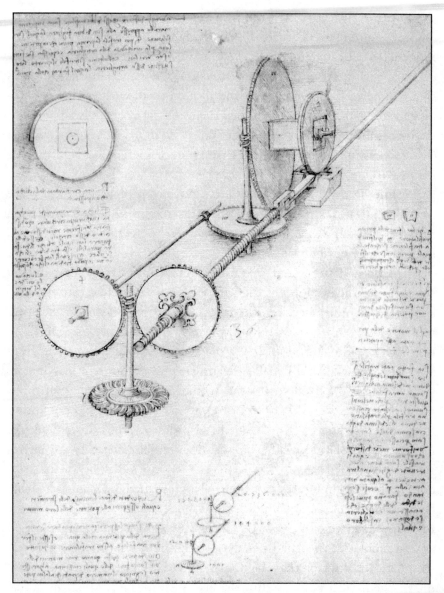

Figure 8-3: Water-powered rolling mill, Codex Atlanticus, folio 10r

vision,[21] Leonardo derived a theory of perspective that went well beyond Alberti, Piero della Francesca, and other leading artists of the
early Renaissance. "There are three kinds of perspective," he declared.
"The first is concerned with the reason for the diminution [of] things

as they recede from the eye. The second contains the way in which colors vary as they recede from the eye. The third and last encompasses the declaration of how objects should appear less distinct the more distant they are." He specified that the first, traditional kind was called "linear perspective" (*lineare*), the second "perspective of color" (*di colore*), and the third the "perspective of disappearance" (*di spedizione*).[22]

As an object recedes into the distance, its image will diminish simultaneously in those three ways. Its size will decrease, its color will become fainter, and the definition of its detail will deteriorate until all three "disappear" at the vanishing point. According to Leonardo, a painter had to master all three kinds of perspective, and in addition he had to take into account a fourth kind, the "aerial perspective" (*aerea*) caused by the effects of the atmosphere on colors and other aspects of visual perception.[23] Leonardo demonstrated his mastery at rendering these subtle aspects of perspective in many of his paintings. Indeed, it is often the misty atmosphere and dreamy nature of their distant mountain landscapes that give his masterworks their special magic and poetic quality.

LIGHT AND SHADOW

Together with the effects of perspective in painting, Leonardo also explored the geometry of light, now known as geometrical optics, as well as the interplay of light and shadow under natural and artificial illumination. The study of optics had already been well developed in the Middle Ages. It had tremendous prestige among medieval philosophers, who associated light with divine power and glory.[24] They knew that light traveled in straight lines, and that its paths obeyed geometrical laws as the light rays passed through lenses and were reflected in mirrors. To the medieval mind, this association of optics with the eternal mathematical laws of geometry was further proof of the divine origin of light.

The dominant figure in medieval optics was the Arab mathematician Alhazen,[25] who wrote a seven-volume work, *Kitab al-Manazir* (*Book of Optics*), published in Arabic in the eleventh century and widely available in Latin translation as *Opticae Thesaurus* from the thirteenth century on. Alhazen's treatise included detailed discussions of vision and the anatomy of the eye. He introduced the idea that light rays emanate from luminous objects in straight lines in all directions and discovered the laws of reflection and refraction. He paid special attention to the problem of finding the point on a curved mirror where a ray of light will be reflected to pass from a given source to an observer, which subsequently came to be known as "Alhazen's problem." Alhazen's *Optics* inspired several European thinkers, who added original observations of their own, including the Polish philosopher Witelo of Silesia as well as John Pecham and Roger Bacon in England. It was from these authors that Leonardo first learned about Alhazen's pioneering work.[26]

From his earliest years in Verrocchio's workshop, Leonardo was familiar with the grinding of lenses and the use of concave mirrors to focus sunlight for welding.[27] Throughout his life he tried to improve the design of these burning mirrors, and when he became seriously interested in the theory of optics, he undertook careful studies of their geometries. He was fascinated by the intricate intersections of the reflected rays, which he explored in a series of precise and beautiful diagrams, tracing their pathways from parallel beams of light through their reflections to the focal point (or points). He showed that in spherical mirrors, the rays are focused in an area along the central axis (see Fig. 8-4), whereas parabolic mirrors are true "mirrors of fire," focusing all the rays in a single point. He also made several attempts to solve Alhazen's problem, and late in his life, while experimenting with parabolic mirrors in Rome, found an ingenious solution by employing an instrument with hinged rods.[28]

In Figure 8-4, Leonardo has constructed the reflected light rays by drawing in each point the radius of the mirror (which is perpendicular to the reflecting surface) and then using the so-called law of reflection, that the angle of incidence is equal to the angle of reflection. This law was already known to Alhazen, but Leonardo realized that it applies not only to the reflection of light, but also to the mechanical rebound of a ball thrown against a wall, and to the echo of sound.[29] "The line of percussion and that of its rebound," he writes in Manuscript A, "will make an angle on the wall . . . between two equal angles." And then he adds: "The voice is similar to an object seen in a mirror."[30] Several years

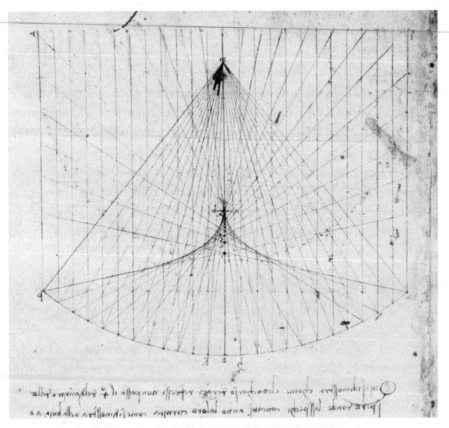

Figure 8-4: Study of concave spherical mirror,
Codex Arundel, folio 87v

later he applied the same reasoning to the rebound of a jet of water
from a wall, noting, however, that some of the water peels off as an
eddy after the reflection.[31]

By far the largest part of Leonardo's optical studies concerned the
effects of light falling on objects and the nature of different kinds of
shadows. As a painter, he was famous for his subtle use of light and
shade,[32] so it is not surprising that the longest section, part 5, of his
Treatise on Painting is titled "On Shadow and Light." Based on his earlier notes in Manuscript C, these chapters contain practical advice to
the painter on how to render gradations of light and shadow in landscapes, and on trees, drapery, and human faces, as well as abstract discussions on the nature of shadow, the difference between luster and

light, the nature of contrasts, the juxtaposition of colors, and many related subjects.

According to Leonardo, shadow is the central element in the science of painting. It allows the painter to effectively represent solid bodies in relief, emerging from the backgrounds of the painted surface. His poetic definition of shadow in the Codex Atlanticus is clearly written from the artist's point of view:

> Every opaque body is surrounded, and its whole surface is enveloped, in shadow and light. . . . Besides this, shadows have in themselves various degrees of darkness, because they are caused by the absence of a variable amount of the luminous rays. . . . They clothe the bodies to which they are applied.[33]

In order to fully understand the intricacies of the interplay between light and shadow, Leonardo designed a series of elaborate experiments with lamps shining on spheres and cylinders, their rays intersecting and being reflected to create an endless variety of shadows. As in his experiments on linear perspective, he systematically varied the relevant variables—in this case the size and shape of the lamp, the size of the illuminated object, and the distance between the two. He distinguished between "original shadows" (formed on the object itself) and "derived shadows" (cast by the object through the air and onto other surfaces).[34]

Figure 8-5, for example, shows a diagram of a sphere illuminated by light falling through a window. Leonardo has traced light rays emanating from four points (labeled a, b, c, and d). He shows four gradations of primary shadows on the sphere (labeled n, o, p, and q), and the corresponding gradations of derived shadows, cast between the boundary lines of the eight light rays behind the sphere (labeled by the letters along the base of the diagram).

In these experiments Leonardo uses extended light sources (such as windows) as well as point sources (for example, the flame of a candle), and he considers the combined effects of direct sunlight and ambient light—"the universal light of the sky," as he calls it.[35] He also introduces several lamps, studies how the gradations of the shadows change with each new lamp, and examines how the shadows move when the lamps and the object are moved. As Kenneth Clark has remarked, "The

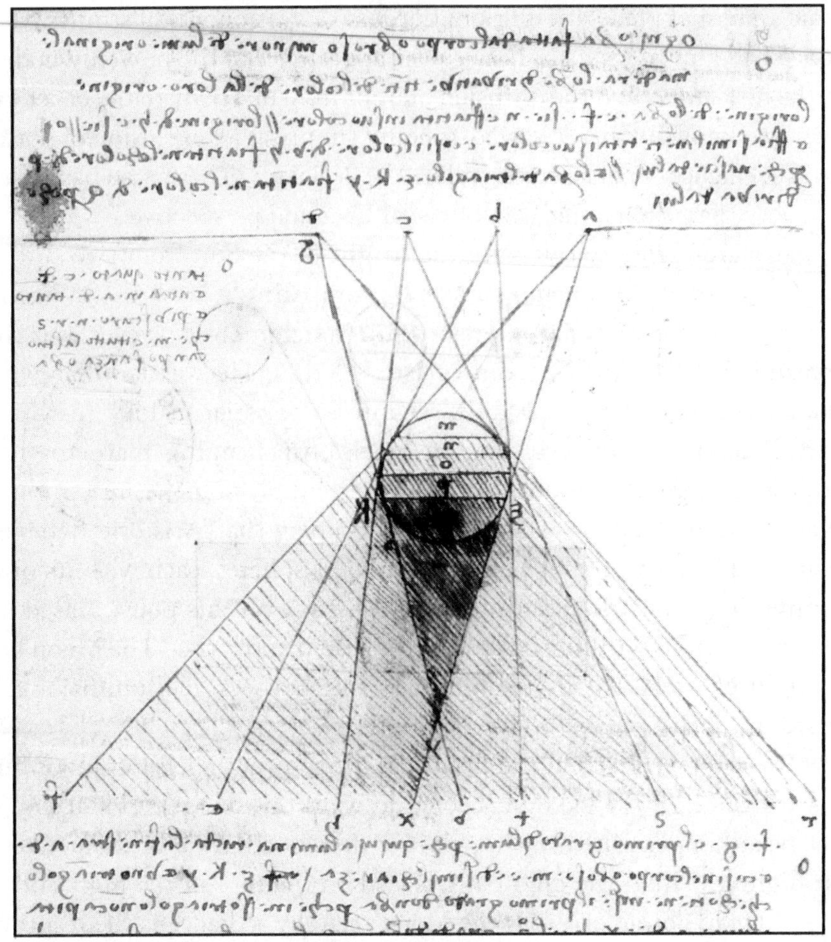

Figure 8-5: Gradations of primary and derived shadows, Ms. Ashburnham II, folio 13v

calculations are so complex and abstruse that we feel in them, almost for the first time, Leonardo's tendency to pursue research for its own sake, rather than as an aid to his art."[36]

OPTICS AND ASTRONOMY

Leonardo's optical observations also included observations of the heavenly bodies, especially the Sun and the Moon. He was well aware of the Ptolemaic system of planetary motion, but his own astronomical studies were concerned almost exclusively with the appearance of the heavenly bodies to the human eye and the diffusion of light from one body to the other. As far as we know, Leonardo saw astronomy simply as an extension of optics and the science of perspective. Indeed, he declared: "There is no part of astronomy that is not a function of visual lines and perspective."[37]

Leonardo tried to calculate the height of the Sun from two different angles of elevation, and its size by comparing it with the image in a camera obscura.[38] What interested him much more, however, was the transmission of light between celestial bodies. He was familiar with the ancient division of the universe into a "celestial realm," in which perfect bodies move according to precise, unchanging mathematical laws, and an "earthly realm," in which natural phenomena are complex, ever changing, and imperfect.[39] He also knew that Aristotle believed that the Moon and the planets were flawless spheres, each with its own luminosity. Leonardo disagreed with Aristotle on this point. Based on his observations with the naked eye, he stated correctly: "The Moon has no light of itself, but so much of it as the Sun sees, it illuminates. Of that luminosity, we see as much as faces us."[40]

Having convinced himself that the Moon is not itself luminous but reflects the light of the Sun, Leonardo went on to argue that it could not be an unblemished sphere, since it does not show a brilliant circular highlight like "the gold balls placed on the tops of the high buildings." He hypothesized that the Moon's patchy radiance is the result of multiple reflections of sunlight from the waves on its waters. "The skin, or surface, of the water that makes up the sea of the Moon," he wrote, "is always ruffled, little or much, more or less; and this roughness is the cause of the proliferation of the innumerable images of the Sun, which are reflected in the ridges and concavities, and sides and fronts, of the innumerable wrinkles."[41]

He then reasoned that there could be no waves in the lunar sea unless the surface of its waters was ruffled by air, and hence he concluded that the Moon, like the Earth, has its own set of four elements.[42] And in the final flourish of these interdependent observations and arguments, Leonardo pointed out that reflected sunlight from the waters of the sea must be transmitted also in the opposite direction, from the

Earth to the Moon. This reasoning led him to the astonishing and prophetic statement that "to anyone standing on the Moon . . . this our Earth with its element of water would appear and function just as the Moon does to us."[43]

Leonardo's ideas about astronomy, even though only partly correct, were certainly remarkable, and it is hard to believe that he was not interested in celestial mechanics at all. We know that he possessed a copy of Ptolemy's *Cosmography* and that he held it in high regard. He also owned a volume by the Arab astronomer Albumazar, and several other sources on astronomy are mentioned in the Notebooks.[44] But no notes on the movements of the planets have come down to us.

It is also interesting that Leonardo did not subscribe to the ancient belief that the stars influence life on Earth. In the Renaissance, astrology enjoyed a high reputation. The professions of astronomer and astrologer were inseparably connected, and even Leonardo used the word *astrologia* when he referred to astronomy. Renaissance princes, including Ludovico Sforza in Milan, often consulted court astrologers about matters of health, and even about political decisions. Thus Leonardo probably kept his views about astrologers to himself at court, but in his Notebooks he showed great contempt for them, describing their practices as "that deceptive opinion by means of which (begging your pardon) a living is made from fools."[45] The main focus of Leonardo's studies was the terrestrial realm of living, and its ever-changing forms, and he believed that its processes were not influenced by the stars but followed their own "necessities," which he intended to understand and explain by means of reasoning, based on direct experience.

THE NATURE OF LIGHT RAYS

Leonardo's studies of perspective and of light and shadow not only found artistic expression in his mastery of rendering subtle visual complexities, but also stimulated his scientific mind to investigate the very nature of the rays that carried light in pyramids from the objects to the eye. With his empirical method of systematic observation and with highly ingenious experiments that used only the most rudimentary instruments, he observed optical phenomena and formulated concepts about the nature of light that would take hundreds of years to be rediscovered.

His starting point was the accepted contemporary knowledge that light is emitted by luminous objects in straight lines. To test this assertion, Leonardo used the principle of the camera obscura, which had been known since antiquity. Here is how he describes his experiment:

> If the front of a building, or any piazza or field, which is illuminated by the sun, has a dwelling opposite to it, and if in the front that does not face the sun you make a small round hole, all the illuminated objects will send their images through that little hole and will appear inside the dwelling on the opposite wall, which should be white. And there they will be, exactly and upside down. . . . If the bodies are of various colors and shapes, the rays forming the images will be of various colors and shapes, and of various colors and shapes will be the representations on the wall.[46]

Leonardo repeats this experiment many times with various combinations of objects and with several holes in the camera obscura, as clearly illustrated on a folio in the Windsor Collection.[47] Having performed a series of tests, he then confirms the traditional knowledge: "The lines from . . . the sun, and other luminous rays passing through the air, are obliged to keep in a straight direction."[48] He also specifies that these lines are infinitely thin, like geometrical lines. He calls them "spiritual," by which he means simply without material substance.[49] And finally, Leonardo asserts that light rays are rays of power—or, as we would say today, of energy[50]—which radiate from the center of a luminous body, such as the sun. "It will appear clear to the experimenters," he writes, "that every luminous body has in itself a hidden center, from which and to which . . . arrive all the lines generated by the luminous surface."[51]

Thus, in essence, Leonardo identifies three basic properties of light rays: They are rays of energy generated at the center of luminous bodies; they are infinitely thin and without material substance; and they always travel in straight lines. Before the discovery of the electromagnetic nature of light in the nineteenth century, nobody could have improved on Leonardo's description, and even then contradictions concerning the nature of light waves persisted until they were resolved by Albert Einstein in the twentieth century.[52] On the other hand, the view of light rays as straight geometrical lines is still considered an excellent approximation for understanding a broad range of optical phenomena and is taught to physics students in our colleges and universities as geometrical optics.

THE WAVE NATURE OF LIGHT

The idea that light rays emanate from luminous objects in straight lines in all directions was known to Leonardo from Alhazen's treatise on optics before he tested it experimentally. Another idea that was popular in medieval optics, which he adopted from John Pecham (who, in turn, was influenced by Alhazen), was the concept of pyramids of light filling the air with images of solid objects:

> The body of the air is full of infinite pyramids composed of radiating straight lines which emanate from the edges of the surfaces of the solid bodies placed in the air; and the further they are from their cause the more acute are the pyramids, and although their converging paths intersect and interweave, nevertheless they never blend but proliferate independently, infusing all the surrounding air.[53]

With this poetic description, Leonardo simply rephrased Alhazen's original insight, but he added the significant observation that the pyramids of light "intersect and interweave" without interfering with each other. In a remarkable display of systemic thinking, Leonardo used this observation as a key argument to speculate about the wave nature of light. Here is how he proceeded.

First, he combines the fact that light is radiated equally in all directions, which he has tested repeatedly, with the image of visual pyramids. He draws a diagram that shows a spherical body radiating equal pyramids (represented by triangles) in different directions, and he notes in the accompanying text that their tips are enclosed by a circle: "The equidistant perimeter of converging rays of the pyramid will give to their objects angles of equal size."[54] In other words, if observers were placed at the tips of these pyramids around the circle, their visual angles would be the same (see Figure 8-6). In the same diagram, Leonardo extends one pyramid to show that the visual angle at its apex decreases as the pyramid becomes longer.

From this exercise, he concludes that light spreads in circles, and he immediately associates this circular pattern with the circular spread of ripples of water and the spread of sound in air: "Just as the stone thrown into the water becomes the center and cause of various circles, and the sound made in the air spreads out in circles, so every object placed within the luminous air diffuses itself in circles and fills the surroundings with an infinite number of images of itself."[55]

Having linked the circular pattern of the spread of light to the similar spread of ripples in water, Leonardo then sets out to study the details of the phenomenon in a pond in order to learn something about the radiation of light. In doing so, he uses, at the very beginning of his scientific explorations, a technique that would become an integral part of the scientific method in subsequent centuries. Since he cannot actually see the circular (or, more correctly, spherical) propagation of light, he takes the similar pattern in water as a model, hoping that it will reveal to him something about the nature of light under close study. And he does indeed study it very closely.

In Manuscript A, the very same Notebook that contains his analysis of perspective and many of his optical diagrams, Leonardo records his detailed investigations of the circular spread of water waves:

> If you throw two small stones at the same time onto a sheet of motionless water at some distance from one another, you will see that around those two percussions two separate sets of circles are caused, which will meet as they increase in size and then interpenetrate and intersect one another, while always maintaining as their centers the places struck by the stones.[56]

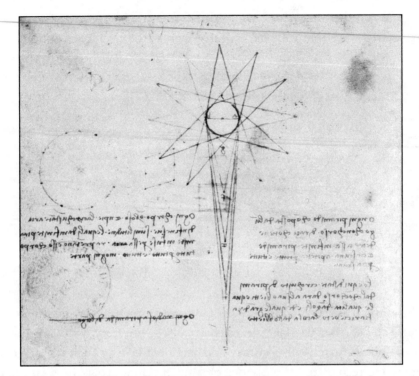

*Figure 8-6: Visual pyramids radiated from a spherical body,
Ms. Ashburnham II, folio 6v*

Leonardo illustrates this phenomenon with a diagram (Fig. 8-7), and to understand its exact nature, he focuses on the precise movement of the water particles, making it easier for the eye to follow them by throwing small pieces of straw into the pond and watching their movements. Here is what he observes.

> Although there seems to be some demonstration of movement, the water does not depart from its place, because the openings made by the stones are closed again immediately. And that motion, caused by the sudden opening and closing of the water, makes in it a certain shaking, which one could call a tremor rather than a movement.

> And so that what I say may be more evident to you, pay attention to those blades of straw which, because of their lightness,

float on the water and are not moved from their original position by the wave that rolls underneath them as the circles arrive.

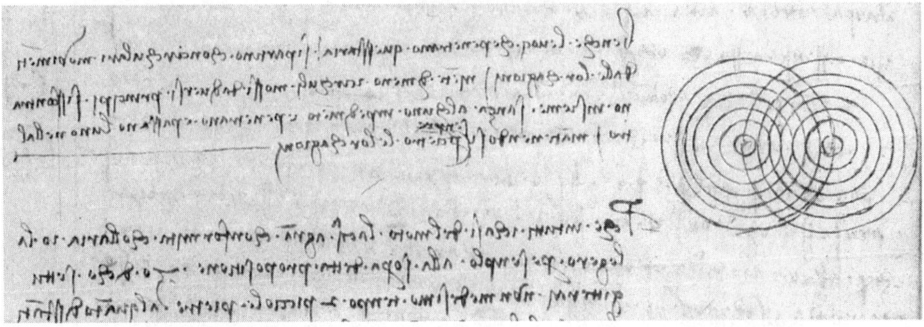

Figure 8-7: Intersection of circular water waves, Ms. A, folio 61r

Throughout history, countless people have thrown pebbles into ponds and watched the circular ripples they caused, but very few would have been able to match the accuracy and fine details of Leonardo's observations. He recognized the essence of wave motion—that the water particles do not move along with the wave but merely move up and down as the wave passes by.[57] What is transported along the wave is the disturbance causing the wave phenomenon—the "tremor," as Leonardo calls it—but not any material particles: "The water, though remaining in its position, can easily take this tremor from neighboring parts and pass it on to other adjacent parts, always diminishing its power until the end." And this is the reason, he concludes correctly, why the circular waves intersect smoothly without disturbing each other:

> Therefore, the disturbance of the water being a tremor rather than a movement, the circles cannot break one another as they meet, because, water being of the same quality in all its parts, it follows that these parts transmit the tremor from one to another without moving from their place.

This smooth intersection of water waves is the key property that suggests to Leonardo that light and sound, too, propagate in waves. He has noted that the pyramids of light "intersect and interweave" without interfering with each other,[58] and he applies the same reasoning to sound: "Although the voices that penetrate the air spread in circular motion from their causes, nevertheless the circles moved from different origins meet without any impediment, penetrate and pass into one another, always keeping their causes at their centers, because in all cases of motion, there is great conformity between water and air."[59] In other words, just as the intersecting circular ripples in the pond retain their distinct identities, we can see the images of different objects, or hear the sounds of different voices, and still distinguish them clearly.

From these observations, Leonardo draws the momentous conclusion that both light and sound are waves. A few years later he extends his insight to elastic waves in the earth and concludes that wave motion, caused by initial vibrations (or "tremors"), is a universal form of propagation of physical effects. "The movement of earth against earth, crushing it," he writes, "moves the affected parts only slightly. Water struck by water creates circles round the place where it is struck; the voice in the air goes further, [and the tremor] in fire further still."[60]

The realization that wave motion is a universal phenomenon in all four elements—earth, water, air, and fire (or light)—was a revolutionary insight in Leonardo's time. It took another two hundred years before the wave-nature of light was rediscovered by Christian Huygens; the wave-nature of sound was first clearly articulated by Marin Marsenne during the first half of the seventeenth century, and earthquakes were associated with elastic waves only in the eighteenth century.[61]

In spite of Leonardo's impressive insights into the nature of wave motion and its widespread occurrence in nature, it would be an overstatement to say that he developed a wave theory of light similar to that presented by Huygens two hundred years later. To do so would have meant to understand the mathematical representation of a wave and relate its amplitude, frequency, and other characteristics to observed optical phenomena. These concepts were not used in science until the seventeenth century, when the mathematical theory of functions was developed.

Leonardo gave a correct description of transverse waves, in which the direction of energy transfer (the spreading of the circles) is at right angles to the direction of the vibration (the "tremor"), but he never considered longitudinal waves, in which the vibrations and energy transfer go in the same direction. In particular, he did not realize that sound waves are longitudinal. He appreciated that waves in different media (or "elements") travel at different velocities, but believed erroneously that the wave velocity is proportional to the power of the percussion that sets it off.[62]

He marveled at the swift velocity of light: "Look at the light of the candle and consider its beauty," he wrote. "Blink your eye and look at it again. What you see of it was not there before, and what was there before is not anymore."[63] But he also realized that, however fast light moves, its velocity is not infinite. He asserted that the speed of sound is greater than that of elastic waves in earth, and that light moves faster than sound, but that the mind moves even faster than light. "The mind jumps in an instant from the East to the West," he noted, "and all the other immaterial things have velocities that are by a long way inferior."[64]

Even though Leonardo did not state explicitly that the velocity of light is finite, it is clear from his Notebooks that he held that view. This is quite extraordinary, since the traditional view, handed down from antiquity, was that the propagation of light is instantaneous. Even Huygens and Descartes subscribed to that traditional view, and it was not until the end of the seventeenth century that the finite velocity of light was established.[65]

Leonardo was well aware of the phenomenon of refraction (the deflection of a light ray upon passing obliquely from air into glass, for instance). He performed several ingenious experiments to explore it, without, however, relating the effect to the wave-nature of light as Descartes and others would do some 150 years later. Leonardo even used refraction in a primitive prism to split white light into components of different colors, as Isaac Newton would do again in a celebrated experiment during the 1660s. But unlike Newton, Leonardo did not go much further than accurately recording the effect.[66]

On the other hand, Leonardo found the correct explanation for a phenomenon that had intrigued people throughout history—the blue color of the sky. In the years of his optical experiments, he climbed one of the giant peaks of Monte Rosa and noticed the deep blue of the sky at high altitude.[67] During the long climb, he apparently pondered the age-old question, "Why is the sky blue?"—and with amazing intuition came up with the correct answer:

> The blue displayed by the atmosphere is not its own color, but is caused by moisture that has evaporated into minute and imperceptible atoms on which the solar rays fall, rendering them luminous against the immense darkness of the region of fire that forms a covering above them. And this may be seen, as I myself saw it, by anyone who climbs Monte Rosa.[68]

The modern explanation of this phenomenon was given about four hundred years later by Lord Rayleigh, and the effect is now known as Rayleigh scattering. Sunlight is scattered by the molecules of the atmosphere (Leonardo's "minute and imperceptible atoms") in such a way that blue light is absorbed much more than other frequencies and is then radiated in different directions all around the sky. Hence, whichever way we look, we will see more of the scattered blue light than light of any other color. It is evident that Leonardo's explanation of solar rays falling on the molecules and "rendering them luminous" is a perfectly accurate qualitative description of the effect. This must certainly rank among his finest achievements in optics.

SOUND WAVES

Leonardo also explored the nature of sound, and from experiments with bells, drums, and other musical instruments, he observed that sound is always produced by "a blow on a resonant object." He correctly deduced that this causes an oscillating movement in the surrounding air, which he called "fanning movement" (*moto ventilante*) in association with the oscillating movement of a handheld fan.[69] "There cannot be any sound," he concluded, "where there is not movement and percussion of air; there cannot be percussion of that air where there is no instrument."[70]

Leonardo then proposed that, as in water, the initial percussion propagates in the form of circular waves, "since in all cases of movement water has great conformity with air."[71] As noted earlier, he was unaware that sound travels via longitudinal waves, but he noticed the phenomenon of resonance, demonstrating it with small pieces of straw, as he had demonstrated the transverse movement of water waves:

> The blow given to the bell will make another bell similar to it respond and move somewhat. And the string of a lute, as it sounds, produces response and movement in another similar string of similar tone in another lute. And this you will perceive by placing a straw on the string which is similar to that sounded.[72]

The observations of resonating bells and lute strings suggested to Leonardo the general mechanism for the propagation and perception of sound—from the initial percussion and the resulting waves in the air to the resonance of the eardrum.

Lacking the appropriate mathematical language, Leonardo was not able to develop a proper wave theory of light, nor a corresponding wave theory of sound.[73] He observed that the loudness of the sound generated depended on the power of percussion, but he failed to associate it with the amplitude of the sound wave; nor did he relate the pitch of sound to the wave's frequency. However, many years later, during the time he was reviewing the contents of all his Notebooks,[74] he came close to understanding the relation between pitch and frequency by studying the sound made by flies and other insects.

Whereas the common belief in his time was that flies produce sound with their mouths, Leonardo correctly observed that the sound is generated by their wings and proceeded with a clever experiment: "That flies have their voice in the wings," he recorded, "you will see by . . . daubing them with a little honey in such a way that they are not entirely prevented from flying. And you will observe that the sound made by the movement of their wings . . . will change from high to low pitch in direct proportion to the degree that their wings are more impeded."[75]

One of Leonardo's most impressive discoveries in the field of acoustics was his observation that, "If you tap a board covered with dust, that dust will collect in diverse little hills."[76] Having enhanced the vibrations of lute strings by putting small pieces of straw on them, he now concluded correctly that the dust was flying off the vibrating parts of the board and settling at the nodes, that is, in the areas that were not vibrating. He did not stop at that observation, but carefully continued tapping the vibrating surface while observing the fine movements of the little hills of dust. Next to a sketch representing one such hillock as a pyramid, he recorded his observations. "The hills will always pour down that dust from the tips of their pyramids to their base," he wrote. "From there, it will re-enter underneath, ascend through the center, and fall back again from the top of that little hill. And so the dust will circulate again and again . . . as long as the percussion continues."[77]

The attention to detail in these observations is truly remarkable. The phenomenon of nodal lines of dust or sand on vibrating plates was rediscovered in 1787 by the German physicist Ernst Chladni. They are now commonly called "Chladni patterns" in physics textbooks, where it is generally not mentioned that Leonardo da Vinci discovered them almost three hundred years earlier.

VISION AND THE EYE

To complete his science of perspective, Leonardo studied not only the external pathways of light rays, together with various optical phenomena, but also followed them right into the eye. Indeed, during the 1480s, he pursued his anatomical studies of the eye and the physiology of vision simultaneously with his investigations of perspective and the interplay of light and shadow.

At that time there was a debate among Renaissance artists and philosophers about the exact location of the tip of the visual pyramid in the eye. Most artists followed Alberti, who paid little attention to the actual physiology of vision and located the apex of the visual pyramid in a geometric point at the center of the pupil. Most philosophers, by contrast, took the position of Alhazen, who asserted that the eye's visual faculty must reside in a finite area rather than in an infinitely small point.[78]

In the beginning of his investigations of perspective and the anatomy of the eye, Leonardo adopted Alberti's view, but during the 1490s, as his research became more sophisticated, he came to embrace

Alhazen's position, arguing that "if all the images that come to the eye converged in a mathematical point, which is proved to be indivisible, then all the things seen in the universe would appear as one, and that one would be indivisible."[79]

In his late optical writings in Manuscript D, finally, he asserted repeatedly and confidently that "every part of the pupil possesses the faculty of vision (virtù visiva), and . . . this faculty is not reduced to a point, as the perspectivists wish."[80] In this Notebook, Leonardo offers three simple but very elegant experiments, involving the shadowy perception of small objects held near the eye, as persuasive proofs of Alhazen's position.[81] From then on he distinguished between two kinds of perspective. The first, "perspective made by art," is a geometric technique for representing objects located in three-dimensional space on a flat surface, while the second, "perspective made by nature," needs a proper science of vision to be understood.[82]

Having convinced himself that in such a science of vision, the geometric apex of the visual pyramid in the eye needs to be replaced by much more complex pathways of the sensory impressions, Leonardo then traced these pathways through the lens and the eyeball to the optic nerve, and from there all the way to the center of the brain where he believed he had found the seat of the soul.

NINE

The Eye, the Senses, and the Soul

The structure of the eye and the process of vision were natural wonders for Leonardo that never ceased to amaze him. "What language can express this marvel?" he writes about the eyeball, before continuing with a rare expression of religious awe: "Certainly none. This is where human discourse turns directly to the contemplation of the divine."[1] In the *Treatise on Painting*, Leonardo waxes enthusiastic about the human eye:

> Don't you see that the eye embraces the beauty of the whole world? It is the master of astronomy, it practices cosmography, it counsels and corrects all human arts; it transports man to different parts of the world. [The eye] is the prince of mathematics; its sciences are most certain. It has measured the heights and sizes of the stars, it has discovered the elements and their locations. . . . It has created architecture, perspective, and

divine painting. . . . [The eye] is the window of the human body, through which [the soul] contemplates and enjoys the beauty of the world.[2]

It is not surprising that Leonardo spent more than twenty years investigating the anatomy and physiology of the eye by carefully dissecting the eyeball and associated muscles and nerves. One of his earliest drawings, made around 1487, shows the human head and brain surrounded by several membranes, like layers of an onion (Fig. 9-1). In fact, this onion analogy was widely used by leading medieval anatomists.[3] Beneath the layers of the scalp Leonardo shows two membranes (known today as dura mater and pia mater) surrounding the brain and then extending to form the eyeball, which contains a round lens. The pupil is formed by a transparent gap in the membranes in front of the lens, which appears to lie unattached, presumably floating in some clear fluid. This crude drawing is a faithful illustration of the medieval view of the eye, which was based almost entirely on imagination rather than on empirical knowledge.

With his own anatomical dissections, Leonardo soon progressed far beyond these traditional ideas. The "onion drawing" already shows one of his discoveries, the frontal sinus above the eyeball, and in the subsequent years he would gradually add many fine details concerning the anatomy of the eye and the pathways of visual perception.

He was well aware of the novelty of his discoveries. "The eye has until now been defined by countless writers in a certain way," he noted in the Codex Atlanticus, "but I find through experience that it works in a different manner."[4]

LEONARDO'S ANATOMY OF THE EYE

Leonardo's study of visual perception was an extraordinary program of scientific investigation, combining optics, anatomy of the eye, and neuroscience. He explored these fields without any inhibitions, applying the same meticulous empirical method to them that he used to explore everything else in nature, never fearing that some phenomenon might be beyond his grasp.

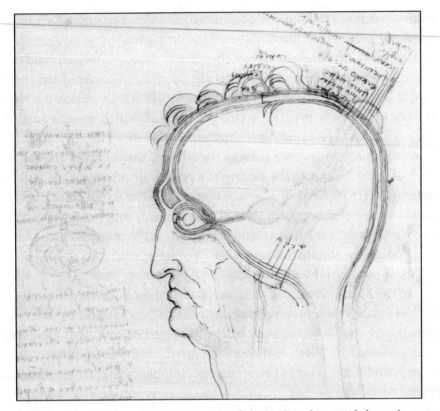

*Figure 9-1: Leonardo's illustration of the medieval view of the scalp,
brain, and eyeball, Anatomical Studies, folio 32r*

One of the first things Leonardo noticed when he studied the structure of the eye in detail was its ability to change the size of the pupil according to its exposure to light. He first observed this phenomenon while painting a portrait, and then tested it in a series of experiments in which he exposed subjects to varying amounts of light. "The pupil of the eye," he concluded, "changes to as many different sizes as there are differences in the degrees of brightness and darkness of the objects which present themselves before it. . . . Nature has equipped the visual faculty, when irritated by excessive light, with the contraction of the pupil . . . , and here nature works like someone who, having too much light in his house, closes half of a window, and more or less according to necessity." And then he added: "You can observe that in nocturnal animals such as cats, screech owls, tawny owls and others, which have the pupil small at midday and very large at night."[5]

When he investigated the mechanism of these contractions and dilations in his dissections of the eyeball, Leonardo discovered the delicate sphincter of the pupil. "I find by experiment," he recorded, "that the black, or nearly black, crinkled rough color, which appears around the pupil, serves no other function than to increase or decrease the size of that pupil."[6] In another passage, he likened the action of the radial folds of the sphincter to the closing of a purse with a string.[7] Leonardo's detailed description of the "nearly black, crinkled rough color" of the pupillary muscles is amazingly accurate. Indeed, it is almost identical to that of modern medical textbooks, in which the muscles on the central opening of the iris, the so-called "pupillary ruff," are described as a dark brown, wrinkled rim.[8]

In the Middle Ages and the Renaissance, most natural philosophers believed that vision involved the emission of "visual rays" by the eye, which were then reflected back by the perceived objects. This view was first proposed by Plato and was supported by Euclid, Ptolemy, and Galen. Only the great experimental philosopher Alhazen expounded the opposite view—that vision was triggered when visual images, carried by light rays, entered the eye.

Leonardo debated the merits of both points of view at great length before agreeing with Alhazen.[9] His principal argument in favor of the theory of "intromission" was based on his discovery of the pupil's adaptation to changing illumination. In particular, he saw the fact that sudden bright sunlight produces pain in the eye as decisive proof that light not only enters the eye, but can also cause harm to it and, in extreme cases, even its destruction. An additional argument for the entry of light into the eye was Leonardo's observation of afterimages. "If you look at the sun or another luminous body and then shut your eyes," he noted, "you will see it similarly inside your eye for a long space of time. This is evidence that images enter the eye."[10]

After a hiatus of almost twenty years, Leonardo returned to the study of vision around 1508 to explore further details of the eye's anatomy and its visual pathways.[11] This time, he also made use of his new technique of embedding the eyeball in egg white during dissections.[12] He recognized the cornea as a transparent membrane and noticed its prominent curvature, concluding correctly that this extends the visual field beyond 180 degrees: "Nature made the surface of the cornea in the eye convex in order to allow surrounding objects to imprint their images at greater angles."[13]

Leonardo realized that the extension of the visual field by the prominence of the cornea's curvature is due to the refraction of light rays when they pass from the air into the denser medium of the cornea, and he carefully illustrated this phenomenon in several sketches. In addition, he tested the refractions experimentally by building a crystal model of the cornea.[14]

Leonardo was quite familiar with lenses from his optical experiments as well as from his own use of spectacles, which he had to wear by the time he studied the lens of the eye.[15] Naturally, he applied his knowledge of refraction to his investigations of both the cornea and the lens. However, he always presented the lens, which he called the "crystalline humor," as spherical and located in the center of the eyeball, suspended in a clear fluid, rather than right behind the pupil. Kenneth Keele has pointed out that Leonardo's sophisticated technique of dissection of the eyeball, developed around 1509, would certainly have enabled him to recognize the true shape and location of the lens, and Keele has speculated that Leonardo either did not continue his dissections of the eye after that time, or that more accurate drawings have been lost.[16]

The detailed optics of the light rays inside the eyeball presented great difficulties for Leonardo, as they did for all his contemporaries. Today we know that the rays are refracted by the convex lens in such a way that they cross each other behind the lens and form an inverted image of the perceived object on the retina. How the brain then corrects the inversion to produce normal vision is still not fully understood.

Since Leonardo could not know that a second inversion of the image is performed in the brain, he had to construct two consecutive inversions of the light rays within the eyeball to produce an upright image. He came up with a brilliant though incorrect idea. The first inversion of the rays, he postulated, occurs between the pupil and the lens, caused by the small opening of the pupil, which turns the image upside down like a camera obscura.[17]

The inverted rays then enter the lens where they are inverted a second time, resulting in an upright image at the end. Leonardo built a simple but very ingenious model of the eye to test this idea and illustrated it clearly with a charming drawing in Manuscript D (Fig. 9-2). In the lower part of the drawing, he has sketched the visual pathways according to his theory. The light rays, entering the eye from below, are slightly refracted by the cornea (except for the central ray), proceed through the small opening of the pupil and, as in a camera obscura, produce an inverted image on the spherical lens. There, the rays are inverted again before they form a proper image on the back of the lens, from where they would enter the optic nerve.

The upper part of the drawing shows Leonardo's model. He has filled a transparent globe, representing the eyeball, with water and at the front has fitted a plate with a small hole in the middle, representing the pupil. Suspended in the center of the globe is a "ball of thin glass," representing the lens, behind which Leonardo places his own eye underwater in the position of the optic nerve. "Such an instrument," he explains in the accompanying text, "will send the images . . . to the eye just as the eye sends them to the visual faculty."[18]

Leonardo's construction of the visual pathways was certainly ingenious, but it also had some serious problems. The camera-obscura effect would work only if the size of the pupil were much smaller and its distance from the lens greater than they actually are. And even if that were the case, the images of objects on the retina would be affected by the contractions and dilations of the pupil in response to varying exposures to light. Leonardo considered that possibility and also experimented with alternative visual paths, but he was never able to resolve the inconsistencies inherent in his construction.[19] Nevertheless, his discoveries of many fine details of the eye's anatomy are truly remarkable.

Leonardo was the first to distinguish between central and peripheral vision. "The eye has a single central line," he observed, "and all the things that come to the eye along this line are seen well. Around this central line, there are an infinite number of other lines, which are of less value the further they are from the central line."[20] He was also the first to explain binocular vision—the way in which we see things

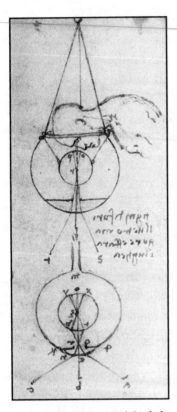

Figure 9-2: Model of the eye and diagram of visual pathways, Ms. D, folio 3v

stereoscopically by fusing the separate images of the visual field formed in each eye. To explore the details of binocular vision, he placed objects of various sizes at varying distances from the eyes, from very close to very far, and looked at them alternatively with the right and left eye and with both eyes. His conclusion was unequivocal and correct: "One and the same object is clearly comprehended when seen with two concordant eyes. These eyes refer it to one and the same point inside the head. . . . But if you displace one of those eyes with the finger, you will see one perceived object converted into two."[21]

FROM THE OPTIC NERVE TO THE SEAT OF THE SOUL

From his earliest studies of sensory perception, Leonardo did not limit his investigations of vision to the optics of the eye, but followed the paths of sensory impressions through the nerves into the brain. Indeed, even his early "onion drawing" of the scalp and eyeball (Fig. 9-1), which represents the medieval conception of the eye, shows the optic nerve leading to the center of the brain, where the vague outlines of three cavities can be seen. According to Aristotelian and medieval philosophy, these were the areas in the brain where different stages of perception took place. The first cavity, named *sensus communis* (common sense) by Aristotle, was the place where all the senses came together to produce an integrated perception of the world, which was then interpreted and partly committed to memory in the other two cavities.

These hollow spaces do exist in the central portion of the brain, but their shapes and functions are quite different from those imagined by medieval natural philosophers. They are called cerebral ventricles by today's neuroscientists; there are actually four of them, all interconnected. They support and cushion the brain and produce a clear, colorless fluid that circulates over the surfaces of the brain and spinal cord, transporting hormones and removing metabolic waste products.

Leonardo embraced the Aristotelian idea of the ventricles as centers of sensory perception, expanded it, and, by employing his skills as an anatomist and empirical scientist, integrated it with his ideas about the nature of light and the physiology of vision. To begin with, he determined the exact shape of the cerebral ventricles by carefully injecting wax into them.[22]

He recorded his results in several drawings, for example, the one shown in Figure 9-3, which also exhibits the pathways of several sensory nerves to the brain. Comparison of this drawing (which is based on the dissection of the brain of an ox) with those in a modern medical textbook makes it evident that Leonardo reproduced the shapes and locations of the cerebral ventricles with tremendous accuracy. The two anterior, so-called lateral ventricles, the third (central) ventricle, and the fourth (posterior) ventricle can easily be recognized.

Leonardo's neurological theory of visual perception must be ranked as one of his greatest scientific achievements. It has been analyzed in admirable detail by the eminent Leonardo scholar and physician Kenneth Keele.[23]

In Leonardo's anatomy, the optic nerve is pictured as expanding gradually where it enters the eyeball and attaching itself directly to the back of the spherical lens, forming a kind of restricted retina. This is where the visual images are transformed into nerve impulses. He saw this process as a percussion of the optic nerve by the light rays, which triggers sensory impulses (sentimenti) that travel through the nerves in the form of waves, just as the "tremors" triggered by stones thrown into a pond propagate in the form of water waves.[24] However, Leonardo specified that the sensory, or nervous, impulses are not material. He called them "spiritual," by which he simply meant that they were incorporeal and invisible. Following Galen, he thought that the optic nerve, like all nerves, was hollow, "perforated" by a small central tube through which the wave fronts formed by sensory impulses travel toward the center of the brain.

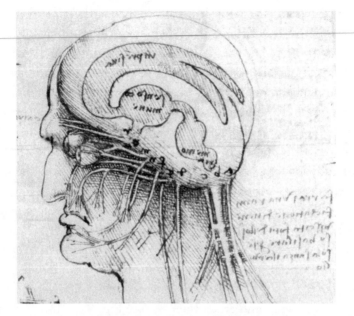

*Figure 9-3: Cerebral ventricles and pathways of cranial
nerves, "Weimar Blatt," in Anatomical Studies,
between folios 54 and 55*

Kenneth Keele concludes that Leonardo's physiology of sensory
perception is "thoroughly mechanistic," because it prominently features movement and percussion.[25] I disagree with this assessment in
view of Leonardo's explicit emphasis on the nonmaterial nature of the
nervous impulses. According to modern neuroscience, the nerve impulses are of electromagnetic nature, wave fronts of ions moving along
the nerves—and, as Leonardo stated, invisible to the naked eye. The
neurons form long, thin fibers (called axons), surrounded by cell membranes, for which Leonardo's term "perforated tubes" does not seem a
bad description. Inside these tubes, the wave fronts of ions move in the
fluid of the nerve cells. These are phenomena in the realms of microbiology and biochemistry, which were inaccessible to Leonardo. As a
good empiricist, he simply stated that the sensory impulses are invisible and did not further speculate about their nature. No scientist could
have done better before the development of the microscope and the
theory of electromagnetism several centuries later.

From his very first anatomical studies, Leonardo paid special attention to the pathways of the sensory nerves in the human skull, in particular the optic nerve. Indeed, as Keele points out, "Leonardo's
personal investigations of the anatomy of the eye and optic nerves . . .
formed the central motive for his beautiful perspectival demonstrations
of the structure of the human skull."[26] These stunning pictures of the
skull are famous for their delicate renderings of light and shade and
their masterful application of visual perspective (see Fig. 8-2 on p.
216). In addition, the trained eye of the physician sees in them amazingly accurate depictions of the skull's cavities and nerve openings—
the eye socket, its neighboring sinuses, the tear ducts, and the
openings (foramina) for the optic and auditory nerves.[27]

When Leonardo followed the optic nerves from each eyeball into
the brain, he noticed that they intersect in an area now known as the optic chiasma ("crossing").[28] He documented this discovery in all his
drawings of the optic and cranial nerves (see Fig. 9-3). Leonardo speculated that the crossing of the optic nerves served to facilitate "the equal
movement of the eyes" in the process of visual perception.[29] He was
on the right track, but he did not know that the process of synchroniz-
ing the visual perception of the two eyes is much more complex, involving the subtle interplay of several sets of muscles and nerves.

By the time Leonardo drew the so-called Weimar Blatt (Fig. 9-3),
around 1508, his knowledge of the nature and course of the cranial
nerves had reached its peak. He still maintained that all the nerves carrying the sensory impressions converge in the anterior ventricle,[30] but
he departed from Aristotle by shifting the location of the *senso comune*
to the central cavity of the brain.[31] In the anterior ventricle, Leonardo
located a special organ not mentioned by anyone before him, which he
called the receptor of impressions *(impressiva)*.[32] He saw it as a relay sta-
tion that collects the wave patterns of sensory impressions, makes
selections by some process of resonance, and organizes them into harmonious rhythmic forms that are then passed on to the *senso comune*,
where they enter consciousness.

HEARING AND THE OTHER SENSES

Although Leonardo considered sight "the best and most noble of the senses,"[33] he investigated the other senses as well, paying particular attention to the pathways of their cranial nerves. From his earliest drawings of the head, he consistently delineated the auditory and olfactory nerves, as well as the optic nerve, and showed how they all converge toward the *senso comune*.

In his famous drawings of the skull in perspective, Leonardo clearly depicted the auditory canal, but in his known manuscripts there is no detailed description of the anatomy of the ear. He was aware of the eardrum and recognized that its percussion by sound waves produces sensory impulses in the auditory nerve. However, he did not document any of the intermediary processes, having convinced himself, perhaps, that the generation of auditory nervous impulses by means of percussion was analogous to that of the impulses in the optic nerve, and that both of them ended up in the *senso comune*.

Leonardo may or may not have recorded more detailed studies of the human perception of sound in manuscripts that have been lost, but we know for certain that he spent considerable time studying the *production* of sound by the human voice. He not only investigated the anatomy and physiology of the entire vocal apparatus to understand the formation of the voice, but extended his studies to phonetics, musical theory, and the functioning and design of musical instruments.[34]

The larynx, or voice box, which contains the vocal cords, is a notoriously complicated organ, and it is not surprising that Leonardo did not fully understand its functioning. However, he produced astonishingly accurate drawings of its detailed anatomy, far beyond anything known in his time, and he also realized that many other parts of the body are involved in the formation of the human voice. In the words of Kenneth Keele, Leonardo realized that

> voice production involved the integrated function of structures
> ranging from the thoracic cage, through lungs, bronchi, trachea,

larynx, pharynx, nasal and mouth cavities to the teeth, lips and tongue; and he considers all these structures, producing unprecedentedly accurate drawings of them all.[35]

In his studies of the human voice, Leonardo frequently used the mechanisms of sound production in flutes and trumpets as models. In fact, he always used the word *voce* (voice) for the sounds produced by these instruments. His investigations of the variation of pitch in wind instruments naturally led him to study scales and develop elements of musical theory.

Leonardo's musical talent was well known by his contemporaries and played an important role in his early success at the Sforza court in Milan.[36] We also have contemporary reports that he composed pieces of music for the theatrical performances and other spectacles he produced at court.[37] Unfortunately, no musical score by Leonardo has been preserved. On the other hand, we can find numerous drawings of musical instruments in his Notebooks, most of them with designs for improving existing instruments. These designs include keyboards for wind instruments, tuned drums, glissando flutes (like Swanee whistles), and a *viola organista* (organ violin), a kind of organ with timbre similar to a string instrument.[38]

Leonardo's dissections of the cranial nerves and the central nervous system convinced him that all five senses are associated with special nerves that carry sensory impressions to the brain, where they are selected and organized by the receptor of impressions *(impressiva)* and passed on to the *senso comune*. There, in the central ventricle of the brain, the integrated sensory impressions are judged by the intellect and influenced by the imagination and memory.

In several of his drawings of the human skull, Leonardo indicated the position of the third cerebral ventricle by three intersecting coordinates, with complete spatial accuracy in three dimensions (see Fig. 8-2). This cavity in the center of the brain he identified not only as the location of the *senso comune*, but also as the seat of the soul. "The soul appears to reside in the judicial part," he concluded, "and the judicial part appears to be in the place where all the senses come together, which is called *senso comune*. . . . The *senso comune* is the seat of the soul, the memory is its store, and the receptor of impressions is its informant."[39] With this statement, Leonardo links his elaborate theory of sensory perception to the ancient idea of the soul.

COGNITION AND THE SOUL

In early Greek philosophy, the soul was conceived as the ultimate moving force and source of all life.[40] Closely associated with this moving force, which leaves the body at death, was the idea of knowing. From the beginning of Greek philosophy, the concept of the soul had a cognitive dimension. The process of animation was also a process of knowing. Thus Anaxagoras, in the fifth century B.C., called the soul *nous* (reason) and saw it as a world-moving rational substance.

During the period of Hellenistic-Roman philosophy, Alexandrian thought gradually separated the two characteristics that had originally been united in the Greek conception of the soul—that of a vital force and that of the activity of consciousness. Side by side with the soul, which moves the body, now appears "spirit" as an independent principle expressing the essence of the individual, and also of the divine personality. Alexandrian philosophers introduced the triple division of the human being into body, soul, and spirit, but the boundaries between "soul" and "spirit" were fluctuating. The soul was situated somewhere between the two extremes, matter and spirit.

Leonardo adopted the integrated view of the soul that was held by Aristotle and the early Greek philosophers, who saw it both as the agent of perception and knowing and as the force underlying the body's formation and movements. Unlike the Greek philosophers, however, he did not merely speculate about the nature of the soul, but tested the ancient views empirically. In his delicate dissections of the brain and the nervous system, he traced the sensory perceptions from the initial impressions on the sense organs, especially the eye, through the sensory nerves to the center of the brain. He also followed the nerve impulses for voluntary movement from the brain down the spinal cord, and through the peripheral motor nerves out to the muscles, tendons, and bones; and he illustrated all these pathways in precise anatomical drawings (see, e.g., Fig. 9-4).[41]

From his thorough investigations of the brain and the nervous system, Leonardo concluded that the soul evaluated sensory impressions and transferred them to the memory, and that it was also the origin of voluntary bodily movement, which he associated with reason and judgment.

In Leonardo's view, all material movement originated in the immaterial and invisible movements of the soul. "Spiritual movement," he reasoned, "flowing through the limbs of sentient animals, broadens their muscles. Thus broadened, these muscles become shortened and draw back the tendons that are connected to them. This is the origin of force in the human limbs. . . . Material movement arises from the immaterial."[42] With this concept of the soul, Leonardo expanded the traditional Aristotelian idea according to his empirical evidence. In this, he was far ahead of his time.

During the subsequent centuries, Leonardo's Notebooks remained hidden in ancient European libraries and many of them were lost, and the integrated Aristotelian view of the soul gradually disappeared from philosophy. The idea of spirit as a disembodied divine principle became the dominant theme of religious metaphysics, and the soul, accordingly, was seen as being independent from the body and endowed with immortality. For other philosophers, the concept of the soul became increasingly synonymous with that of the rational mind, and in the seventeenth century, René Descartes postulated the fundamental division of reality into two independent and separate realms—that of mind, the "thinking thing" (res cogitans), and that of matter, the "extended thing" (res extensa).

This conceptual split between mind and matter has haunted Western science and philosophy for more than three hundred years. Following Descartes, scientists and philosophers continued to think of the mind as an intangible entity and were unable to imagine how this "thinking thing" is related to the body. In particular, the exact relationship between mind and brain is still a mystery to most psychologists and neuroscientists.

During the last two decades of the twentieth century, however, a novel conception of the nature of mind and consciousness emerged in the life sciences, which finally overcame the Cartesian division between mind and body. The decisive advance has been to reject the view of mind as a thing; to realize that mind and consciousness are not entities

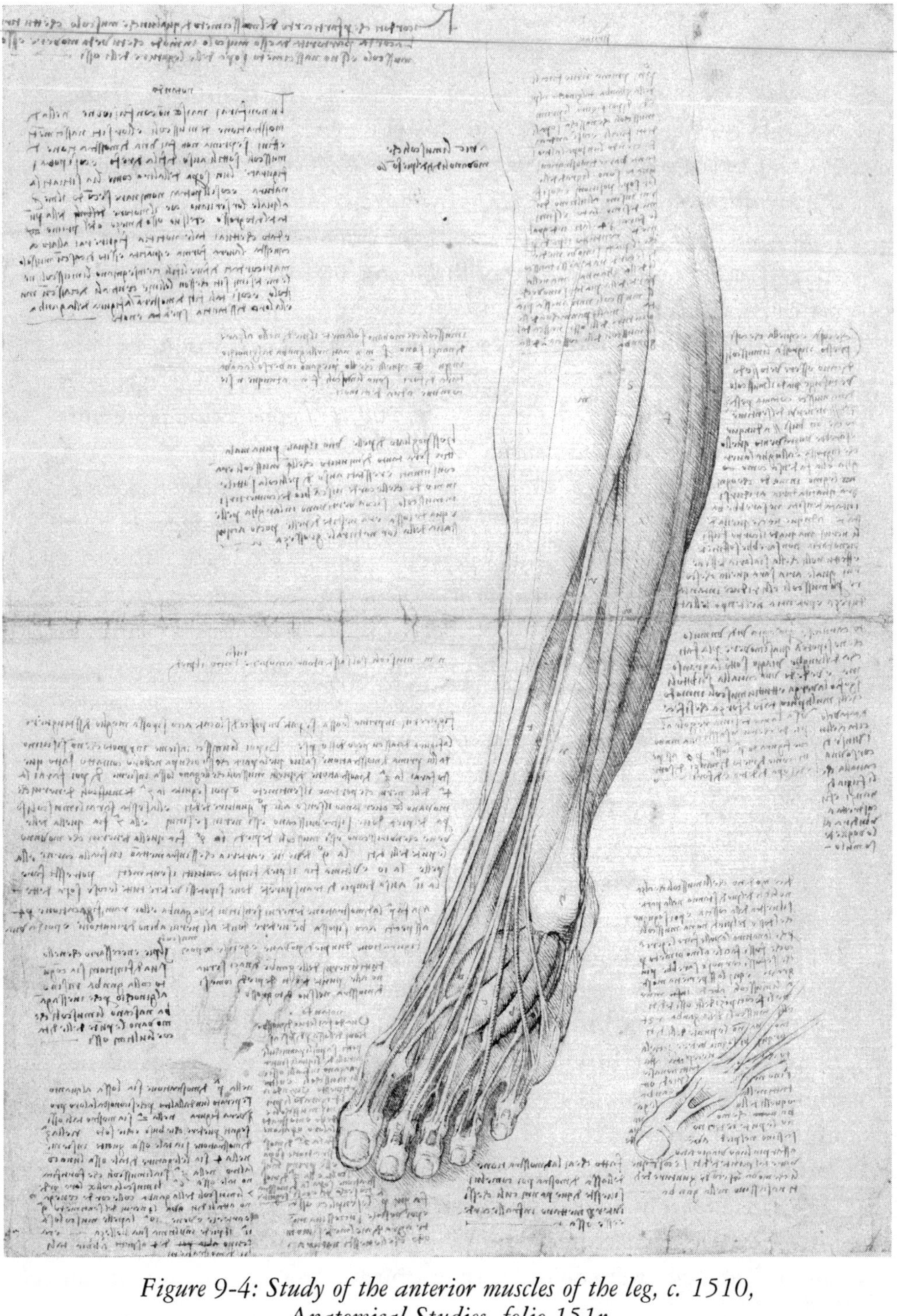

Figure 9-4: Study of the anterior muscles of the leg, c. 1510,
Anatomical Studies, folio 151r

but processes. In the past twenty-five years the study of mind from this new perspective has blossomed into a rich interdisciplinary field known as cognitive science, which transcends the traditional frameworks of biology, psychology, and epistemology.[43]

One of the central insights of cognitive science is the identification of cognition, the process of knowing, with the process of life. Cognition, according to this view, is the organizing activity of living systems at all levels of life. Accordingly, the interactions of a living organism—plant, animal, or human—with its environment are understood as cognitive interactions. Thus life and cognition become inseparably connected. Mind—or, more accurately, mental activity—is immanent in matter at all levels of life. This new conception represents a radical expansion of the concept of cognition and, implicitly, the concept of mind. In the new view, cognition involves the entire process of life—including perception, emotion, and behavior—and does not even necessarily require a brain and a nervous system.

It is evident that the identification of mind, or cognition, with the process of life, although a novel idea in science, comes very close to Leonardo's concept of the soul. Like Leonardo, modern cognitive scientists see cognition (or the soul) both as the process of perception and knowing and as the process that animates the movements and organization of the body. There is a conceptual difference. Whereas cognitive scientists understand cognition clearly as a process, Leonardo saw the soul as an entity. However, when he wrote about it, he always described it in terms of its activities.

How close Leonardo's conception of the soul comes to the modern concept of cognition can be seen in his notes on the flight of birds, in which he compares the movements of the living bird with those of the flying machine he is designing. Over many hours of intense observations of birds in flight in the hills surrounding Florence, Leonardo became thoroughly familiar with their instinctive capacity to maneuver in the wind, keeping their equilibrium by responding to changing air currents with subtle movements of their wings and tails.[44]

In his notes, he explained that this capacity was a sign of the bird's intelligence—a reflection of the actions of its soul.[45] In modern scientific language, we would say that a bird's interactions with the air currents and its delicate maneuvers in the wind are cognitive processes, as Leonardo clearly recognized and accurately described. He also realized that these delicate cognitive processes of a bird in flight would always be superior to those of a human pilot steering a mechanical device:

> It could be said that such an instrument designed by man is lacking only the soul of the bird, which must be counterfeited with the soul of the man. . . . [However], the soul of the bird will certainly respond better to the needs of its limbs than would the soul of the man, separated from them and especially from their almost imperceptible balancing movements.[46]

Following Aristotle, Leonardo saw the soul not only as the source of all bodily movements, but also as the force underlying the body's formation. He called it "the composer of the body."[47] This is completely consistent with the views of today's cognitive scientists who understand cognition as a process involving the self-generation and self-organization of living organisms.

The main difference between Leonardo's concept of the soul and modern cognitive science seems to be that Leonardo gave the human soul a specific location in the brain. Today we know that reflective consciousness—the special kind of cognition that is characteristic of the great apes and humans—is a widely distributed process involving complex layers of neural networks. Without access to the brain's microscopic structures, chemistry, and electromagnetic signals, Leonardo had no way of discovering these extended networks of neurons; and since he observed that the pathways of various sensory nerves seem to converge toward the brain's central ventricle, he decided that this had to be the seat of the soul.

At the time of the Renaissance, there was no agreement about the soul's location. Whereas Democritus and Plato had recognized the importance of the brain, Aristotle regarded the heart as the seat of the *sensus communis*. Averroës, the great Arab commentator on Aristotle whose teachings were very influential in Italy during the Renaissance,[48] had expounded yet another view. He identified the soul with the form of

the entire living body, which meant that it did not have a specific location. Leonardo, after considering such opinions, in view of the empirical evidence he had gathered, confidently located the soul in the
central cavity of the brain.

Body and soul formed one indivisible whole for Leonardo. "The
soul desires to stay with its body," he explained, "because without the
organic instruments of that body it can neither carry out nor feel anything."[49] Again, this is completely consistent with modern cognitive
science, where we have come to understand the relationship between
mind and body as one between (cognitive) process and (living) structure, which represent two complementary aspects of the phenomenon
of life. Indeed, as Leonardo wrote of the soul, so cognitive scientists today speak of the mind as being fundamentally embodied. On the one
hand, cognitive processes continually shape our bodily forms, and on
the other, the very structure of reason arises from our bodies and
brains.[50]

Remarkably, for his time, Leonardo repeatedly argued against the
existence of disembodied spirits. "A spirit can have neither voice, nor
form, nor force," he declared. "And if anyone should say that, through
air collected together and compressed, a spirit assumes bodies of various forms, and by such instrument speaks and moves with force, to that
I reply that, where there are neither nerves nor bones, there can be no
force exerted in any movement made by such imaginary spirits."[51]

In Leonardo's view, the essential unity of body and soul arises at the
very beginning of life, and it dissolves with the demise of both at
death. On the two folios that contain his most beautiful drawings of
the human embryo in the womb (Fig. E-1), we find the following inspired thoughts on the relationship between the souls of mother and
child:

> One and the same soul governs these two bodies; and the desires,
> fears and pains are common to this creature as to all other ani-
> mated parts. . . . The soul of the mother . . . in due time awakens
> the soul which is to be its inhabitant. This at first remains asleep
> under the guardianship of the soul of the mother who nourishes
> and vivifies it through the umbilical vein.[52]

This extraordinary passage is completely compatible with modern cognitive science. In poetical language, the artist and scientist describes the gradual development of the embryo's mental life together with its body. At the end of life, the reverse process takes place. "While I thought I was learning how to live, I have been learning how to die," Leonardo wrote movingly late in his life.[53] In a striking departure from Christian doctrine, Leonardo da Vinci never expressed a belief that the soul would survive the body after death.

A THEORY OF KNOWLEDGE

My last two chapters outline what amounts to an extensive theory of knowledge, testifying to Leonardo's genius as an integrative, systemic thinker. Approaching perception and knowledge as a painter, he began by exploring the appearance of things to the eye, the nature of perspective, the phenomena of optics, and the nature of light. He not only used the ancient metaphor of the eye as the window of the soul, but took it seriously and subjected it to his empirical investigations, following the rays of the "pyramids of light" into the eye, tracing them through the lens and the eyeball to the optic nerve. He described how in that area, known today as the retina, the percussion of light rays generates sensory impulses, and he followed these sensory impulses along the optic nerve all the way to the "seat of the soul" in the central cavity of the brain.

Leonardo also developed a detailed theory of how the sensory impressions enter consciousness. He remained vague on how exactly the nerve impulses come under the influence of the intellect, memory, and imagination, glossing over the relationship between conscious experience and neurological processes. However, even today our leading neuroscientists can do no better.[54]

That Leonardo was able to develop a sophisticated and coherent theory of perception and knowledge based on empirical evidence but without any knowledge of cells, molecules, biochemistry, or electromagnetism is certainly extraordinary. Many facets of his explanations later became separate scientific disciplines, including optics, cranial anatomy, neurology, brain physiology, and epistemology. During the last decade of the twentieth century, these subjects began to converge again within the interdisciplinary field of cognitive science, showing striking similarities to Leonardo's systemic conception of the process of knowing.

Once again, I cannot help but wonder how differently Western science would have developed if Leonardo had published his treatises during his lifetime, as he had intended. Galileo, Descartes, Bacon, and Newton—the giants of the Scientific Revolution—lived and worked in intellectual milieus that were much closer to that of the Renaissance than ours. I believe they would have understood Leonardo's language and reasoning much better than we do today. These natural philosophers, as they were still called, struggled with the very same problems that occupied and fascinated Leonardo during his life, and for which he often found original solutions. How would they have incorporated his insights into their theories?

Alas, such questions have no answers. While Leonardo's paintings had a decisive influence on European art, his scientific treatises remained hidden for centuries, disconnected from the development of modern science.

"Read me, O reader, if in my words

you find delight"

L eonardo's science cannot be understood within the mechanistic paradigm of Galileo, Descartes, and Newton. Although he was a mechanical genius who designed countless machines, his science was not mechanistic. He fully recognized and extensively studied the mechanical aspects of the human and animal bodies, but he always saw them as instruments, used by the soul for the organism's self-organization. Trying to understand those processes of self-organization—the growth, movements, and transformations of nature's living forms—was at the very core of Leonardo's science. It was a science of qualities and proportions, of organic forms shaped and transformed by underlying processes. Nature as a whole was alive and animated for Leonardo, a world in continual flux and development, in the macrocosm of the Earth as in the microcosm of the human body.

While his contemporaries deferred to the authorities of Aristotle and the Church, Leonardo developed and practiced an empirical approach to acquiring independent knowledge, which became known as the scientific method many centuries after him. It involved the systematic and careful observation of natural phenomena, ingenious experiments, the formulation of theoretical models, and many attempts at mathematical generalizations.

Leonardo used his empirical method—together with his exceptional powers of observation and his "sublime left hand"—to analyze, draw, and paint "with philosophic and subtle speculation . . . all the qualities of forms."[1] The records he left of his lifelong investigations are superb testimonies of both his art and his science.

In recent decades, scholars have given us comprehensive analyses of some areas of Leonardo's science (albeit often from perspectives somewhat different from mine), while other areas remain largely unexplored. Leonardo's entire corpus of anatomical studies has been analyzed in impressive detail in a magnificent book, *Leonardo da Vinci's Elements of the Science of Man*, by the historian of medicine and Leonardo scholar Kenneth Keele.[2]

Leonardo's original contributions to landscape and garden design as well as his outstanding work in botany are discussed in great detail in an insightful volume by botanist William Emboden, *Leonardo da Vinci on Plants and Gardens*.[3] Unfortunately, there is no comparable volume about Leonardo's voluminous writings on "the motion of the waters," which include his pioneering studies of fluid flow, as well as his many original thoughts on the ecological dimension of water as the medium and nurturing fluid of life. His related geological observations, centuries ahead of their time, also remain largely unexplored.

Leonardo's contributions to mechanics and engineering are discussed extensively in several books, including the beautiful volume on *Renaissance Engineers from Brunelleschi to Leonardo da Vinci* by science historian Paolo Galluzzi.[4] His precise observations and analyses of the flight of birds and his persistent attempts to design workable flying machines are evaluated in a captivating, richly illustrated monograph by science historian Domenico Laurenza, *Leonardo on Flight*.[5] However, no overall assessment of Leonardo's wide-ranging works in architecture and engineering from the modern perspective of design has been offered so far.[6] This would certainly be a fascinating subject.

Leonardo's studies of the living forms of nature began with their outward appearance and then turned to methodical investigations of their intrinsic nature. Life's patterns of organization, its organic structures, and its fundamental processes of metabolism and growth are the unifying conceptual threads that interlink his knowledge of macro- and microcosm. Throughout his life he studied, drew, and painted the rocks and sediments of the Earth, shaped by water; the growth of plants shaped by their metabolism; and the anatomy of the animal body in motion. He used his scientific understanding of the forms of nature as the intellectual underpinning of his art, and he used his drawings and paintings as tools of scientific analysis. Thus Leonardo's studies of nature's living forms represent a seamless unity of art and science.

In the Italian Renaissance, it was not unusual to find painters who were also accomplished sculptors, architects, or engineers. The *uomo universale* was the great ideal of the time. Nevertheless, Leonardo da Vinci's synthesis of art and science, and its brilliant applications in numerous fields of design and engineering, were absolutely unique. In subsequent centuries, Leonardo's scientific concepts and observations were gradually rediscovered, and his vision of a science of organic forms reemerged several times in different epochs. Never again, however, was so much intellectual and artistic genius embodied in a single human being.

Leonardo himself never boasted about his unique talents and skills, and in his thousands of pages of manuscripts he never vaunted the originality of so many of his ideas and discoveries. But he was well aware of his exceptional stature. In the Codex Madrid, in the midst of extensive discussions of the laws of mechanics, we find two lines that can stand as his own definitive epitaph:

> *Read me, O reader, if in my words you find delight,*
> *for rarely in the world will one such as I be born again.*[7]

For over forty years, Leonardo relentlessly pursued his scientific explorations, driven by his restless and intense intellectual curiosity, his love of nature, and his passion for all living things. His magnificent drawings often reflect that passion with great delicacy and sensitivity. For example, his famous picture of a fetus in utero (Fig. E-1) is accompanied by several smaller sketches that liken the womb to the embryo sac of a flower, picturing the peeled-off layers of the uterine membranes in an arrangement of flower petals. The entire set of drawings vividly shows Leonardo's tremendous care and respect for all forms of life. They exude a tenderness that is deeply moving.

Leonardo's science was a gentle science. He abhorred violence and had a special compassion for animals. He was a vegetarian because he did not want to cause animals pain by killing them for food. He would buy caged birds in the marketplace and set them free, and would observe their flight not only with a sharp observational eye but also with great empathy. Browsing through the Notebooks, one may suddenly get the impression that a single bird has flown right onto the page while Leonardo was discussing something else, followed by a whole flock of fluttering creatures on the subsequent folios.[8]

In the designs of his flying machines, Leonardo tried to imitate the flight of birds so closely that he almost gives the impression of wanting to become a bird. He called his flying machine *uccello* (bird), and when he drew its mechanical wings, he mimicked the anatomical structure of a bird's wing so accurately and, one almost feels, lovingly, that it is often hard to tell the difference (see Fig. E-2).

Instead of trying to dominate nature, as Francis Bacon advocated in the seventeenth century, Leonardo's intent was to learn from her as much as possible. He was in awe of the beauty he saw in the complexity of natural forms, patterns, and processes, and aware that nature's ingenuity was far superior to human design. "Though human ingenuity in various inventions uses different instruments for the same end," he declared, "it will never discover an invention more beautiful, easier, or more economical than nature's, because in her inventions nothing is wanting and nothing is superfluous."[9]

This attitude of seeing nature as a model and mentor is now being rediscovered in the practice of ecological design. Like Leonardo da Vinci five hundred years ago, ecodesigners today study the patterns and

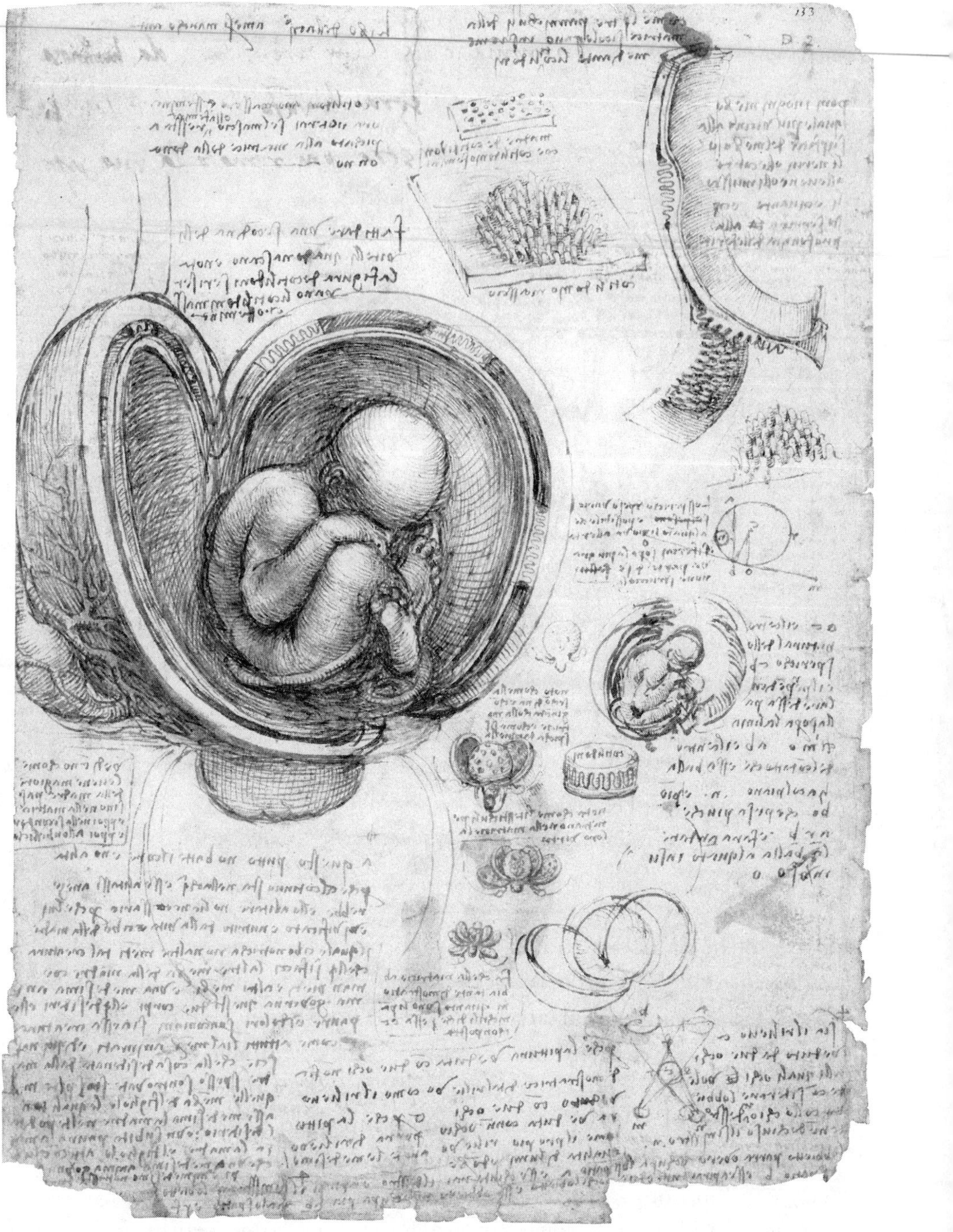

Figure E-1: The fetus within the womb, c. 1510–12,
Anatomical Studies, folio 198r

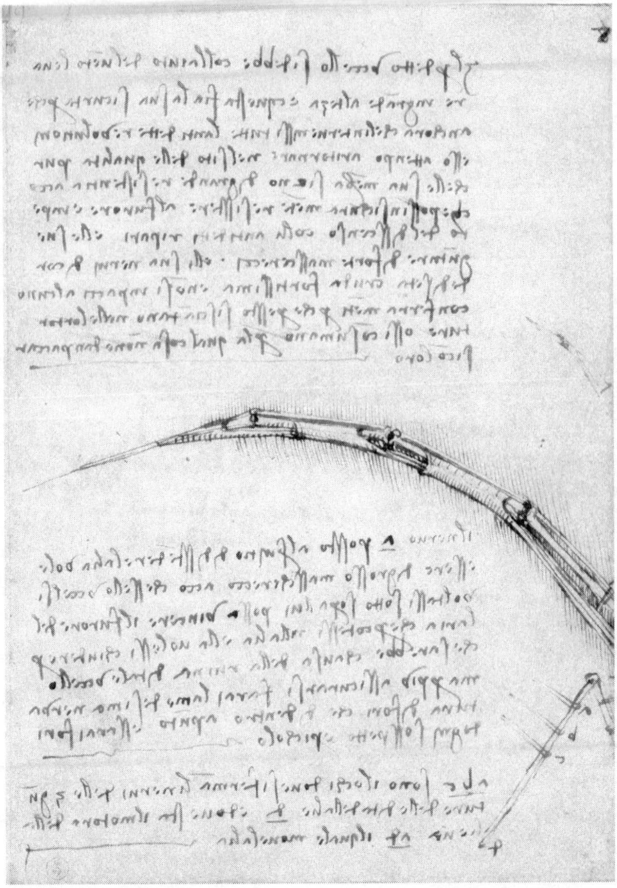

*Figure E-2: Study for a mechanical wing imitating
the wing of a bird, Codex sul volo, folio 7r*

flows in the natural world and try to incorporate the underlying principles into their design processes.[10] When Leonardo designed villas and
palaces, he paid special attention to the movements of people and
goods through the buildings, applying the metaphor of metabolic
processes to his architectural designs.[11] He also considered gardens as
parts of buildings, always attempting to integrate architecture and nature. He applied the same principles to his designs of cities, viewing a
city as a kind of organism in which people, material goods, food, water, and waste need to flow with ease for the city to be healthy.[12]

In his extensive projects of hydraulic engineering, Leonardo carefully studied the flow of rivers in order to gently modify their courses by inserting relatively small dams in the right places and at the optimal angles. "A river, to be diverted from one place to another, should be coaxed and not coerced with violence," he explained.[13]

These examples of using natural processes as models for human design, and of working with nature rather than trying to dominate her, show clearly that as a designer, Leonardo worked in the spirit that the ecodesign movement is advocating today. Underlying this attitude of appreciation and respect of nature is a philosophical stance that does not view humans as standing apart from the rest of the living world, but rather as being fundamentally embedded in, and dependent upon, the entire community of life in the biosphere.

Today this philosophical stance is promoted by a school of thought and cultural movement known as "deep ecology."[14] The distinction between "shallow" and "deep" ecology is now widely accepted as a useful terminology for referring to a major division within contemporary environmental thought. Shallow ecology views humans as above or outside the natural world, as the source of all value, and ascribes only instrumental, or "use," value to nature. Deep ecology, by contrast, does not separate humans—or anything else—from the natural environment. It sees the living world as being fundamentally interconnected and interdependent and recognizes the intrinsic value of all living beings. Amazingly, Leonardo's Notebooks contain an explicit articulation of that view: "The virtues of grasses, stones, and trees do not exist because humans know them. . . . Grasses are noble in themselves without the aid of human languages or letters."[15]

Ultimately, deep ecological awareness is spiritual or religious awareness. When spirituality is understood as a way of being that flows from a deep sense of oneness with all, a sense of belonging to the universe as a whole, it becomes clear that ecological awareness is spiritual in its deepest essence.[16] It seems that Leonardo da Vinci's view of the world had that kind of spiritual dimension. Unlike most of his contemporaries, he hardly ever referred to God's creation, but preferred to speak of the infinite works and marvelous inventions of nature. The Notebooks are full of passages in which he describes how nature "has ordained" that animals should experience pain, how she has created stones, made the surface of the cornea convex, given movement to animals, and formed their bodies.

In all of these passages, one senses Leonardo's great reverence for nature's boundless creativity and wisdom. They are not couched in religious language, but are deeply spiritual nonetheless.

During the centuries after Leonardo's death, while his Notebooks remained hidden, the Scientific Revolution and the Industrial Revolution replaced the organic worldview of the Middle Ages and the Renaissance with the altogether different conception of the world as a machine. The resulting mechanistic paradigm—formulated in scientific language by Galileo, Descartes, Newton, and Locke—has dominated our culture for over three hundred years, during which it has shaped modern Western society and significantly influenced the rest of the world.[17]

This paradigm consists of a number of deeply entrenched ideas and values, among them the view of the universe as a mechanical system composed of elementary building blocks, the view of the human body as a machine, the view of life in society as a competitive struggle for existence, and the belief in unlimited material progress to be achieved through economic and technological growth. All of these assumptions have been fatefully challenged by recent events, and a radical revision of them is now occurring.

As our new century unfolds, it is becoming increasingly apparent that the major problems of our time—whether economic, environmental, technological, social, or political—are systemic problems that cannot be solved within the current fragmented and reductionist framework of our academic disciplines and social institutions. We need a radical shift in our perceptions, thinking, and values. And, indeed, we are now at the beginning of such a fundamental change of worldview in science and society.

During the last few decades, the mechanistic Cartesian view of the world has begun to give way to a holistic and ecological view not unlike that expressed in the science and art of Leonardo da Vinci. Instead of seeing the universe as a machine composed of elementary building blocks, scientists have discovered that the material world, ultimately, is a network of inseparable patterns of relationships; that the planet as a whole is a living, self-regulating system. The view of the human body as a machine and of the mind as a separate entity is being replaced by one that sees not only the brain, but also the immune system, the bodily tissues, and even each cell as a living, cognitive system. Evolution is no longer seen as a competitive struggle for existence, but rather a cooperative dance in which creativity and the constant emergence of novelty are the driving forces. And with the new emphasis on complexity, networks, and patterns of organization, a new science of quality is slowly emerging.[18]

Naturally, this new science is being formulated in a language that is quite different from that of Leonardo's, as it incorporates the latest achievements of biochemistry, genetics, neuroscience, and other advanced scientific disciplines. However, the underlying conception of the living world as being fundamentally interconnected, highly complex, creative, and imbued with cognitive intelligence is quite similar to Leonardo's vision. This is why the science and art of this great sage of the Renaissance, with their integrative scope, sublime beauty, and life-affirming ethics, are a tremendous inspiration for our time.

APPENDIX

Leonardo's Geometry of Transformations

In this appendix, I shall discuss some of the more technical details of Leonardo's geometry of transformations, which may be of interest to readers familiar with modern mathematics.

There are three types of curvilinear transformations that Leonardo uses repeatedly in various combinations.[1] In the first type, a given figure with one curvilinear side is translated into a new position in such a way that the two figures overlap (see Fig. A-1). Since the two figures are identical, the two parts remaining when the part they have in common (B) is subtracted must have equal areas (A = C). This technique allows Leonardo to transform any area bounded by two identical curves into a rectangular area, that is, to "square" it.

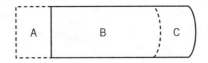

Figure A-1: Transformation by translation

However, in accordance with his science of qualities, Leonardo is not interested in calculating areas, only in establishing proportions.[2]

The second type of transformation is achieved by cutting out a segment from a given figure, say a triangle, and then reattaching it on the other side (see Fig. A-2). The new curvilinear figure, obviously, has the same area as the original triangle. As Leonardo explains in the accompanying text: "I shall take away portion b from triangle ab, and I will return it at c. . . . If I give back to a surface what I have taken away from it, the surface returns to its former state."[3] He frequently draws such curvilinear triangles, which he calls *falcate* (falcates), deriving the term from *falce*, the Italian word for scythe.

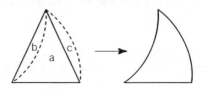

Figure A-2: Transformation of a triangle into a "falcate"

Leonardo's third type of transformation involves gradual deformations rather than movements of rigid figures; for example, the deformation of a rectangle, as shown in Figure A-3. The equality of the two areas can be shown by dividing the rectangle into thin parallel strips and then pushing each strip into a new position, so that the two vertical straight lines are turned into curves.

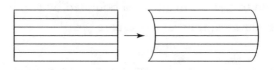

Figure A-3: Deformation of a rectangle

This operation can easily be demonstrated with a deck of cards. However, to rigorously prove the equality of the two areas requires making the strips infinitely thin and using the methods of integral calculus. As Matilde Macagno points out, this example shows again that Leonardo's way of visualizing these mappings and transformations foreshadows concepts associated with the development of calculus.[4]

In addition to these three basic transformations, Leonardo experimented extensively with a geometric theorem involving a triangle and a moon-shaped segment, which is known as the "lunula of

Hippocrates" after the Greek mathematician Hippocrates of Chios. To construct this figure, a rectangular isosceles triangle ABC is inscribed in a circle with radius a, and then an arc with radius b is drawn around point C from A to B (see Fig. A-4). The lunula in question is the shaded area bounded by the two circular arcs.

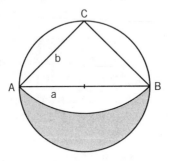

Figure A-4: The lunula of Hippocrates

Hippocrates of Chios (not to be confused with the famous physician Hippocrates of Cos) proved in the fifth century B.C. that the area of the lunula is equal to that of the triangle ABC. This surprising equality can easily be verified with elementary geometry, taking into account that the radii of the two arcs are related by the Pythagorean theorem $2a^2 = b^2$. Leonardo apparently learned about the lunula of Hippocrates from a mathematical compendium by Giorgio Valla, published in Venice in 1501, and made frequent use of the equality in various forms.[5]

On the folio in Codex Madrid II, shown in Fig. 7-6 on p. 206, Leonardo sketched a series of transformations involving the three basic types on a single page, as if he had wanted to record a catalog of his basic transformations. In the top two sketches in the right margin of the page, Leonardo demonstrates how a portion of a pyramid can be detached and reattached on the opposite side to create a curvilinear solid. He frequently uses the term "falcate" for such curvilinear pyramids and cones, as he does for curvilinear triangles. These falcates can also be obtained by a continuous process of gradual deformation, or "flow," which Leonardo demonstrates in the next two sketches with the example of a cone.

The sketch below the cone shows the bending of a cylinder with a cone inscribed in it. It almost looks like a working sketch for a metal shop, which shows that Leonardo always had real physical objects and phenomena in mind when he worked on his geometric transformations. Indeed, the Codex Atlanticus contains a folio filled with instructions for deforming metal pieces into various shapes. Among many others, these deformations include the bending of a cylinder, as shown here.[6]

The last two sketches in the right margin represent examples of so-called parallel shear, which are extended to circular shears in the three sketches in the center of the page. In these examples, rectilinear figures are transformed into spirals, and the conservation of area is far from obvious. To Leonardo, the circular operations evidently looked like legitimate extensions of his linear deformations. Indeed, as Matilde Macagno has shown with the help of elementary calculus, Leonardo's intuition was absolutely correct.[7]

The two sketches below the circular shears, finally, show examples of the "squaring" of surfaces bounded by two parallel curves. There is a striking similarity between these surfaces and those in the three sketches just above, which suggests that Leonardo probably thought of the two techniques as alternative methods for squaring surfaces bounded by parallel curves.

As I have discussed, Leonardo's geometric transformations of planar figures and solid bodies may be seen as early forms of topological transformations.[8] Leonardo restricted them to transformations in which area or volume are conserved, and he called the transformed figures "equal" to the original ones. Topologists call the figures related by such transformations, in which very general geometric properties are preserved, topologically equivalent.

Modern topology has two main branches, which overlap considerably. In the first, known as point-set topology, geometric figures are regarded as collections of points, and topological transformations are seen as continuous mappings of those points. The second branch, called combinatorial topology, treats geometric figures as combinations of simpler figures, joined together in an orderly manner.

Leonardo experimented with both of these approaches. The operations shown in Figure 7-6 can all be seen as continuous deformations or, alternatively, as continuous mappings. On the other hand, his ingenious transformation of a dodecahedron into a cube (Fig. 7-5 on p. 202) is a beautiful and elaborate example of combinatorial topology.

The concept of continuity, which is central to all topological transformations, has to do, ultimately, with very basic properties of space and time. Hence topology is seen today as a general foundation of mathematics and a unifying conceptual framework for its many branches. In the early sixteenth century, Leonardo da Vinci saw his geometry of continuous transformations in a similar vein—as a fundamental mathematical language that would allow him to capture the essence of nature's ever-changing forms.

The double folio in the Codex Atlanticus (see p. 209) represents the culmination of Leonardo's explorations of topological transformations. These drawings were intended for a comprehensive treatise, for which he proposed several titles—*Treatise on Continuous Quantity, Book of Equations*, and *De ludo geometrico (On the Game of Geometry)*.

The diagrams shown on the two sheets display a bewildering variety of geometric forms built from intersecting circles, triangles, and squares, which look like playful variations of floral patterns and other aesthetically pleasing motifs, but turn out to be rigorous "geometric equations" based upon topological principles.

The double folio is divided equally by nine horizontal lines on which Leonardo has placed a regular array of semicircles (and, in the last now, some circles), filled with his geometric designs.[9] The starting point for each diagram is always a circle with an inscribed square. Depending on how the circle is cut in half, two equivalent basic diagrams are obtained (see Fig. A-5), one with a rectangle and the other with a triangle inside the semicircle.

Since the white areas in the two diagrams are equal, both representing half of the inscribed square, the shaded areas must also be

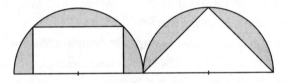

Figure A-5: The two basic diagrams, from Codex Atlanticus, folio 455, row 3

equal. As Leonardo explains in the accompanying text, "If one removes equal parts from equal figures, the remainder must be equal."[10]

The two figures are then filled with shaded segments of circles, *bisangoli* ("double angles" shaped like olive leaves), and falcates (curvilinear triangles) in a dazzling variety of designs. In all of them, the ratio between the shaded areas (also called "empty") and the white areas (also called "full") is always the same, because the white areas—no matter how fragmented they may be—are always equal to the original inscribed half square (rectangle or triangle), and the shaded areas are equal to the original shaded areas outside the half square.

These equalities are by no means obvious, but the text underneath each diagram specifies how parts of the figure can successively be "filled in" (i.e., how shaded and white parts can be interchanged) until the original rectilinear half square is recovered and the figure has thus been "squared." The same principle is always repeated: "To square [the figure], fill in the empty parts."[11]

In Figure A-6, I have selected a specific diagram from the double folio to illustrate Leonardo's technique. The text under the diagram

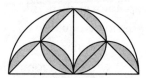

Figure A-6: Sample diagram (number 7 in row 7, Codex Atlanticus, folio 455)

reads: "To square, fill in the triangle with the four falcates outside."[12] I have redrawn the diagram in Figures A-7 a and b so as to make its geometry explicit. Inside the large half circle with radius R, Leonardo has generated eight shaded segments B by drawing four smaller half circles with half the radius, r = R/2 (see Fig. A-7 a). The falcates he mentions are the white areas marked F.

By specifying that the four "empty" (shaded) areas inside the triangle are to be "filled in" with the four falcates, Leonardo indicates that the areas F and B are equal. Here is how he might have reasoned. Since he knew that the area of a circle is proportional to the square of its ra-

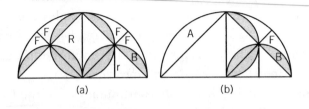

Figure A-7: Geometry of the sample diagram

dius,[13] he could show that the area of the large half circle is four times that of each small half circle, and that consequently the area of the large segment A is four times that of the small segment B (see Fig. A-7 b). This means that, if two small segments are subtracted from the large segment, the area of the remaining curved figure (composed of two falcates) will be equal to the area subtracted, and hence the area of the falcate F is equal to that of the small segment B.

For the other figures, the squaring procedure can be more elaborate, but eventually the original diagrams are always recovered. This is Leonardo's "game of geometry." Each diagram represents a geometric—or, rather, topological—equation, and the accompanying instruction describes how the equation is to be solved to square the curvilinear figure. This is why Leonardo proposed *Book of Equations* as an alternative title for his treatise. The successive steps of solving the equations can be depicted geometrically, as shown (for example) in Figure A-8.[14]

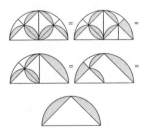

Figure A-8: Squaring the sample diagram

Leonardo delighted in drawing endless varieties of these topological equations, just as Arab mathematicians in previous centuries had been fascinated by exploring wide varieties of algebraic equations. Occasionally he was carried away by the aesthetic pleasure of sketching fanciful geometric figures. But the deeper significance of his game of geometry was never far from his mind. The infinite variations of geometric forms in which area or volume were always conserved were meant to mirror the inexhaustible transmutations in the living forms of nature within limited and unchanging quantities of matter.

NOTES

Citations of Leonardo's manuscripts refer to the scholarly editions listed in the Bibliography. I have retranslated some of the passages by staying closer to the original texts, so as to preserve their Leonardesque flavor.

❧ PREFACE ❧

1. Kenneth Clark, *Leonardo da Vinci*, Penguin, 1989, p. 258.
2. Ibid., p. 255.
3. Martin Kemp, "Leonardo Then and Now," in Kemp and Jane Roberts, eds., *Leonardo da Vinci: Artist, Scientist, Inventor*, Catalogue of Exhibition at Hayward Gallery, Yale University Press, 1989.

❧ INTRODUCTION ❧

1. See p. 130.
2. *Trattato*, chapter 19; "sensory awareness" is my translation of Leonardo's term *senso comune*, which I discuss on p. 248.
3. Ms. Ashburnham II, folio 19v.
4. *Trattato*, chapters 6 and 12.
5. Codex Leicester, folio 34r.
6. Daniel Arasse, *Leonardo da Vinci: The Rhythm of the World*, Konecky & Konecky, New York, 1998, p. 80.
7. Fritjof Capra, *The Web of Life*, Doubleday, New York, 1996, p. 100.
8. For a detailed account of the history and characteristics of systemic thinking, see Capra (1996).
9. Ibid., p. 112.
10. See p. 207.
11. See p. 195.
12. See p. 243.
13. See p. 252.

14. Ms. A, folio 3r.
15. Arasse (1998), p. 311.
16. See p. 227.
17. Arasse (1998), p. 20.
18. *Trattato*, chapter 367.
19. Irma Richter, ed., *The Notebooks of Leonardo da Vinci*, Oxford University Press, New York, 1952, p. 175.
20. See p. 254.
21. Anatomical Studies, folio 153r.
22. See p. 250.
23. See p. 260.
24. Anatomical Studies, folio 173r.

℘ CHAPTER I ℘

1. Giorgio Vasari, *Lives of the Artists*, published originally in 1550; trans. George Bull, 1965; reprinted as *Lives of the Artists*, vol. 1, Penguin, 1987.
2. Paolo Giovio, "The Life of Leonardo da Vinci," written around 1527, first published in 1796; translation from the original Latin by J. P. Richter, 1939; reprinted in Ludwig Goldscheider, *Leonardo da Vinci*, Phaidon, London, 1964, p. 29.
3. Vasari (1550), pp. 13–14.
4. Serge Bramly, *Leonardo*, HarperCollins, New York, 1991, p. 6.
5. Anonimo Gaddiano, "Leonardo da Vinci," written around 1542; trans. Kate Steinitz and Ebria Feigenblatt, 1949; reprinted in Goldscheider (1964), pp. 30–32. This manuscript, now in the Biblioteca Nazionale in Florence, was formerly housed in the Biblioteca Gaddiana, the private library of the Florentine Gaddi family.
6. *Trattato*, chapter 36.
7. Giorgio Nicodemi, "The Portrait of Leonardo," in *Leonardo da Vinci*, Reynal, New York, 1956.
8. Ibid.
9. Clark (1989), p. 255.
10. *Trattato*, chapter 50.
11. Ms. H, folio 60r.
12. Bramly (1991), p. 342.
13. Ms. Ashburnham II, folios 31r and 30v.
14. See Arasse (1998), p. 430.

15. See Martin Kemp, *Leonardo da Vinci: The Marvellous Works of Nature and Man*, Harvard University Press, Cambridge, Mass., 1981, p. 152.

16. Bramly (1991), p. 115.

17. Vasari (1550); translation of this passage by Daniel Arasse; see Arasse (1998), p. 477.

18. See, e.g., Bramly (1991), p. 119.

19. See Michael White, *Leonardo: The First Scientist*, St. Martin's/Griffin, New York, 2000, pp. 132–33.

20. See Bramly (1991), p. 241.

21. Ibid., p. 133.

22. Charles Hope, "The Last 'Last Supper'," *New York Review of Books*, August 9, 2001.

23. Kenneth Keele, *Leonardo da Vinci's Elements of the Science of Man*, Academic Press, New York, 1983 p. 365.

24. See Penelope Murray, ed., *Genius: The History of an Idea,* Basil Blackwell, New York, 1989.

25. Quoted by Wilfrid Mellers, "What is Musical Genius?," Murray (1989), p. 167.

26. See Andrew Steptoe, ed., *Genius and the Mind*, Oxford University Press, 1998.

27. See David Lykken, "The Genetics of Genius," in Steptoe (1998).

28. Kenneth Clark, quoted by Sherwin B. Nuland, *Leonardo da Vinci*, Viking Penguin, New York, 2000, p. 4.

29. Quoted by David Lykken in Steptoe (1998).

30. Quoted by Bramly (1991), p. 281.

31. Quoted by Richter (1952), p. 306.

32. Murray (1989), p. 1.

❦ CHAPTER 2 ❦

1. See Jacob Burckhardt, *The Civilization of the Renaissance in Italy*, original German edition published in 1860, Modern Library, New York, 2002.

2. See Bramly (1991), p. 100.

3. *Trattato*, chapter 79.

4. See Robert Richards, *The Romantic Conception of Life*, University of Chicago Press, 2002.

5. See Fritjof Capra, *Uncommon Wisdom*, Simon & Schuster, New York, 1988, p. 71.

6. *Trattato*, chapter 42.

7. Ibid., chapter 33.

8. Ibid., chapter 13.

9. Kemp (1981), p. 161.

10. *Trattato*, chapter 68.

11. Anatomical Studies, folio 50v.

12. See Fritjof Capra, *The Hidden Connections*, Doubleday, New York, 2002, p. 119.

13. See Penny Sparke, *Design and Culture in the Twentieth Century*, Allen & Unwin, London, 1986.

14. Codex Atlanticus, folio 323r.

15. *Trattato*, chapter 23.

16. Clark (1989), p. 63.

17. See Arasse (1998), p. 274.

18. Quoted by Arasse (1998), p. 275.

19. Anatomical Studies, folio 139v.

20. Arasse (1998), p. 202.

21. Ibid., p. 283.

22. Kemp (1981), p. 56.

23. Arasse (1998), p. 284.

24. See Capra (2002), pp. 13–14 and p. 116.

25. See Claire Farago, "How Leonardo Da Vinci's Editors Organized His *Treatise on Painting* and How Leonardo Would Have Done It Differently," in Lyle Massey, ed., *The Treatise on Perspective: Published and Unpublished*, National Gallery of Art, Washington, distributed by Yale University Press, 2003.

26. See Claire Farago, *Leonardo da Vinci's Paragone: A Critical Interpretation with a New Edition of the Text in the Codex Urbinas*, E. J. Brill, Leiden, 1992.

27. *Trattato*, chapters 14, 19.

28. Ibid., chapter 29.

29. Ibid., chapters 38, 41.

30. See Bram Kempers, *Painting, Power and Patronage*, Allen Lane, London, 1992; Steptoe (1998), p. 255.

31. See Arasse (1998), p. 293.

32. See p. 3.

33. Clark (1989), p. 167.

34. Kemp (1981), p. 97.

35. *Trattato*, chapter 412.

36. Clark (1989), p. 129. In the history of Italian art, the fifteenth century

is known as the quattrocento (four hundred), the sixteenth century is called the cinquecento (five hundred), and so on.

37. *Trattato*, chapter 124.

38. See p. 8.

39. See p. 212.

40. These notes are in Manuscripts C and Ashburnham II.

41. Kemp (1981), p. 98.

42. See Bramly (1991), pp. 101–2.

43. Ibid., p. 106.

44. See Kemp (1981), pp. 94–96.

45. See Ann Pizzorusso, "Leonardo's Geology: The Authenticity of the Virgin of the Rocks," *Leonardo*, vol. 29, no. 3, pp. 197–200, MIT Press, 1996.

46. See William Emboden, *Leonardo da Vinci on Plants and Gardens*, Dioscorides Press, Portland, Ore., 1987, p. 125.

47. *Trattato*, chapter 38.

48. Bramly (1991), p. 228.

49. This Roman equestrian statue of the Gothic king Odoacer no longer exists. It was destroyed in the eighteenth century; see Bramly (1991), p. 232.

50. Codex Atlanticus, folio 399r.

51. This treatise, mentioned by Vasari and by Lomazzo, has been lost.

52. Kemp (1981), p. 205.

53. Codex Madrid II, folio 157v.

54. See Bramly (1991), pp. 234–35.

55. Codex Atlanticus, folio 914ar.

56. Bramly (1991), p. 250.

57. See p. 36.

58. I am grateful to ecodesigner Magdalena E. Corvin for illuminating discussions and correspondence on the nature of design.

59. See Bramly (1991), p. 232.

60. See Clark (1989), p. 139.

61. See Bramly (1991), p. 219.

62. Codex Atlanticus, folio 21r.

63. See Bramly (1991), p. 272.

64. See Pierre Sergescu, "Léonard de Vinci et les mathématiques," cited in Arasse (1998), p. 65.

65. See Kemp (1981), p. 88.

66. See Paolo Galluzzi, *Renaissance Engineers*, Giunti, Florence, 1996, p. 187.

67. Clark (1989), p. 110.

68. Ludwig H. Heydenreich, "Leonardo and Bramante: Genius in Architecture," in C. D. O'Malley, ed., *Leonardo's Legacy: An International Symposium*, University of California Press, Berkeley and Los Angeles, 1969; Carlo Pedretti, *Leonardo, Architect*, Rizzoli, New York, 1985.

69. See Pedretti (1985) for a full account of Leonardo's architectural work; see also Jean Guillaume, "Léonard et l'architecture," in Paolo Galluzzi and Jean Guillaume, eds., *Léonard de Vinci: ingénieur et architecte*, Musée des Beaux-Arts de Montréal, 1987.

70. Arasse (1998), p. 173.

71. Heydenreich (1969).

72. Arasse (1998), pp. 179–80. Mannerism is a style of art and architecture developed in the late sixteenth century and characterized by spatial incongruity and elegant, elongated figures.

73. Kemp (1981), p. 110.

74. See, for example, White (2000), p. 124.

75. Codex Atlanticus, folio 730r.

76. See Guillaume (1987); see also Arasse (1998), pp. 165–68.

77. Anatomical Studies, folio 97r.

78. Emboden (1987).

79. Ms. B, folio 38r.

80. Codex Atlanticus, folio 184v.

81. Ms. B, folio 16r; see also Guillaume (1987).

82. Nuland (2000), p. 53.

83. See Bramly (1991), pp. 402–3.

84. See International Healthy Cities Foundation, www.healthycities.org.

85. Arasse (1998), p. 152.

86. Ibid., p. 233.

87. Ibid., pp. 239–40.

88. See Kate Steinitz, "Le dessin de Léonard de Vinci pour la représentation de la Danaé de Baldassare Taccone," in Jean Jacquot, ed., *Le Lieu théâtral à la Renaissance*, Paris, 1968.

89. See Arasse (1998), p. 239.

90. See Bramly (1991), p. 301.

91. See Kemp (1981), p. 182., for a detailed description of the vaulted architecture and Leonardo's matching design.

92. See Arasse (1998), p. 138.

93. Quoted in Fritjof Capra, *The Turning Point*, Simon & Schuster, New York, 1982, p. 68.

❧ CHAPTER 3 ❧

1. See, e.g., Ludwig H. Heydenreich, *Leonardo da Vinci*, 2 vols., Macmillan, New York, 1954; Clark (1989); Bramly (1991).
2. "Ser" was the traditional title of a notary.
3. Codex Atlanticus, folio 888r.
4. See Arasse (1998), pp. 108–9.
5. Ibid., p. 39.
6. Codex Atlanticus, folio 327v.
7. See p. 116.
8. See Bramly (1991), p. 53.
9. See Arasse (1998), p. 502 n. 71.
10. Vasari probably exaggerated when he called Verrocchio "a close friend" of Ser Piero, but it is quite likely that the notary knew the artist, since many of his clients were patrons of the arts.
11. Bramly (1991), pp. 65–66.
12. Ibid., pp. 67–69.
13. Domenico Laurenza, "Leonardo: La scienza trasfigurata in arte," *Le Scienze*, Rome, maggio 2004a, p. 6.
14. See Arasse (1998), p. 54.
15. See Bramly (1991), pp. 71–72; Carlo Pedretti, *Leonardo: The Machines*, Giunti, Florence, 1999, p. 16.
16. See Laurenza (2004a), p. 7.
17. Ms. G, folio 84v.
18. See Jane Roberts, "The Life of Leonardo," in Martin Kemp and Jane Roberts, eds., *Leonardo da Vinci: Artist, Scientist, Inventor*, Catalogue of Exhibition at Hayward Gallery, Yale University Press, 1989.
19. See Keele (1983), p. 9.
20. See Domenico Laurenza, *Leonardo on Flight*, Giunti, Florence, 2004b, p. 16.
21. See Keele (1983), p. 9.
22. See Martin Kemp, *Leonardo*, Oxford University Press, 2004, pp. 13–14.
23. See Bramly (1991), p. 144.
24. Clark (1989), p. 59.
25. See Bramly (1991), p. 156.
26. Ibid., p. 91.
27. Ibid., p. 157; see also White (2000), p. 83.
28. See White (2000), p. 81.
29. See Pedretti (1999), p. 16.
30. See Keele (1983), pp. 9–11.

31. See Arasse (1998), pp. 350–61.
32. Clark (1989), pp. 74–75.
33. See p. 23.
34. See Clark (1989), p. 78.
35. Roberts (1989).
36. Arasse (1998), p. 361.
37. Anonimo Gaddiano (1542).
38. Ludovico's official title was Duke of Milan and, like other powerful rulers of the Renaissance, he was often referred to as a prince.
39. See Pedretti (1999), p. 32.
40. See Bramly (1991), p. 158.
41. See p. 26.
42. Codex Atlanticus, folio 1082r.
43. See Clark (1989), p. 85.
44. Keele (1983), p. 11.
45. See Bramly (1991), pp. 183–84.
46. See p. 44.
47. See Kemp (1981), pp. 93–94.
48. For the comparison of the two paintings, based on the analysis of Leonardo's geology, see Pizzorusso (1996); for the corresponding botanical analysis, see Emboden (1987), p. 125.
49. Clark (1989), p. 93.
50. See p. 58.
51. Laurenza (2004a), p. 23.
52. See Arasse (1998), p. 43.
53. See Keele (1983), p. 20.
54. See Laurenza (2004a), p. 24.
55. Codex Atlanticus, folio 888r.
56. See Arasse (1998), p. 37.
57. See Emboden (1987), p. 21; Kemp (2004), pp. 165–66.
58. Clark (1989), p. 129.
59. See p. 246.
60. Laurenza (2004a), p. 27.
61. See Guillaume (1987).
62. See p. 57.
63. See Bramly (1991), p. 192.
64. See Heydenreich (1969).
65. See Arasse (1998), p. 397.

66. See p. 48.
67. See White (2000), pp. 127–28.

✎ CHAPTER 4 ✎

1. See Kemp (2004), pp. 38–40.
2. See Keele (1983), p. 22.
3. Ibid., p. 22.
4. See Keele (1983), p. 22; Fazio Cardano was the father of the famous mathematician Girolamo Cardano, the founder of probability theory.
5. See Laurenza (2004b), p. 40.
6. See Ladislao Reti, ed., *The Unknown Leonardo*, McGraw-Hill, New York, 1974, pp. 272–73.
7. See Kemp (1981), p. 194.
8. Quoted in Richter (1952), p. 322.
9. See p. 197.
10. For a discussion of the golden section and its connection with the Platonic solids, see Mario Livio, *The Golden Ratio*, Broadway Books, New York, 2002.
11. Luca Pacioli, *De divina proportione*, Paganinum de Paganinis, Venice, 1509; fascsimile edition of the ms. in the Biblioteca Ambrosiana di Milano published by Fontes Ambrosiani XXXi, G. Biggiogero and F. Riva, eds., Milan, 1966.
12. See p. 30.
13. See Bramly (1991), pp. 294–95.
14. Clark (1989), p. 146.
15. See Hope (2001).
16. Clark (1989), p. 149.
17. The portrait, now in the Louvre, is also known as *La Belle Ferronière*.
18. See p. 61.
19. See Codex Leicester, folio 4r.
20. See p. 20.
21. See Bramly (1991), p. 308.
22. See p. 51.
23. Ludovico briefly regained possession of Milan in 1500 before being captured and taken to France as prisoner, where he remained until his death in 1508.
24. See Keele (1983), p. 25.

25. See Bramly (1991), p. 307.

26. See Arasse (1998), p. 210.

27. Ibid., p. 417.

28. Kemp (1981), p. 218.

29. See Bramly (1991), p. 310.

30. The drawing is now in the Louvre; see Arasse (1998), p. 398.

31. See Codex Atlanticus, folio 638vd.

32. See Keele (1983), pp. 28–29.

33. See also p. 22.

34. Codex Leicester, folio 22v.

35. See Keele (1983), p. 28.

36. These rooms, with fading frescoes on their walls, may have been identified recently in a building in central Florence; see *International Herald Tribune*, January 19, 2005.

37. See Arasse (1998), p. 448.

38. See White (2000), pp. 208–9.

39. See Keele (1983), pp. 30–32.

40. See Bramly (1991), pp. 330–31.

41. Ibid., p. 332.

42. Codex Arundel, folio 272r.

43. See p. 23.

44. Codex Forster I, folio 3r.

45. See p. 205.

46. See Laurenza (2004b).

47. Ibid., p. 96.

48. See Bramly (1991), pp. 348–49.

49. See Emboden (1987), pp. 62–65.

50. See p. 19.

51. See Kemp (1981), p. 270.

52. See Bramly (1991), pp. 356–58.

53. This bronze group, *Saint John the Baptist Preaching to a Levite and a Pharisee*, can still be seen above the Baptistery's north door. The life-size statues do seem to exhibit Leonardesque features.

54. Codex Arundel, folio 1r.

55. Anatomical Studies, folio 154r.

56. Ibid., folio 113r.

57. Ibid., folio 69v.

58. See Keele (1983), pp. 321–22.

59. See Farago (2003).

60. See Emboden (1987), p. 24.
61. See Bramly (1991), pp. 370–71.
62. See Laurenza (2004a), p. 87.
63. See Emboden (1987), pp. 65–68.
64. See p. 19.
65. See Bramly (1991), pp. 385–86.
66. See p. 254.
67. Historians long believed that the dissections themselves got Leonardo into trouble with the pope. However, Domenico Laurenza has documented that there were no religious or ethical objections to dissections in Italy at the time. According to Laurenza, it was the clash between Leonardo's Aristotelian view of the soul and Leo X's Thomistic view that was at the root of the pope's ban; see Domenico Laurenza, "Leonardo nella Roma di Leone X," *XLIII Lettura Vinciana*, Biblioteca Leonardiana, Vinci, 2003.
68. See Bramly (1991), pp. 384–85.
69. See p. 23.
70. Drawings and Miscellaneous Papers, vol. I, folio 67r.
71. The *Leda* was lost or destroyed in the early eighteenth century; see Bramly (1991), p. 465 n. 49.
72. Arasse (1998), p. 462.
73. *Trattato*, chapter 25.
74. See Bramly (1991), p. 397.
75. See Arasse (1998), p. 152.
76. See Bramly (1991), p. 398.
77. Ibid., p. 399.
78. Quoted by Kemp (1981), p. 349.
79. Quoted by Bramly (1991), p. 400.
80. See p. 39.
81. Quoted by Bramly (1991), p. 400.
82. See Keele (1983), p. 41.
83. See p. 3.
84. See p. 197.
85. Anatomical Studies, folio 113 r.
86. Codex Atlanticus, folio 673 r.
87. See p. 58.
88. See Keele (1983), p. 40.
89. See p. 58.
90. Codex Trivulzianus, folio 27r.

91. See Bramly (1991), pp. 406–7.
92. Quoted by Bramly (1991), pp. 411–12.
93. See Carlo Pedretti and Marco Cianchi, *Leonardo: I codici*, Giunti, Florence, 1995; see also Bramly (1991), p. 417.
94. See Reti (1974).

❧ CHAPTER 5 ❧

1. Thomas S. Kuhn, *The Structure of Scientific Revolutions*, University of Chicago Press, 1962; see also Capra (1996), p. 5.
2. See, e.g., George Sarton, *The Appreciation of Ancient and Medieval Science during the Renaissance*, University of Pennsylvania Press, Philadelphia, 1955; Marie Boas, *The Scientific Renaissance*, Harper & Brothers, New York, 1962.
3. "Byzantine Empire" is the term commonly used to refer to the Greek-speaking Eastern Roman Empire during the Middle Ages. Its capital was Constantinople, today's Istanbul.
4. See Karen Armstrong, *Islam: A Short History*, Modern Library, New York, 2000, pp. 5–6.
5. See pp. 120–21.
6. See Sarton (1955), p. 4.
7. See Pedretti (1999), p. 83.
8. Ibid., p. 91.
9. See p. 39.
10. Anatomical Studies, folio 139v.
11. See George Sarton, "The Quest for Truth: A Brief Account of Scientific Progress during the Renaissance," in Robert M. Palter, ed., *Toward Modern Science*, vol. 2, Noonday Press, New York, 1961.
12. See p. 97.
13. See Kemp (1981), pp. 159–60.
14. See Fritjof Capra, *The Tao of Physics*, Shambhala, Berkeley, 1975; 25th Anniversary Edition by Shambhala, Boston, 2000, pp. 55–56.
15. See Capra (1996), p. 18.
16. See Wilhelm Windelband, *A History of Philosophy*, published originally in 1901 by Macmillan; reprinted by The Paper Tiger, Cresskill, N.J., 2001, p. 149.
17. See p. 249.
18. See p. 225.
19. See, for example, p. 197.

20. Sarton (1955), p. 171.
21. Irrational numbers, e.g., square roots, cannot be expressed as ratios, or quotients, of integers.
22. *Al jabr* refers to the process of reducing the number of unknown mathematical quantities by binding them together in equations.
23. See Capra (1996), p. 114.
24. See Sarton (1955), p. 52.
25. See Capra (1982), p. 306.
26. Ibid., p. 311.
27. See Sarton (1955), p. 7.
28. Ibid., pp. 169–70.
29. Anatomical Studies, folio 136r.
30. See Boas (1962), p. 131.
31. See p. 85.
32. See p. 95.
33. See Kemp (1981), p. 323.
34. See Emboden (1987), p. 141.
35. See p. 118.

❧ CHAPTER 6 ❧

1. See, for example, Kuhn (1962).
2. Quoted in Capra (1982), p. 101.
3. For the classical work on Leonardian paleography, see Gerolamo Calvi, *I manoscritti di Leonardo da Vinci dal punto di vista cronologico storico e biografico*, Bramante, Busto Arsizio, 1982; first published in 1925, republished in 1982 with a foreword by Augusto Marinoni.
4. A list of the scholarly editions of Leonardo's Notebooks is given in the Bibliography on pp. 299–301.
5. Codex Trivulzianus, folio 20v.
6. Codex Forster III, folio 14r.
7. *Trattato*, chapter 33.
8. Codex Atlanticus, folio 323r.
9. Ibid., folio 534v.
10. Ms. E, folio 55r.
11. See pp. 2 and 37.
12. Clark (1989), p. 255.
13. E. H. Gombrich, preface to *Leonardo da Vinci: Artist, Scientist, Inventor*, Catalogue of Exhibition at Hayward Gallery, Yale University Press, 1989.

14. Ms. A, folio 47r, and Ms. M, folio 57r; see also Keele (1983), pp. 132–33.
15. See Keele (1983), pp. 136–37.
16. Ibid., p. 141.
17. See Codex Atlanticus, folio 1b.
18. See Keele (1983), p. 135.
19. Anatomical Studies, folio 104r.
20. Nuland (2000), p. 131.
21. Keele (1983), pp. 244–45.
22. Ibid., p. 301.
23. See Enzo Macagno, "Lagrangian and Eulerian Descriptions in the Flow Studies of Leonardo da Vinci," *Raccolta Vinciana*, Fasc. XXIV, 1992a.
24. See p. 85.
25. See Augusto Marinoni, introduction to Leonardo da Vinci, *Il codice atlantico della Biblioteca ambrosiana di Milano*, vol. 1, pp. 18–25, Giunti, Florence, 1975.
26. See Capra (1996), p. 18.
27. Ibid., p. 22.
28. Codex Atlanticus, folio 1067.
29. See Capra (1982).
30. See Frank Zöllner and Johannes Nathan, *Leonardo da Vinci: The Complete Paintings and Drawings*, Taschen, 2003, pp. 384–99.
31. See Keele (1983), p. 142.
32. *Trattato*, chapter 501.
33. See Bramly (1991), p. 257.
34. Anatomical Studies, folio 69v.
35. See, for example, Martin Kemp (1999a), "Analogy and Observation in the Codex Hammer," in Claire Farago, ed., *Leonardo's Science and Technology*, Garland Publishing, New York, 1999; Arasse (1998), p. 74.
36. Arasse (1998), p. 19.
37. Ms. C, folio 26v.
38. See Capra (1996), p. 169.
39. Codex Atlanticus, folio 813.
40. Ibid., folio 508v.
41. See p. 48; see also Stephen Jay Gould, "The Upwardly Mobile Fossils of Leonardo's Living Earth," in Stephen Jay Gould, *Leonardo's Mountain of Clams and the Diet of Worms*, Harmony Books, New York, 1998.
42. Codex Arundel, folio 172v.
43. See p. 48.

44. See Emboden (1987), p. 163.
45. See Keele (1983), p. 316.
46. See Emboden (1987), p. 171.
47. *Trattato*, chapter 21.
48. See p. 11.
49. Anatomical Studies, folio 153r.
50. Codex *sul volo*, folio 3r.
51. See Marshall Clagett, "Leonardo da Vinci: Mechanics," in Farago (1999).
52. Codex Atlanticus, folio 481.
53. See Clagett (1999).
54. See p. 37.
55. See Pedretti (1999); also see Domenico Laurenza, Mario Taddei, and Edoardo Zanon, *Le Macchine di Leonardo*, Giunti, Florence, 2005.
56. See, for example, Kemp and Roberts (1989), pp. 218–41.
57. See p. 92.
58. For a detailed description of the purpose and functioning of this machine, see Bern Dibner, "Leonardo: Prophet of Automation," in O'Malley (1969).
59. See, for example, Kemp (1989), p. 227.
60. For a detailed description of this mechanism, see Dibner (1969).
61. Codex Forster II, folios 86r and 87r.
62. Codex Madrid I, cover.
63. Ibid., folio 95r.
64. Codex Leicester, folio 25r.
65. Ms. E, folio 54r.
66. For a comprehensive account of Leonardo's studies on flight, see Laurenza (2004b).
67. See p. 91.
68. Codex Atlanticus, folio 1058v.
69. In Newton's formulation, the law reads: "For any action there is an equal and opposite reaction."
70. Laurenza (2004b), p. 44.
71. See Kemp and Roberts (1989), p. 236.
72. See p. 111.
73. Codex *sul volo*, folio 16r.
74. See Kemp (2004), pp. 127–29.
75. Kemp (1989), p. 239.
76. Kenneth Keele, *Leonardo da Vinci on Movement of the Heart and Blood*, Lippincott, Philadelphia, 1952, p. 122.

77. Anatomical Studies, folio 81v.
78. Ibid., folio 198v.
79. Nuland (2000), p. 161.
80. Ms. I, folio 18r.
81. Clark (1989), p. 250.

❧ CHAPTER 7 ❧

1. Ms. G, folio 96v.
2. Anatomical Studies, folio 116r.
3. See p. 150.
4. See p. 44.
5. See p. 237.
6. Quoted in Capra (1982), p. 55.
7. An arithmetic progression is a sequence of numbers such that the difference between successive terms is a constant. For example, the sequence 1, 3, 5, 7, . . . is an arithmetic progression with common difference 2. Functions are relationships between unknown variable numbers, or "variables," denoted by letters. For example, in the equation $y = 2x + 1$, the variable y is said to be a function of x. In linear functions, such as in this example, the variables are raised only to the first power. The graphs corresponding to these functions are straight lines; hence the term "linear." Arithmetic progressions are special cases of linear functions in which the variables are discrete numbers. Thus, in the example above, the equation $y = 2x + 1$ turns into the sequence 1, 3, 5, 7, . . . if x is restricted to positive integers.
8. Ms. A, folio 10r; see also p. 214. It should be noted that, like many medieval and Renaissance writers, Leonardo uses the word "pyramid" to describe all solids that have regular or irregular bases and one apex, including cones; see Keele (1983), p. 153.
9. Ms. M, folio 59v.
10. Ibid.
11. Ms. M, folio 45r.
12. See Keele (1983), pp. 113–14.
13. See Morris Kline, *Mathematical Thought from Ancient to Modern Times*, Oxford University Press, New York, 1972, p. 338.
14. Keele (1983), p. 157.
15. See E. H. Gombrich, "The Form of Movement in Water and Air," in O'Malley (1969).

16. See p. 39.

17. Arasse (1998), p. 271.

18. See pp. 92 and 95.

19. Clark (1989), p. 38.

20. Codex Madrid II, folio 67r.

21. The theory of functions deals with relationships among continuous variable numbers, or variables. Differential calculus is a branch of modern mathematics used to calculate the rate of change of a function with respect to the variable on which it depends.

22. Codex Arundel, folios 190v and 266r.

23. From The Notebooks of Paul Klee (1961), quoted in Francis Ching, *Architecture: Form, Space, and Order*, 2nd ed., John Wiley, New York, 1996, p. 1.

24. Codex Arundel, folio 190v.

25. Matilde Macagno, "Geometry in Motion in the Manuscripts of Leonardo da Vinci," *Raccolta Vinciana*, Fasc. XXIV, 1992b, and "Transformation Geometry in the Manuscripts of Leonardo da Vinci," *Raccolta Vinciana*, Fasc. XXVI, 1995.

26. Codex Madrid II, folio 107r.

27. See Kline (1972), p. 340.

28. Ms. M, folio 66v.

29. See Keele (1983), p. 276.

30. Codex Atlanticus, folio 781ar.

31. See p. 109.

32. Codex Forster I, folio 3r.

33. Codex Madrid II, folio 72r.

34. Ibid., folio 112r.

35. Anatomical Studies, folio 121r.

36. Codex Atlanticus, folio 124v.

37. Ms. G, folio 96r.

38. See Macagno (1995).

39. Ibid.

40. See Kline (1972), p. 349.

41. For detailed discussions of Leonardo's three basic types of curvilinear transformations, see appendix, pp. 267–74.

42. For a more detailed discussion of the transformations sketched on this folio, see appendix, pp. 269–71.

43. Kemp (1981), p. 253.

44. Kline (1972), p. 1158.

45. Ibid., p. 1170.
46. See p. 60.
47. See Pedretti (1985), p. 296.
48. See p. 55.
49. See Arassse (1998), p. 212.
50. See p. 122.
51. Codex Atlanticus, folio 455; see also Arasse (1998), pp. 122–23.
52. Clark (1989), p. 39.
53. See appendix, pp. 271–74.
54. Today we would qualify this assertion by saying that the causal relationships in nature can be represented by *approximate* mathematical models.
55. Codex Forster III, folio 43v.
56. See Capra (1996), p. 128.

❦ CHAPTER 8 ❦

1. See p. 160.
2. See George Lakoff and Mark Johnson, *Philosophy in the Flesh*, Basic Books, New York, 1999, p. 94; see also p. 252 in present text.
3. Codex Trivulzianus, folio 20v.
4. See pp. 80 and 84.
5. See p. 91.
6. The treatise on perspective is contained in Ms. A, folios 36–42; the diagrams of geometrical optics are in Manuscripts A and C.
7. See p. 44.
8. James Ackerman, "Science and Art in the Work of Leonardo," in O'Malley (1969).
9. Ms. A, folio 1v.
10. Ms. A, folio 10r. As noted above, Leonardo, like many of his contemporaries, used the word "pyramid" to also describe cones and other solids that have a single apex; see p. 193, footnote 8.
11. Ms. A, folio 1v.
12. See Keele (1983), p. 46.
13. Ms. Ashburnham II, folio 23r.
14. Ms. A, folio 8v.
15. See p. 95.
16. See p. 246.
17. See p. 41.
18. Arasse (1998), pp. 300–301.

19. See p. 93.
20. Ms. A, folio 3r.
21. See p. 238.
22. Ms. Ashburnham II, folio 18r.
23. Ibid., folio 25.
24. See Kemp (1981), p. 33.
25. See p. 150.
26. See Kemp (1981), p. 35.
27. See p. 74.
28. Codex Arundel, folio 70v.
29. See Keele (1983), pp. 55–56.
30. Ms. A, folio 19r.
31. See Keele (1983), p. 141.
32. See p. 44.
33. Codex Atlanticus, folio 676r.
34. Ibid.
35. *Trattato*, chapters 681–82.
36. Clark (1989), p. 129; quoted also on p. 87 in present text.
37. *Trattato*, chapter 17.
38. See Keele (1983), p. 132; see also p. 226 in present text about Leonardo's use of the camera obscura.
39. See p. 146.
40. Codex Arundel, folio 94v.
41. Ibid.
42. See Keele (1983), pp. 91–92.
43. Ms. F, folio 41v.
44. See Kemp (1981), p. 323; see also p. 155 in present text.
45. *Trattato*, chapter 25.
46. Codex Atlanticus, folio 372v.
47. Anatomical Studies, folio 118v.
48. Ibid., folio 22v.
49. It would be wrong to read any occult meaning into Leonardo's frequent use of the term "spiritual." He defines it clearly to mean simply "invisible and immaterial" and uses it consistently in this sense; see p. 244.
50. The concept of energy was defined precisely only in the seventeenth century. Leonardo uses both *potentia* and *virtù* to mean power, or energy.
51. Anatomical Studies, folio 22v.
52. See Capra (1975), p. 61.
53. Ms. Ashburnham II, folio 6v.

54. Ibid.

55. Ms. A, folio 9v.

56. Ibid., folio 61r.

57. More precisely, the water particles move in small circles; see Capra (1975), p. 152.

58. See p. 227.

59. Ms. A, folio 61r.

60. Ms. H, folio 67r.

61. There is even some speculation that Huygens may have been aware of Leonardo's research when he published his famous work on optics, *Traité de la lumière*, in 1690; see White (2000), p. 177.

62. See Kenneth Keele, "Leonardo da Vinci's Physiology of the Senses," in O'Malley (1969).

63. Ms. F, folio 49v.

64. Codex Atlanticus, folio 545v.

65. See White (2000), p. 182.

66. Ibid., p. 183.

67. See p. 97.

68. Codex Leicester, folio 4r.

69. See Keele (1983), p. 215.

70. Ms. B, folio 4v.

71. Ms. A, folio 61r.

72. Ibid., folio 22v.

73. See p. 231.

74. See p. 114.

75. Anatomical Studies, folio 148v.

76. Codex Madrid I, folio 126v.

77. Ibid.

78. See Martin Kemp (1999b), "Leonardo and the Visual Pyramid," in Farago (1999).

79. Ms. F, folio 34r.

80. Ms. D, folio 4v.

81. See Kemp (1999b).

82. Ms. E, 16v.

❧ CHAPTER 9 ❧

1. Codex Atlanticus, folio 949v.

2. *Trattato*, chapter 28.

3. See Keele (1983), p. 61.

4. Codex Atlanticus, folio 327v.

5. Ms. D, folio 5v.

6. Codex Atlanticus, folio 345r.

7. Ms. F, folio 39v.

8. See Keele (1983), pp. 73–74.

9. Ibid., p. 69.

10. Codex Atlanticus, folio 545r.

11. See p. 213.

12. See p. 163.

13. Ms. D, folio 1r.

14. See Keele (1983), pp. 74–75.

15. Spectacles were well known in Leonardo's day. They were of two kinds, those "for the young" (concave lenses) and those "for the old" (convex lenses); see Keele (1983), p. 210.

16. Ibid., p. 204.

17. See p. 226.

18. Ms. D, folio 3v.

19. See Keele (1983), p. 201.

20. Anatomical Studies, folio 115r. Leonardo was unaware that central vision actually takes place at the macula on the periphery of the optic disk.

21. Codex Atlanticus, folio 546r.

22. See p. 163.

23. Keele (1969), and Keele (1983), p. 60.

24. See p. 228.

25. Keele (1969).

26. Keele (1983), p. 63.

27. Ibid., pp. 64–65.

28. The optic chiasma is actually a partial crossing in which each nerve separates into two branches, and the inner branch from each eye crosses over to join the outer branch from the other eye.

29. Codex Atlanticus, folio 832v.

30. The anterior ventricle consists of two almost completely separated lateral wings and is therefore also described as two lateral ventricles.

31. Following Kenneth Keele, I am using Leonardo's Italian term *senso comune* for this region of the brain, since the English "common sense" has quite a different meaning; see Keele (1983), p. 62.

32. Leonardo may have coined the term *impressiva* (or *imprensiva*) in analogy

to related terms like *apprensiva* and *comprensiva*, used by medieval schol-ars; see Farago (1992), pp. 301–2. "Receptor of impressions" is the translation proposed by Martin Kemp; see Kemp (1981), p. 127.

33. *Trattato*, chapter 28.
34. For more extensive discussions of Leonardo's studies of the human voice, phonetics, and music, see Giulio Panconcelli-Calzia, "Leonardo's Work in Phonetics and Linguistics," and Enrico Magni-Dufflocq, "Da Vinci's Music," in *Leonardo da Vinci*, Reynal, New York, 1956; and especially Keele (1983), p. 215.
35. Keele (1983), p. 219.
36. See p. 82.
37. See p. 60.
38. See Arasse (1998), p. 222.
39. Anatomical Studies, folio 39r.
40. See Windelband (2001), p. 62; see also p. 145 in present text.
41. See Keele (1983), p. 267.
42. Codex Arundel, 151r,v.
43. See Capra (2002), p. 33.
44. See p. 111.
45. See Laurenza (2004b), pp. 86–88.
46. Codex Atlanticus, 434r.
47. Anatomical Studies, folio 114v.
48. See p. 140.
49. Codex Atlanticus, folio 166r.
50. See Capra (2002), p. 61.
51. Ms. B, folio 4v.
52. Anatomical Studies, folios 198r and 114v.
53. Codex Atlanticus, folio 680r.
54. See Capra (2002), pp. 40–41.

✵ EPILOGUE ✵

1. See p. 3.
2. Keele (1983); see also Nuland (2000).
3. Emboden (1987).
4. Galluzzi (1996); see also Pedretti (1999); Laurenza, Taddei, and Zanon (2005).
5. Laurenza (2004b).
6. Leonardo's engineering and architecture are both covered extensively in

the beautiful catalog of an exhibit at the Musée des Beaux-Arts de Montréal; see Galluzzi (1987).

7. Codex Madrid I, folio 6r.
8. See, e.g., Ms. E, folios 38ff.
9. Anatomical Studies, folio 114v.
10. See Capra (2002), pp. 229ff.
11. See p. 57.
12. See p. 58.
13. Codex Leicester, folio 13r; see also folio 32r.
14. See Capra (1996), pp. 6–7.
15. *Trattato*, chapter 34.
16. See Fritjof Capra and David Steindl-Rast, *Belonging to the Universe*, HarperSanFrancisco, 1991.
17. See Capra (1982).
18. See Capra (1996), and Capra (2002).

≫ APPENDIX ≪

1. See Macagno (1992b).
2. See p. 169.
3. Codex Madrid II, folios 107r and 111v.
4. Macagno (1992b).
5. See Kemp (1981), p. 250.
6. Codex Atlanticus, folio 82r.
7. Macagno (1992b).
8. See pp. 205–8.
9. See analysis by Pedretti, and Marinoni; Codex Atlanticus, folio 455.
10. Codex Atlanticus, folio 455.
11. Ibid.
12. Ibid.
13. See Keele (1983), p. 154.
14. Leonardo, apparently, did not feel the need to record the solutions of his topological equations graphically. If he had done so, he would probably have used a different notation, as the equal sign (=) came into common usage only in the seventeenth century; see Kline (1972), p. 260.

LEONARDO'S NOTEBOOKS

Facsimiles and Transcriptions

❧ ANATOMICAL STUDIES (WINDSOR COLLECTION) ❧

Kenneth Keele and Carlo Pedretti, *Leonardo da Vinci: Corpus of the Anatomical Studies in the Collection of Her Majesty the Queen at Windsor Castle*, 3 vols., Harcourt Brace Jovanovich, New York, 1978–80.

❧ DRAWINGS AND MISCELLANEOUS PAPERS (WINDSOR COLLECTION) ❧

Carlo Pedretti, *The Drawings and Miscellaneous Papers of Leonardo da Vinci in the Collection of Her Majesty the Queen at Windsor Castle*, 2 vols., Harcourt Brace Jovanovich, New York, 1982.
  Volume I: Landscapes, Plants, and Water Studies
  Volume II: Horses and Other Animals
Complete edition to comprise four volumes; volumes 3 and 4 not yet published.

❧ CODEX ARUNDEL ❧

Leonardo da Vinci, *Il Codice Arundel 263 nella British Library: edizione in facsimile nel riordinamento cronologico dei suoi fascicoli; a cura di Carlo Pedretti; trascrizioni e note critiche a cura di Carlo Vecce*, Giunti, Florence, 1998.

❧ CODEX ATLANTICUS ❧

Leonardo da Vinci, *Il codice atlantico della Biblioteca ambrosiana di Milano, trascrizione diplomatica e critica di Augusto Marinoni*, Giunti, Florence, 1975–80.

❧ CODEX SUL VOLO ❧

Leonardo da Vinci, *The codex on the flight of birds in the Royal Library at Turin*, edited by Augusto Marinoni, Johnson Reprint, New York, 1982.

❧ CODICES FORSTER I, II, III ❧

Leonardo da Vinci, *I codici Forster del Victoria and Albert Museum di Londra; trascrizione diplomatica e critica di Augusto Marinoni, edizione in facsimile*, 3v., Giunti, Florence, 1992.

❧ CODEX LEICESTER (FORMERLY CODEX HAMMER) ❧

Leonardo da Vinci, *The Codex Hammer*, translated into English and annotated by Carlo Pedretti, Giunti, Florence, 1987.

❧ CODICES MADRID I, II ❧

Leonardo da Vinci, *The Madrid Codices*, transcribed and translated by Ladislao Reti, McGraw-Hill, New York, 1974.

❧ MANUSCRIPTS AT INSTITUT DE FRANCE ❧

Leonardo da Vinci, *I manoscritti dell'Institut de France, edizione in facsimile sotto gli auspici della Commissione nazionale vinciana e dell'Institut de France, trascrizione diplomatica e critica di Augusto Marinoni*, Giunti, Florence, 1986–90. (Mss. A, B, C, D, E, F, G, H, I, K, L, M; Ms. A includes as a supplement Ashburnham II, also listed as B.N. 2038; Ms. B includes as a supplement Ashburnham I, also listed as B.N. 2037.)

❧ CODEX TRIVULZIANUS ❧

Leonardo da Vinci, *Il codice di Leonardo da Vinci nella Biblioteca trivulziana di Milano, trascrizione diplomatica e critica di Anna Maria Brizio*, Giunti, Florence, 1980.

❧ TRATTATO DELLA PITTURA (CODEX URBINAS) ❧

Leonardo da Vinci, *Libro di pittura, Codice urbinate lat. 1270 nella Biblioteca apostolica vaticana, a cura di Carlo Pedretti, trascrizione critica di Carlo Vecce,* Giunti, Florence, 1995.

BIBLIOGRAPHY

Ackerman, James. "Science and Art in the Work of Leonardo." In C. D. O'Malley, ed., *Leonardo's Legacy: An International Symposium*. University of California Press, Berkeley and Los Angeles, 1969.

Anonimo Gaddiano. "Leonardo da Vinci." Written around 1542; translation by Kate Steinitz and Ebria Feigenblatt, 1949; reprinted in Ludwig Goldscheider, *Leonardo da Vinci*. Phaidon, London, 1964.

Arasse, Daniel. *Leonardo da Vinci: The Rhythm of the World*. Konecky & Konecky, New York, 1998.

Armstrong, Karen. *Islam: A Short History*. Modern Library, New York, 2000.

Boas, Marie. *The Scientific Renaissance*. Harper & Brothers, New York, 1962.

Bramly, Serge. *Leonardo: Discovering the Life of Leonardo da Vinci*. HarperCollins, New York, 1991.

Burckhardt, Jacob. *The Civilization of the Renaissance in Italy*. Original German edition published in 1860; Modern Library, New York, 2002.

Calvi, Gerolamo. *I manoscritti di Leonardo da Vinci dal punto di vista cronologico storico e biografico*. Bramante, Busto Arsizio, 1982; first published in 1925, republished in 1982 with a foreword by Augusto Marinoni.

Capra, Fritjof. *The Tao of Physics*. Shambhala, Berkeley, 1975; 25th Anniversary Edition by Shambhala, Boston, 2000.

———. *The Turning Point*. Simon & Schuster, New York, 1982.

———. *Uncommon Wisdom*. Simon & Schuster, New York, 1988.

———. *The Web of Life*. Doubleday, New York, 1996.

———. *The Hidden Connections*. Doubleday, New York, 2002.

———, and David Steindl-Rast. *Belonging to the Universe*, HarperSanFrancisco, 1991.

Ching, Francis. *Architecture: Form, Space, and Order*. 2nd Edition. John Wiley, New York, 1996.

Clagett, Marshall. "Leonardo da Vinci: Mechanics." In Claire Farago, ed., *Leonardo's Science and Technology*. Garland, New York, 1999.

Clark, Kenneth. *Leonardo da Vinci*. Penguin, 1989.

Dibner, Bern. "Leonardo: Prophet of Automation." In C. D. O'Malley, ed., *Leonardo's Legacy: An International Symposium*. University of California Press, Berkeley and Los Angeles, 1969.

Emboden, William. *Leonardo da Vinci on Plants and Gardens*. Dioscorides Press, Portland, Ore., 1987.

Farago, Claire. *Leonardo da Vinci's Paragone: A Critical Interpretation with a New Edition of the Text in the Codex Urbinas*. E. J. Brill, Leiden, 1992.

———, ed. *Leonardo's Science and Technology*. Garland, New York, 1999.

———. "How Leonardo da Vinci's Editors Organized his *Treatise on Painting* and How Leonardo Would Have Done It Differently," in Lyle Massey, ed., *The Treatise on Perspective: Published and Unpublished*. National Gallery of Art, Washington, distributed by Yale University Press, 2003.

Galluzzi, Paolo. *Renaissance Engineers*. Giunti, Florence, 1996.

———, and Jean Guillaume, eds. *Léonard de Vinci: ingénieur et architecte*. Musée des Beaux-Arts de Montréal, 1987.

Giovio, Paolo. "The Life of Leonardo da Vinci." Written around 1527, first published in 1796; translation from the original Latin by J. P. Richter, 1939; reprinted in Goldscheider (1964), p. 29.

Goldscheider, Ludwig. *Leonardo da Vinci*. Phaidon, London, 1964.

Gombrich, E. H. "The Form of Movement in Water and Air." In C. D. O'Malley, ed., *Leonardo's Legacy: An International Symposium*. University of California Press, Berkeley and Los Angeles, 1969.

———. Preface to *Leonardo da Vinci: Artist, Scientist, Inventor*. Catalogue of Exhibition at Hayward Gallery, Yale University Press, 1989.

Gould, Stephen Jay. "The Upwardly Mobile Fossils of Leonardo's Living Earth." In Stephen Jay Gould, *Leonardo's Mountain of Clams and the Diet of Worms*. Harmony Books, New York, 1998.

Guillaume. Jean. "Léonard et l'architecture." In Paolo Galluzzi and Jean Guillaume, eds., *Léonard de Vinci: ingénieur et architecte*. Musée des Beaux-Arts de Montréal, 1987.

Heydenreich, Ludwig H. *Leonardo da Vinci*. 2 vols. Macmillan, New York, 1954.

———. "Leonardo and Bramante: Genius in Architecture." In C. D.

O'Malley, ed., *Leonardo's Legacy: An International Symposium*. University of California Press, Berkeley and Los Angeles, 1969.

Hope, Charles. "The Last 'Last Supper'." *New York Review of Books,* August 9, 2001.

Jacquot, Jean, ed. *Le Lieu théâtral à la Renaissance.* Paris, 1968.

Keele, Kenneth. *Leonardo da Vinci on Movement of the Heart and Blood.* Lippincott, Philadelphia, 1952.

———. "Leonardo da Vinci's Physiology of the Senses." In C. D. O'Malley, ed., *Leonardo's Legacy: An International Symposium*. University of California Press, Berkeley and Los Angeles, 1969.

———. *Leonardo da Vinci's Elements of the Science of Man.* Academic Press, New York, 1983.

Kemp, Martin. *Leonardo da Vinci: The Marvellous Works of Nature and Man.* Harvard University Press, Cambridge, Mass., 1981.

———. "Leonardo Then and Now." In Kemp and Jane Roberts, eds., *Leonardo da Vinci: Artist, Scientist, Inventor*. Catalogue of Exhibition at Hayward Gallery, Yale University Press, 1989.

———. "Analogy and Observation in the Codex Hammer." In Claire Farago, ed., *Leonardo's Science and Technology*. Garland Publishing, New York, 1999a.

———. "Leonardo and the Visual Pyramid." In Claire Farago, ed., *Leonardo's Science and Technology*. Garland Publishing, New York, 1999b.

———. *Leonardo.* Oxford University Press, 2004.

———, and Jane Roberts, eds. *Leonardo da Vinci: Artist, Scientist, Inventor.* Catalogue of Exhibition at Hayward Gallery. Yale University Press, 1989.

Kempers, Bram. *Painting, Power and Patronage.* Allen Lane, London, 1992.

Kline, Morris. *Mathematical Thought from Ancient to Modern Times.* Oxford University Press, New York, 1972.

Kuhn, Thomas S. *The Structure of Scientific Revolutions.* University of Chicago Press, 1962.

Lakoff, George, and Mark Johnson. *Philosophy in the Flesh.* Basic Books, New York, 1999.

Laurenza, Domenico. "Leonardo nella Roma di Leone X." *XLIII Lettura Vinciana.* Biblioteca Leonardiana, Vinci, 2003.

———. "Leonardo: La scienza trasfigurata in arte." *Le Scienze.* Rome, maggio 2004a.

———. *Leonardo on Flight.* Giunti, Florence, 2004b.

————, Mario Taddei, and Edoardo Zanon. *Le Macchine di Leonardo*. Giunti, Florence, 2005.

Leonardo da Vinci. Reynal, New York, 1956.

Livio, Mario. *The Golden Ratio*. Broadway Books, New York, 2002.

Macagno, Enzo. "Lagrangian and Eulerian Descriptions in the Flow Studies of Leonardo da Vinci." *Raccolta Vinciana,* Fasc. XXIV, 1992a.

Macagno, Matilde. "Geometry in Motion in the Manuscripts of Leonardo da Vinci." *Raccolta Vinciana*, Fasc. XXIV, 1992b.

————. "Transformation Geometry in the Manuscripts of Leonardo da Vinci." *Raccolta Vinciana*, Fasc. XXVI, 1995.

Magni-Dufflocq, Enrico. "Da Vinci's Music." In *Leonardo da Vinci*. Reynal, New York, 1956.

Marinoni, Augusto. Introduction to Leonardo da Vinci, *Il codice atlantico della Biblioteca ambrosiana di Milano*. Vol. 1. Giunti, Florence, 1975.

Massey, Lyle, ed. *The Treatise on Perspective: Published and Unpublished*. National Gallery of Art, Washington. Distributed by Yale University Press, 2003.

Murray, Penelope, ed. *Genius: The History of an Idea*. Basil Blackwell, New York, 1989.

Nicodemi, Giorgio. "The Portrait of Leonardo." In *Leonardo da Vinci*. Reynal, New York, 1956.

Nuland, Sherwin B. *Leonardo da Vinci*. Viking Penguin, New York, 2000.

O'Malley, C. D., ed. *Leonardo's Legacy: An International Symposium*. University of California Press, Berkeley and Los Angeles, 1969.

Pacioli, Luca. *De divina proportione*. Paganinum de Paganinis, Venice, 1509; facsimile edition of the manuscript in the Biblioteca Ambrosiana di Milano, published by Fontes Ambrosiani XXXi, G. Biggiogero and F. Riva, eds., Milan, 1966.

Palter, Robert M., ed. *Toward Modern Science*. Vol. 2. Noonday Press, New York, 1961.

Panconcelli-Calzia, Giulio. "Leonardo's Work in Phonetics and Linguistics." In *Leonardo da Vinci*. Reynal, New York, 1956.

Pedretti, Carlo. *Leonardo, Architect*. Rizzoli, New York, 1985.

————. *Leonardo: The Machines*. Giunti, Florence, 1999.

————, and Marco Cianchi. *Leonardo: I codici*. Giunti, Florence, 1995.

Pizzorusso, Ann. "Leonardo's Geology: The Authenticity of the Virgin of the Rocks." *Leonardo*, Vol. 29, No. 3. MIT Press, 1996.

Reti, Ladislao, ed. *The Unknown Leonardo*. McGraw-Hill, New York, 1974.

Richards, Robert. *The Romantic Conception of Life*. University of Chicago Press, 2002.

Richter, Irma, ed. *The Notebooks of Leonardo da Vinci*. Oxford University Press, New York, 1952.

Roberts, Jane. "The Life of Leonardo." In Martin Kemp and Roberts, *Leonardo da Vinci: Artist, Scientist, Inventor*. Catalogue of Exhibition at Hayward Gallery, Yale University Press, 1989.

Sarton, George. *The Appreciation of Ancient and Medieval Science during the Renaissance*. University of Pennsylvania Press, Philadelphia, 1955.

———."The Quest for Truth: A Brief Account of Scientific Progress during the Renaissance." In Robert M. Palter, ed., *Toward Modern Science*, Vol. 2. Noonday Press, New York, 1961.

Sparke, Penny. *Design and Culture in the Twentieth Century*. Allen & Unwin, London, 1986.

Steinitz, Kate. "Le dessin de Léonard de Vinci pour la représentation de la Danaé de Baldassare Taccone." In Jean Jacquot, ed., *Le Lieu théâtrial à la Renaissance*. Paris, 1968.

Steptoe, Andrew, ed. *Genius and the Mind*. Oxford University Press, 1998.

Vasari, Giorgio. *Lives of the Artists*. Published originally in 1550; translation by George Bull, 1965; reprinted as *Lives of the Artists: Volume I*. Penguin, 1987.

White, Michael. *Leonardo: The First Scientist*. St. Martin's/Griffin, New York, 2000.

Windelband, Wilhelm. *A History of Philosophy*. Published originally in 1901 by Macmillan; reprinted by The Paper Tiger, Cresskill, N.J., 2001.

Zöllner, Frank, and Johannes Nathan. *Leonardo da Vinci: The Complete Paintings and Drawings*. Taschen, 2003.

INDEX

Page numbers in italics refer to illustrations.

THE HIDDEN CONNECTIONS
A Science for Sustainable Living

Fritjof Capra explores another frontier in the human significance of scientific ideas—applying complexity theory to large-scale social interactions. In the 1980s, complexity theory emerged as a powerful alternative to classic, linear thought. A forerunner of that revolution, Fritjof Capra now continues to expand the scope of the theory by establishing a framework in which we can understand and solve some of the most important issues of our time. Capra posits that in order to sustain life, the principles underlying our social institutions must be consistent with the broader organization of nature. Discussing pertinent contemporary issues ranging from the controversial practices of the World Trade Organization (WTO) to the Human Genome Project, he concludes with an authoritative, often provocative plan for designing ecologically sustainable communities and technologies as alternatives to the current economic globalization.

Science/978-0-385-49472-4

THE WEB OF LIFE
A New Scientific Understanding of Living Systems

The vitality and accessibility of Fritjof Capra's ideas have made him one of our most eloquent spokespersons on the latest discoveries emerging at the frontiers of scientific, social, and philosophical thought. In *The Web of Life*, Capra offers a brilliant synthesis of such scientific breakthroughs as the theory of complexity, Gaia theory, chaos theory, and other explanations of the properties of organisms, social systems, and ecosystems. Capra's surprising findings stand in stark contrast to accepted paradigms of mechanism and Darwinism, and provide an extraordinary new foundation for ecological policies that will allow us to build and sustain communities without diminishing the opportunities for future generations.

Science/978-0-385-47676-8